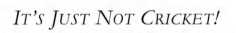

IT'S JUST NOT CRICKET!

Also by Henry Blofeld

Cakes and Bails: Henry Blofeld's Cricket Year

IT'S JUST NOT CRICKET!

HENRY BLOFELD'S
CRICKET YEAR

SIMON & SCHUSTER
A VIACOM COMPANY

First published in Great Britain by Simon & Schuster UK Ltd, 1999
A Viacom company

1 3 5 7 9 10 8 6 4 2

Simon & Schuster UK Ltd
Africa House
64–78 Kingsway
London WC2B 6AH

Simon & Schuster Australia
Sydney

A CIP catalogue record for this book is available from the British Library

ISBN 0-684-85152-0

Printed and bound in Great Britain by
The Bath Press, Bath

For Bitten and Suki
who somehow managed to
bring me back to life.

Contents

CHAPTER ONE

A Very Near Thing

T his book came within a whisker of not getting beyond what is now Chapter Eight.

Having survived England's failure to regain the Ashes in Australia and six weeks rehabilitation back in England, I then flew to New Zealand for a most enjoyable three weeks. The only drawback was that I had to suffer a small part of two of the most boring Test Matches – New Zealand were playing South Africa – it has ever been my lot to watch. As you will later see, this was more than made up for by some extensive research into the extraordinary and increasingly high standard of New Zealand wine. I was lucky enough to visit a number of wineries in both the North and the South Islands and this included two nights in the winery house at Clayvin, just outside Blenheim at the top of the South Island. My old friends, Richard and Johnny Wheeler, whose family wine merchants are perhaps the only good reason for enduring Colchester's daily traffic jams, have invested in half the 35-acre winery, which is producing Pinot Noir and Chardonnay of a formidable quality. A long flight home by way of Sydney and Frankfurt, in both places changing aeroplanes, brought me back to England on the last day of March along with a few bottles that somehow managed to survive the journey.

It was getting on for half past five on the afternoon of Tuesday, 13 April that my year and my life irrevocably changed. I was walking down the King's Road in southwest London to the World's End Nurseries to discuss with James Lotery the possibilities of our minuscule garden just up the road. James runs the Nurseries with good humour, an encouragingly resonant laugh, a well-stocked fridge, considerable knowledge, any number of young Australians to do the donkey work and, of course, a rod of iron. It is conveniently tucked in alongside the World's End pub, and the higgledy-piggledy half an acre or so is full of flowers, plants, trees, pots and ornaments of all shapes and sizes; in fact. anything that might be of use in a London garden. It is marvellous that those benighted planners, who love to ruin any oasis of character in towns and cities, have not yet grasped this with their tenacious claws. I hope James has a cast iron lease.

The Nurseries are not much more than a five-minute walk from where we live and while strolling through Westfield Park on my way to the King's Road, I felt my chest tighten and I had a strange hollow pain on the inside of both forearms. In the King's Road I mercifully came across a passing green bench and gratefully sat down for a few minutes while my chest eased. Then I set off again but after three hundred yards it all came back. This time I propped myself up against a lamp post not more than a stone's throw from James. After a bit I continued, none too confidently, and my mind was not on the job when we began to discuss the merits of small trees over creepers and the different varieties of climbing roses. I was grateful when Bitten arrived and took charge. After taking a number of crucial horticultural decisions, she drove me back home and when Suki, my daughter, turned up, we set off to walk the minute and a half to the Chelsea Ram for dinner.

We were still well short of this splendid watering hole when my chest tightened again. We had a conference of war and as a result walked back home and I rang Trevor Hudson, my doctor. He said, with a chilling finality, 'You've got angina of the heart. Go straight up to bed and don't move unless you want to spend a penny. Stay there until half past nine in the morning when I shall ring you again.' The next day, 14 April, was Bitten's birthday and the year before this festive occasion had also been mucked up when I had to go into hospital in Norwich to have a bucketful of poison removed from my right knee. Poor girl.

Looking back on that evening, I am rather surprised that I was not in more of a panic as I was fairly sure even then that something dramatic had gone wrong. I even remember thinking that bypass surgery, should it come to that, is an operation that has been brought down to such a fine art that there was no need to worry. John, my brother, had emerged unscathed from an angioplasty, which is when they shove a tube, with a tiny deflated balloon on the end, up a main artery from your groin to your heart. When it reaches the place in the artery which is partially blocked, the balloon is blown up and pushed through removing all the gubbins that is causing the blockage. I did as I was told and went straight to bed and slept pretty well. Inevitably, Bitten's birthday got off to a less than celebratory start the next morning.

I waited for the telephone and, being impatient, eventually rang Trevor myself at twenty past nine. He told me that he had arranged a room at the Harley Street Clinic – thank goodness for medical insurance – and I was to be in the care of a heart specialist, a cardiologist, called John Muir whom I would meet later that afternoon. Meanwhile I had to get myself there as soon as I could and with as little effort as possible. Bitten nobly left her office and came back to drive me. I do remember wondering as I locked the front door of the house what sort of condition I would be in when I next walked through it.

Over the following few days I was to have plenty of such thoughts, although they were not prompted by pain as much as by a growing realisation that something rather nasty was going to happen uncomfortably soon. There were some bad moments when I wondered if I was going to survive but, thank goodness, they did not come too often, and I found that I was quite good at shutting them out of my mind. It was alright in the daytime when there was plenty to distract you, but at night, when I tend to get almost everything, from my overdraft downwards, wrong, it was harder. It was no good just turning over and hoping such thoughts would go away. I had to turn on the light and then pick up whichever P. G. Wodehouse I had on the go. As always, he provided the perfect remedy. A book like *A Pelican at Blandings* would raise a smile even in a condemned cell.

In the car, I concentrated on directing Bitten to Weymouth Street. My wife invariably takes on the parking meter brigade and left the car outside the front door on goodness knows how many yellow lines. We did at least leave a note on the windscreen, not that they ever seem to do much good. I strode up the steps into the entrance hall and it felt a little like going to school for the first time. Once I had left my name at the reception desk, Bitten and I sat nervously and rather obviously in a couple of upright chairs and waited while trying to make jolly conversation, without significant success. There was a constant stream of people going in and out and a good proportion were obviously from the Middle East. There was a bustle in the air but it was not an altogether jolly bustle.

After a time, a good-looking foreign lady emerged from a

door behind the reception desk and, with a not very encouraging smile, asked me to go with her into her office. I sat across from her desk and she asked me all the *pro forma* questions. 'Nationality?'

'English.' She gave me a quick look and I think wrote 'British'.

'Date of birth?'

'Much too long ago.' Another look, this time accompanied by a frowning question mark.

'Sorry. 23 September, 1939.'

'Next of kin?'

'My wife.'

Another look. 'Her name?'

'Mrs Blofeld.' Even then she paused slightly before she wrote. I fear she thought I was being difficult. After one or two more less penetrative questions, she slid a form across for me to sign. At the top in block capitals my name was spelt as 'Mr H. Blofield'. I made the gentle suggestion that we should start off on the right foot and told her she had put in one too many 'i's into my name. She took it back, clearly puzzled, studied it minutely and then filled in another form before pushing it back to me across the desk. The bold pronouncement at the top told me that I had now become 'Mr H. Blowfeld'. One too many 'w's this time and back it went again. Eventually we got it right and by the time I left her office, I was in much better spirits.

Bitten and I had a laugh about it all and she bravely did her best to cheer me up. But although it may sound surprising, I was in really rather good order. I think it is much worse for the other halves who have simply to hang around, see you tucked up in bed and listen to the doctors who do not always purvey the cosiest of news. Then, more words of good cheer, a last drink maybe, fond farewells with no one knowing what the future holds, a renegotiation of the lift and a shuffle down the steps to the car and an agonising drive into an eternity of waiting when every possible scenario, particularly the worst ones, flow endlessly through the mind. But Bitten never flickered for an instant. On these occasions, she is an unfailing optimist and she was still sure now that I would be back at home before the day was out. We had planned to go to the new Abba musical that evening and had plans for a super dinner afterwards. I am afraid I was not so confident. I could remember that awful tightness across my chest in the King's Road and I knew this wasn't going to be an outpatient job. I just wished we could get on with it.

All these sort of things were going through my mind as we were sitting there, when an immensely senior looking chap with red epaulettes on his white uniform arrived with a beaming smile and told me in a foreign accent that I had been allotted a room in the old part of the building. He added that it was extremely small but that within the hour he was confident that they would be able to move me to something a trifle bigger just round the corner. At least it was progress of a sort. With the slow assistance of one of those long narrow lifts built to accommodate people on trolleys on their ways to and from the operating theatres, we moved gradually towards the third floor. It was a tiresome lift which spoke to you at every available opportunity, telling you the floor you were leaving and the floor you were about to arrive at and I half expected my batting average to follow. I was mildly surprised it did not wish the occupants good luck as well. It had clearly taken a correspondence course from the lifts at Harrods, but it was still in a different class from that apology for a lift which takes you up to the press box at the Oval and which we come across later. The only surprise was that the lady spoke exclusively in English when it seemed to me that about ninety per cent of those who used the lift were from foreign parts.

The third floor was a veritable rabbit warren and I later

14

discovered the Clinic was a compilation of three or four small houses. In Formula One terms, it was the Monaco Grand Prix through the narrow streets of the Principality rather than the long, wide, scorching straights of, say, Hockenheim. It was uncommonly difficult to overtake in the corridors of the Harley Street Clinic. The only good thing was that the wheelchairs and trolleys had locks that made those on a London taxi look like the answer to question one. Eventually I was pushed triumphantly into a room that made the Black Hole of Calcutta seem rather a desirable spot. I must have sat there with Bitten for about an hour before news arrived of an immediate upgrade, although I think 'upgrade' was perhaps too powerful a word for what actually happened. My next room was certainly bigger but as impressively Spartan. It was also in the old part of the Clinic, which the builders were itching to get their hands on.

I didn't have to get undressed, grateful for the chance to put off for a little bit longer the moment when I would have to reveal that I didn't have any pyjamas. I haven't bothered with them for longer than I can remember although I have vague recollections of a pair in a drawer somewhere in Norfolk, by now, I should think, well and truly corrupted by moth and dust. It also made me think of the countless occasions people had said to me, 'You simply must have one pair of pyjamas in case you ever have to go to hospital.' I kept my fingers crossed that the resources of the Harley Street Clinic might run to a spare pair or two.

It was now that the medics who were going to cope with me began to make an appearance and I felt I was getting a little bit closer to the action. The first to arrive was John Muir, a cardiologist, which to the layman like me is a heart expert who discovers and analyses the problems but who is not a surgeon. John Muir, who is from head to toe one of the most dapper of men and unfailingly charming too, was, I think, my doctor Trevor Hudson's initial contact and was responsible for my berth at the Harley Street Clinic. When I had arrived in my room, I had at once been given an electrocardiograph (ECG) to see what my heart was up to. They attach seven or eight nodules to the top half of your body and sometimes to your wrists and ankles, and miraculously when they turn it on all sorts of squiggles appear on a piece of graph paper on a neighbouring machine and the experts know exactly what is happening. John Muir seemed rather pleased with this first one. Then he asked me to talk him through what had happened in the King's Road the previous afternoon before telling me that I was undoubtedly suffering from angina and that the next morning he would do an angiogram which would reveal all. After that, they would be in a position to decide what to do with me.

Up until now, I had not been in the least scared at what lay ahead but I was definitely squeamish about the angiogram. The mechanics were all too simple. They slip a fine tube into the artery in your groin and feed it up to your heart and when it is in position they release dye. The result is photographed and from this they can see if any arteries are blocked. Miraculously, you don't feel a thing. It all happens in a makeshift television studio and the patient is able to see exactly what is going on. For my part, I kept wishing they could do it without me actually having to watch what was happening. The thought of this made me feel distinctly uneasy and I was grateful for the sleeping pills I was given that night. During the evening, they had been taking frequent ECGs and before turning in, I was fixed up to a more or less permanent form of ECG machine so that the nurses, by looking at a television monitor in their station, could keep an eye on the excesses of my heart through the night. In all medical establishments life seems to begin inordinately early in the morning. At this stage of my internment, the breakfast menu was still new and moderately exciting, not that bananas and plain yoghurt is anything to go overboard about. My tomato soup and pasta had not been too bad the night before but because of my impending angiogram, the breakfast menu was now whipped away from in front of my eyes at the very last moment. There was still plenty of activity and the nurses wasted no time in collecting some more ECGs. John Muir then appeared smiling benevolently in his usual way, but I could still sense that he was in every way rolling up his sleeves for action. I gathered later, long after the operation, that by now my ECGs were beginning to show definite signs of an approaching heart attack, although John Muir did say to me later, that in his opinion, he didn't think it would have killed me. Which was, I suppose, something to be grateful for.

Eventually, the dreaded moment arrived and I was shifted with admirable dexterity and the minimum of discomfort from my bed onto a trolley. I was then pushed and steered to the appropriate venue by an assorted company of attendants who were mostly dressed as if they were about to audition for the part of Banquo's Ghost. John Muir was now wearing a bright blue two-piece outfit with a white V round the neck, which suggested that he had been awarded his first eleven colours, which was, of course, nothing less than I had expected. While I lay on my back, he sat behind a rather dark and almost opaque sheet of glass or Perspex through which I could see him but not what he was doing, and it precluded conversation. He stood up and gave me a brief résumé of what was to follow warning me that it would start with a slight prick in the groin which was the local anaesthetic and might sting. I tried to be frightfully brave about it all but I was not enjoying myself one little bit. But the prick was minimal and there was no sting at all, so at this stage I felt I was ahead of the game. There was a pause for the local to take effect and then there was furious activity on the south side of the opaque screen. I couldn't see any of what was going on but there was never the slightest pain. I could sense from John's movements that he was feeding something into my groin, which must have been the tube on its way up to my heart. It was a strange sensation because I kept thinking that I should be feeling some pain. It was then that I glanced to my left and saw on the television monitor this thin black snake making excellent progress on its way up my body. Then, suddenly, cameras attached to the ceiling on rails began to move backwards and forwards with considerable energy. When I looked back at the monitor, what looked like a puff of black smoke came belching forth from the mouth of the tube and the cameras above me were working like mad as they scooted this way and that across the ceiling.

The first time all this happened, I watched surreptitiously out of the corner of my left eye, not at all sure that it was the wisest thing to do. The process was repeated a number of times and, to my alarm, I began to find it compelling viewing. It was extraordinary that I could feel nothing and yet here I was, fully conscious, watching a tube being pushed through an artery to my heart where it seemed to be behaving as if it was in the pay of MI6. Then it was all over. The cameras went back to their original positions, the monitors were turned off and John Muir reeled me in at a speed which suggested he had caught nothing more impressive than the wretched little tuna which the Commander, Arshed Gilani, had reeled in with considerable histrionics on the Great Barrier Reef the previous January. We shall meet the Commander later on and catch up with his angling achievements in Chapter Eight. I was then wheeled back to my cell while John Muir told me that he would have to go off and look at the pictorial evidence. I could hardly believe that it had all happened so easily. There was, nonetheless, a nagging feeling at the back of my mind that we were coming ever closer to the crunch, but any slight fear that I had was still very much secondary to the comforting knowledge that I was in the hands of real experts. They did this sort of thing for a living on a daily basis and they would surely have been as concerned as I was about their success record. By now, I had persuaded myself that the worst I was in for was an angioplasty. That, too, was a computer game in that you were fully conscious throughout and could follow every detail on the screen. If you wanted to.

I lay in bed with these thoughts going through my mind until a rather pensive John Muir, in another of his immaculate suits, came in brandishing a handful of papers that constituted the photographic evidence. I detected a certain solemnity in his voice as he spoke. He showed me the pictures and tried to explain them. The main arteries to my heart were in fine fettle. The problems lay elsewhere and one artery, which seemed to me hardly smaller than its bigger brothers, was completely blocked with a no-entry sign in position. In addition there were two other smaller ones which were about sixty to seventy per cent bunged up. There were three possible options. The first was to do nothing in the hope that it would be a long time before I was again attacked by angina. From the way I lived my life, this was about the odds that Shadrach, Meshach and Abednego may have felt they faced when they had a good look at the roaring fiery furnace. This was not John Muir's favoured option either, I am glad to say.

The second was an angioplasty, but he made it clear that I would have to have another in nine months at the latest, which meant only the most temporary of reprieves. This left bypass surgery which, if successful, would guarantee me at least fifteen years before it would have to be done again. As far as I was concerned, there was never the slightest doubt. I could no more have lived life with the permanent threat hanging over my shoulder of what amounted really to sudden death, than I could have set off with a cheery whistle to walk unaided through a minefield. My mind was made up before Muir left the room saying that he would soon be back with Christopher Lincoln, the surgeon, who would perform this life-saving operation at eight o'clock the following morning. Lincoln is reckoned to be just about the best in the business at this particular operation. Looking back on that moment, I don't think I was particularly frightened because I had already come to terms with the fact that there was only one viable alternative. In fact, I think I was pretty relieved that we now all knew exactly where we were. The only moment I did not particularly enjoy came at the end of the meeting with Lincoln and Muir when Lincoln unscrewed his black pen, wrote something briefly on a printed sheet of paper and handed it to me telling me that I had to sign. Shortly before, he had said in a slightly matter-of-fact sort of way that only one to two per cent of patients died. I think, to be fair, he called it the 'failure rate', but just for a moment or two it concentrated the mind pretty sharply. The paper was the usual disclaimer in case things went wrong. I started to read, but thought I would feel better if I took it for granted and scribbled my signature. I fear the pen may have shaken a trifle.

Mr Lincoln came across as austere, down-to-earth and practical. He said what he had to say and did not linger. He never did. Later, when I was recovering, a visit from him sometimes seemed to last barely a minute as he did a half circuit of my room, asked two questions, fired the attendant nurse a couple of instructions and was off down the corridor. My main medical trio made an amusing comparison. Christopher Lincoln was six foot tall, ramrod straight, without an ounce of spare flesh, and had steely white hair which went back in waves and glasses thinly rimmed in silver. He had obviously once had a penchant for those colourful striped shirts with attached white collars which were worn so much in the seventies, and which he still put on from time to time. I could see him playing the straight man to David Niven in one of those hysterically funny war films set in the Greek Islands. Alternatively he would have been an ideal rather austere junior officer to Alec Guinness in *The Bridge On The River Kwai*. He would have whistled 'Colonel Bogey' with *brio* and built the bridge with dedication and, given the chance, would have taught the Japs a thing or two of his own.

My abiding impression of John Muir was of his ever impressive displays of the latest Savile Row had to offer, an unquenchable supply of idiosyncratic tie-pins and a splendid and slightly rotund sense of humour. A glance at his feet always revealed his shoes so well polished as to suggest that he had a permanent batman tucked away in his consulting rooms just off Harley Street. He is not a tall man and it would never have surprised me if a cane had suddenly appeared in his hand accompanied by a top hat or a boater and he had set off into a pretty lively song and dance routine. He always walked with a spring in his step. Then there was my own doctor, the avuncular Trevor Hudson who had orchestrated all that was now in front of me without any fuss or bother. He was never anywhere but just off-stage right, but still holding the strings. With more than a look of Gordon Jackson about him (what a happy coincidence that Jackson should have played Hudson, the butler, in *Upstairs Downstairs*), Trevor is everyone's idea of the perfect family doctor, which is exactly what he is. You could never wish to meet a kinder, more friendly and sympathetic human being, nor one who was shrewder or more accurate in his diagnoses with a perfect bedside manner to boot. I had telephoned Trevor on the Tuesday evening at half past seven and by half past nine the next day the team had been assembled.

We had one of those bedside gatherings which are probably best avoided in the rather more civilised room to which I had now been moved in the modernised wing of the Clinic.

Everyone including Bitten, my sister Anthea, a retired doctor, my daughter Suki and Trevor stayed with a glass in their hands to cheer me up and try and gild and burnish my immediate future. I had a glass in my hand, too, make no mistake. We talked in clichés and, to throw in another, the die had been cast. All those present assured me how easy it was going to be, that I would hardly feel anything and would be jumping around in no time at all and back home the day after that. Mmmm. One by one they left. Bitten stayed to the end and we had a happy conversation. As she went out of the door, we both said, 'See you tomorrow,' and meant it, although she later told me she had a horrid premonition that something would go wrong. We had all whistled like mad to keep our collective courage somewhere above zero.

I dipped into P. G. Wodehouse's *Life of the Bodkins* and managed to raise one or two pretty resonant smiles. I had something to eat for dinner, a glass of wine and when the time came, a positive medley of pills of all shapes and sizes and for every possible purpose. I had another full ECG before being fixed up to the battery-operated machine that provided the assembled company of nurses with their midnight watching on the monitor in their room. I was certainly nervous but no more so than when I played cricket at school or at Cambridge and was opening the batting the next morning. In fact, I don't think I was even that nervous, because I most definitely did not regard Christopher Lincoln, my surgeon, in anything like the same bracket as Fred Trueman or Brian Statham back in 1958 or 1959. I can hear the horror in Fred's voice if he ever found out that I had made such a comparison. It would have promised a lively chat on *Test Match Special*. In no time at all, it was six o'clock in the morning and a nurse appeared with two and a half white pills and a tiny amount of water with which to swallow them – I had not been allowed to eat or drink anything after midnight. She was back again an hour later, this time with an injection and after that I can remember nothing. My anaesthetist later asked me if I remembered being taken down to the theatre because she told me that we had had quite an energetic conversation before she had delivered the knock-out punch.

From now on, for the next couple of days, there are any number of sides to the story. What is clear is that it all went wrong, not through anyone's fault, but because nature played its hand and for once got its timing badly wrong. From what I gleaned much later a number of thousand-to-one chances all came home at the same time. Even now I do not fully understand what happened because when I eventually came out of it all, I was given little nuggets of information by all and sundry and it was rather like trying to piece together a recalcitrant and incomplete jigsaw puzzle. However they phrased it or, indeed, tried to skirt round it, I think it is quite clear that I came uncomfortably close to putting my cue in the rack for the last time. But even now none of the medical fraternity has given me a blow by blow account of the precise sequence of events during those two days. Although it is all long past and I am alive and kicking, I still don't think I want to know all the gory details.

As far as I have gathered, the gist of it is that when Christopher Lincoln was most neatly getting on with his needlework in what in the end amounted only to a double-bypass, my heart elected to go into heart attack mode. This apparently means that it battens down the hatches like mad, grows smaller and is nothing like so productive. While the operation was going on, I was on a heart and lung machine and so there was no problem. When it had finished and they tried to return me to my own heart they found that it wasn't in the mood to play ball. Having gone into heart attack mode, it was still waiting for the attack. But because the blocked arteries had now been bypassed and there was no problem, the attack itself never materialised. The trouble was that in these circumstances there was no signal to explain to the heart that it could relax and resume normal service. As a result it began to scratch its head like nobody's business and kept scratching while rigidly maintaining battle formation. I suppose it may have thought that someone was pulling its leg but sadly my heart does not appear to have much of a sense of humour and it continued to stamp its foot, heavily in protest.

The rest of the Friday was fraught with interest. The operation had begun at eight o'clock in the morning and is usually over in two and a half to three hours. During the operation the top half of one's body is kept at a pretty low temperature and when Bitten arrived in the middle of the afternoon, the top half of my body was convulsing violently. Her instinct told her something was wrong although they tried to assure her it was not unusual.

I would not come round from the anaesthetic. Bitten left me that evening in Intensive Care soon after nine not at all happy with the way things were going, after Trevor Hudson had told her they would not now try to bring me round until the next morning. At around half past three the next morning, the telephone at home rang and it was a nurse from Intensive Care telling Bitten to come round to the Clinic as quick as she could as things were not looking good. They had been forced to open me up again because my heart simply would not take over from the machine and, I believe, had packed up altogether. At the same time my other bodily functions were no longer in mid-season form either. They had a look at my heart in case there was an obstructive clot but found none and eventually had to close me up in a hurry as the signs grew worse.

After that dreaded telephone call, Bitten said that she could not remember how she had got dressed or managed to drive herself to Weymouth Street, and had prayed most of the way for me to be kept alive. The porter had met her and told her that Lincoln wanted to see her before she saw me. She was sure this was so that he could tell her I had died. But she went straight through to Intensive Care and I was still alive, just. They had not wanted her to see me as they had operated on me where I was rather than moving me to the theatre and I not yet been cleaned up. Then she saw Lincoln who had realised the urgent need to be there himself for most of the night. He told her that my condition was extremely grave. She went back and looked at me and was horrified when she saw that my blood pressure was down to 59 over 43. Bitten told me later that I had opened my eyes and she had seen a look of abject fear and horror in my face. She had immediately thought back to the accident I had had at Eton forty-two years before when I had ridden a bicycle into a bus with disastrous consequences. She said that she had thought my look then was as if my subconscious was reliving that moment which, thankfully, I have never been able to remember.

Bitten was not going to let me go without a fight. She told the nurses they had to save me. She called the doctors, Lincoln and Muir, to her and told them about me and the sort of person they were dealing with. I wish I could have overheard that one. The medics went into a huddle and John Muir told me later that he had thought I was short of liquid and that they had decided to inject me with something. My kidneys, which were showing distinct signs of calling it a day, suddenly began to show a new interest in life. At last I began to pee, if not like a horse, at least with promise. Much later I heard that my lungs had collapsed as well, but it appears that the injection had provided them with a new inspiration and very gradually their state began to improve.

At this stage my blood pressure was still only 59 over 43

which, in real terms, is about the single-figure level of much of England's recent batting. In what must have been a perfectly ghastly time for everyone as they waited and hoped and feared, it slowly limped up to 60. This hardly rated a standing ovation but everyone breathed a fraction more easily. After what seemed another age, it crept up to 61 and then on and upwards to 62 and beyond. I had been poised to give the bucket the most imperial kick but then a substantial helping hand had given me a significant push in the right direction.

Suki, who had been alerted by Bitten, drove up in the early hours from Hampshire and was there at breakfast time, just after the arrival of my sister, Anthea, and brother-in-law, Anthony Salmon, who is a retired parson. Anthony gave me the last rites and anointed me with holy oil, a little too liberally by all accounts, and said some prayers over my inert body. While Anthony successfully alerted The Almighty to my parlous condition, I would like to think that it was the love, the prayers and the devotion and determination of Bitten that I should live, that made the difference. No one could have had a much worse two days and only her vibrantly strong character, together with her faith and great love, could have enabled her to get through it.

The worst moment had been her conversation with Lincoln in the middle of the night when he told her the severity of the situation and perhaps did not coat this particular pill with as much sugar as he might have done. But then heart surgeons are hugely accomplished and it is their prime function to carry out complex and intricate operations as successfully as they can and to keep their patients alive. If they succeed in that why should they be bothered by the need for a fulsome bedside manner? Theirs is a more demanding job than most and, of course, like everyone else in life, they are going to have their failures. Christopher Lincoln was operating at eight o'clock most mornings often doing bypass surgery on tiny babies weighing no more than a few pounds. Why should he or his colleagues allow themselves to become involved in the emotional side of it all? They have enough on their hands without that. In the situation as it was then, he will probably have been at a complete loss to know why my heart would not take over again. The problem will have been all-consuming and I cannot believe, particularly as I grew to like him very much in the weeks afterwards, that he would have been in any way deliberately uncaring. Four o'clock in the morning with death but a millimetre away is a funny old time for everyone and a great deal must be seen in that perspective. The bottom line was that he got it right in the nick of time. A surgeon dealing with such fundamentals must also be fully entitled to consider that any emotional involvement, however slight, would only make his job more difficult. It is an eternal dichotomy which will never be satisfactorily resolved and who is to say what is wrong and what is right? When I was recovering in hospital, I was told about a well-known heart transplant surgeon who never sees his patients except when he operates on them.

Of course, I knew nothing about the events of that awful night. But I do distinctly remember that more than once on the Saturday, after the second operation when, presumably, I was beginning to pick up a fraction, a sort of a dark grey window appeared in my world of blackness. For a brief moment, I obviously came round. I was unable to speak for, as I later discovered, I was on a ventilator and there was a huge tube going down my throat to my larynx and beyond. I could not open my eyes either, which put me at something of a disadvantage. I suppose the greyness came from whatever light was able to penetrate my closed eyelids. I heard Bitten's voice very clearly asking me how I was and then telling me that Rex was there. Even in my comatose state, I realised she was referring to Rex Neame, who had most nobly driven all the way up from Norfolk. Even then I was not being allowed to forget that wretched hat-trick of Rex's in the 1955 Eton–Harrow match at Lord's when I was his third victim. I most certainly wasn't going to let the memory of that kill me now. In fact, his arrival may have been the turning point. Bitten then asked me if I was in pain and I nodded and someone who must have been a nurse asked me where it hurt and I brought my hand up to my chest. Almost at once, this was followed by a delicious, soothing, all-absorbing and enormously comforting blackness, which must have been caused by the morphine that was then injected. I sort of remember the feeling of lying back against a fabulously soft and luscious velvet cushion and drifting into oblivion.

There were two or three more similar windows as the Saturday wore on. I heard Bitten's voice each time and I can remember her once telling me that her sister Wiveca was another arrival having flown in that morning from Sweden. Hardly surprisingly, Bitten sounded frantic and I wanted to tell her not to worry and that I was on the mend but not to rush me and to let it happen in my own time. My mind was fuddled and my way of communicating this was to use my hands to push her away, which in her situation was the very last thing she wanted to see. It was also the last impression I wanted to create for even in my parlous condition I knew how much I owed to her. Once, I made a sign showing that I wanted to write and a pen was put in my hand and I was shown where to write but was unable to control my hands. It was unbelievably and agonisingly frustrating. I wanted to communicate so much. I was conscious and yet totally unable to get anything across. Then, there was always the final question: 'Is it hurting?' Then came my nod, followed by 'Where?' I pointed and after that the morphine returned me to oblivion. Later I was asked if I had at any stage been aware of my soul trying to part company from my body as has been well documented by some people who have come perilously close to dying. I have no recollection of this happening to me. There was just the delicious all-consuming blackness as I sank back into unconsciousness after each of the brief windows. Maybe the morphine prevented any such recollections.

I woke up properly soon after lunch on the Sunday and although I was extremely sore and obviously confused, my mind was clearing and I could see and recognise those around me. John Muir told me what a dreadful time Bitten had been through. Although I was well aware of what was going on around me, I was still in a heavily drugged state and was kept in the large Intensive Care recovery room. I remember seeing all the washed and shining steel of hospital machinery around me and thinking it was a bit like the cutting-up room in a butcher's shop.

The next day I was moved from this recovery room into the Intensive Care ward and I suppose at that point I became a normal recovery patient. From then on it all seemed to move fast. After a couple of days in Intensive Care being weaned off morphine, I was taken to the third floor. By now my chest hurt like hell whenever I moved for they had opened my sternum up twice in double quick time. The nurses everywhere were unbelievable in their loving care and concern and there was, nothing, however sordid, they did without a smile and nothing was too much trouble either. Gradually, I pieced bits of the story together and realised how lucky I was to be alive. I was soon well enough to complain about the food and my main trouble was that I had to sleep on my back whereas normally I sleep on my tummy. Even with a veritable army of sleeping pills, fitful sleep was the best I ever managed and with pain killers coming along only every four hours, the last hour and a half could often seem to take an unconscionable time in passing.

*　　　*　　　*

There was one other outside attempt on my life. While all this had been happening, it had been announced that the United Cricket Board of South Africa, for whom read Ali Bacher, had sold the radio rights for England's series in South Africa in 1999/2000 to Rupert Murdoch's Talk Radio. This is presided over by a gentleman who edited Murdoch's *Sun* newspaper for a number of years, Kelvin MacKenzie. If what one reads is true, they had paid £150,000 for the privilege. Mr Bacher, a veritable angel as far as cricket's considerable part in the breaking down of apartheid was concerned, but who, like all human angels, needs to be kept an eye on, had not even let BBC's *Test Match Special* make an offer for the rights. Mr MacKenzie's commentary team will be led by Geoffrey Boycott and the sixty-four thousand dollar question is: Is this the end of *TMS*? Will the financial weight of commercial broadcasting yet again defeat the BBC? Or will the charm, the wit, the humour, the camaraderie and the general *joie de vivre* of *TMS* bury Talk Radio under an enormous pyramid of chocolate cakes from which it will never emerge? We shall see. But in spite of this atomic explosion, I still managed to cling on to life. I was also given a copy of *Stick It Up Your Punter,* the uncut story of the *Sun* newspaper which threw some light on Mr MacKenzie and considerably helped my immediate recovery. CMJ and Aggers had both been approached by MacKenzie and asked to join Talk Radio in South Africa and both had kicked him into touch. My account of Geoffrey Boycott's stimulating behaviour in foreign parts in *Cakes and Bails* has meant that I will not be given the chance to record the masterful and idiosyncratic way in which he will undoubtedly marshal his troops in South Africa. One cannot even be ill in peace.

Each day I felt stronger and was soon hoping for an early release, but my wound now began to leak increasingly and it became clear that it had become infected. Instead of an early release, John Muir first told me that I would have to spend the bank holiday weekend in the Clinic and when that was over, he told me I was to have another operation so that Lincoln could thoroughly clean the wound and take away any infection. What I was never told by the medics was that when they had been forced to close me up in a hurry during my second operation, they had not had time to tighten the screws which were holding my sternum together. This accounted for the uncomfortable overlapping, clicking feeling I got in my chest whenever I moved at all extravagantly. The upshot was that I had to have another lengthy operation. I was angry because I felt that I was not being told the real reason for this third operation and it was only after I had had it that I learned the whole truth. John, my brother, came to see me and had heard all about new screws having to be put into my sternum when he had rung up the nurses to hear how I was. It made me cross that none of those in charge had been prepared to tell me about it. I am sure it is bad for some people to know everything but surely that should depend on the type of person lying in the bed. It smacked to me of medical arrogance and I didn't like it. I'm afraid my charming anaesthetist who had come to see me the afternoon before this third operation, got a real mouthful from me about it all. I was glad the next day when they wheeled me down to the theatre that I was conscious and was able to apologise before she gave me yet another knock-out injection – and, happily, the last.

Nevertheless I had to keep my best efforts for when I came round in the recovery room after this third operation. I was not allowed the dosage of morphine I had had the first couple of times and the pain in my chest was agony. By all accounts I let them have my entire vocabulary and at full throttle.

Thank goodness, there were no more infections and I was allowed out six days after this last operation. I spent a week in London and visited Christopher Lincoln twice at the Brompton Hospital so that he could remove the stitches from my chest wound, and John Muir once for an ECG. Then I went down to Norfolk where I had to learn to do nothing and to avoid all stress. A short walk each day, a lie-down after lunch, early bed, not too many visitors and not for too long either – this was the most tiring thing of all – and no lifting or mowing of the lawn, which was a great bit of luck. I was allowed to continue with this book as Lincoln told me that brainwork was a good thing. Getting up in the morning, shaving and having a bath exhausted me and so did even a ten minute walk. During the operations my shoulders had been pinned almost to the point that my shoulder blades were touching and about six weeks after the first operation, the deep bruising came out and for a week or more my shoulders were extremely painful. You quickly learn that there is almost nothing you do that does not involve the shoulders. The main reason that watching the World Cup on television was good for me was that it was just about the only thing that did not. Even so, in two months, believe it or not, I was more or less back on the map although I am not sure my love for limited overs cricket had been significantly boosted.

There was one extraordinary difference to my life. Many times each day, no matter what I was doing, I was pulled up sharp by the realisation that I had come close to dying and might never have seen or done whatever it was I was looking at or doing at that particular moment. To start with, this made me feel nervous and frightened. It made me wonder where I might have been if I had been dead. I also found myself trying to imagine what would have been going on where I now was if I had not survived. It was decidedly eerie. Would God have been at the end of the tunnel, at the bottom of the blackness, or not? After all that I had experienced, I don't think the fact of dying, of which I have always been extremely frightened, will any longer hold quite the same fear for me.

When the moment comes I am sure it will, in the end, be a relief; more of a welcoming home than a full stop. While I can point to nothing to back this up, there was a feeling of serenity that prevented the belief that I was completely alone and on the road to extinction.

I had been recuperating in Norfolk for almost three weeks when I had another sharp and highly amusing reminder of my own mortality. It had not been one of my better days and I was having a kip when the telephone rang. It was the indomitable Ivo Tennant who is very much 'the man from *The Times*'. We spoke of this and that for a moment or two before I realised he was after something. He was using that slightly treacly voice he reserves for these occasions. We came to it by a circuitous route. He asked me if I knew that Johnny Woodcock, of immortal cricket writing fame, had given up writing the cricketing obituaries for *The Times*. Feeling suitably ashamed that I did not (although the information proved to be less than one hundred per cent accurate), I said I feared this was a piece of hot news the *Eastern Daily Press* had unaccountably tucked away on an inside page.

Ivo went on to say that he had taken on the task and that, although he hoped it would not be for immediate use, he was writing my obituary. Which, as conversation stoppers go, is in a particularly high class. After a lot of thought, I gave him what I considered to be a pretty meaningful 'Oh really'. He told me he wanted to know a few things about me and asked if he could ring up Bitten or my brother. Having only a week or two before saved me from death, I thought that if Bitten had been asked to contribute to my obituary so soon afterwards, she might easily have given Ivo a nasty dose of earache. I couldn't completely overcome the feeling that, for once, Ivo had been deserted by his usual impeccable sense of timing. But at least he had had the tact not to ask me to contribute to my own obituary. I am waiting to hear how he got on with my brother.

While this unfortunate interlude had me off the road for much of the 1999 season in England, cricket continued unabated round the world from September 1998 to September 1999 and I was still in the thick of a fair amount of it. First, at the start of October in 1998, Bitten and I retreated to Portugal for a week's sun but even so cricket refused to leave me alone.

CHAPTER TWO

Freaks, Fixers and Fisticuffs

Fair enough. My computer had to go into the overhead locker, but so too did my Panama hat, which I had hoped to dangle on my knee rather than have it squashed out of shape in the small space available. The air hostess was all charmless, grim-faced and sharp-nosed insistence. She wore her rather ostentatious wedding ring in a manner which suggested that if necessary, it could do back-up duty as a knuckle duster. Her Rosa Klebb-like qualities came to the fore again when, just before take-off, I was ordered in irritatingly school mistressy tones not to read a newspaper. When I queried this instruction I was told, in a voice that had already awarded me something much nastier than the dunce's cap, that in an emergency people have been known to slip on newspapers. It was impossible not to laugh and that wasn't popular either.

We had been airborne for an hour when I asked for a second glass of wine and I fully expected to be told that one was more than enough. I decided that to have asked for a third would have tempted Providence one step too far. When we arrived at Faro in the south of Portugal the atmosphere was still one of armed neutrality. My general wellbeing was not helped at the airport, either. After a prolonged search of all those carrying small blackboards freckled with people's names, and the tapping of a good many others on the shoulder, it transpired that the car I had arranged to meet us had failed to put in an appearance. I then took my place in a queue that led to the kiosk of a well-known car hire firm and, in time, I managed to secure a small, nondescript looking machine. It had obviously done noble service for there was more than a touch of the Ancient Mariner about it.

There followed an hysterical twenty minutes while a Portuguese chap tried, with a sparse knowledge of English, to show me how the car worked. He really couldn't tell his brake from his accelerator, but he had a great sense of humour which happily bestraddled the language barrier. It seemed important that he should make a note of all the many dents so that I would not be held responsible when I returned the car at the end of the week. This took time because whenever a dent was identified we discovered another one and by the time we had finished he had written a not inconsiderable essay in no readily discernible language. He was lucky his customer was not Mr Geoffrey Boycott. The next excitement came when I discovered that the directions I had been given to find the Lisbon road, our initial objective, only very approximately coincided with the actual layout of the roads in front of us. It is at moments like these that wives can be less than forgiving.

Having driven three times around the airport car park, I decided to go straight on rather than turn left and that cracked it. From then on, the directions were brilliant. It was with something of a flourish that I eventually turned left off the main road. Then, after going left at the BP station, first left, first left again, and then a couple of first rights, there it was, the second house on the left. Now, only forty-five minutes after leaving the airport (for the fourth time), we found ourselves outside locked gates, which proclaimed that Orchard House, Vilamoura, our destination, lay within. This presented certain difficulties for we had never met our host and hostess, Bill and Sally Sykes. We had talked on the telephone having been put in touch by a mutual friend, Nick Hammill, who is to the Algarve rather as Lawrence was to Arabia, and cricket was our common denominator. Nick had told me, somewhat guardedly, that Bill was trying to run some sort of a cricket operation in the Algarve.

When you've not met someone who has asked you to stay and you arrive and find the drive gates locked and there is no bell to ring, it leaves you in something of a quandary. I peered through the gates and could see across the lawns a long rambling house and plenty of trees. Delightful, but first we had to gain entry. I rattled the gates a bit and coughed loudly a time or two. Nothing much happened so Bitten suggested I should hoot. I didn't really want to as it sounds so rude. The horn seems to be saying, 'What do you mean by making us wait like this?' Anyway, I did as I was told and gave a couple of what I thought were tentative, almost apologetic hoots. Of course, car horns are beyond the grasp of personality. They either hoot or they don't. The noise sounded deeply offensive but, hard as I looked through the gates, I couldn't see anyone who could have taken offence. After a slight pause, I had another go and that did the trick. An extremely elegant lady, who was looking faintly *après-swim* and who had to be Sally, appeared from the right-hand end of the house and walked towards us across the lawn.

There are some people who you know you are going to get on with even before you have said a word to each other, and

Sally was one of them. She opened the gates and couldn't have been less worried about the hooting. She showed us where to go and when I parked the car as instructed at the left-hand end of the house, I saw a bronzed figure in white shorts striding across some more grass on the other side of the house. He was about ten yards away when he spoke: 'I've just been doing a bit of work on the pitch in case you want a bat,' was the promising start and I knew we were going to get on well with him also. I looked past him and saw what appeared to be an artificial pitch in the middle of an expanse of grass. 'It's only just been laid this week,' he went on, 'and we've got eleven prep school boys coming out the weekend after next.'

This was my introduction to a most unusual, if not unique, cricket adventure in an unlikely part of the world, presided over by one of those splendid eccentrics which probably only a combination of cricket and England is able to produce. As you would imagine from his well lived in face, Bill Sykes has done a lot of things and been to a great many places stretching from Hong Kong to the Turks and Caicos Islands. He had made a good deal of money until, like many others, he had got on the wrong end of the insurance world in London. In the good old days he had used Vilamoura as his jumping off spot. It was now more or less his only spot, where he lived with Sally, the natural beauty of the Algarve, and, quite simply, his cricketing dreams.

Bill has always loved cricket and was himself a considerable batsman in club cricket in Hertfordshire, for whom he was unlucky not to play Minor County cricket. He had made his business life in the East, mainly in Hong Kong and, when the going was good, had been attracted to the Algarve because of its lovely climate, the easy-going life style and its proximity to London. The Algarve would not necessarily be everyone's ideal place to fulfil a cricketing dream, but when Bill had arrived he had managed to buy one of the first villas to be built at Vilamoura. In those early days each house had been set in four or five acres of land, which allows a certain room for manoeuvre.

Bill had this hankering for his own cricket ground and also an urge to try to find and develop young talent. His plan had been to build a small but immaculate cricket ground in front of the house and to bring prep school children out from England for a week at a time where, under the supervision of expert coaches, they would be able to play cricket. Several other sports such as tennis, football, swimming, billiards and snooker are also available at Orchard House. But cricket is his main preoccupation and he wants children who have already shown a particular aptitude for the game to come and develop their skills still further. The weekend after we left, which was half-term in England, eleven boys from Aldwickbury School in Harpenden (the famous lyricist, Tim Rice's old prep school) were coming out for a week. In preparation for their visit I helped Bill make a video about the facilities at Orchard House.

It is, of course, a tiny cricket ground. If anything it is even slightly smaller than the magical Valley of Peace just outside Christchurch in New Zealand, about which you will hear more later in the book. Before Bill got to work the area which is now used for cricket was nothing but rough, barren, stony, desiccated wasteland as most of the surrounding countryside still is. Two acres have been cleared and levelled, new topsoil has been put down, an irrigation system installed and the grass planted. Nearly all the work has been done by Bill himself who, subsequently, would have won a gold medal for weeding if one had been available. He used fairway grass which had only been sown two months before we visited Orchard House early in October. Already, it was in prime condition and it was going to be an ideal ground for fielding because it was flat and smooth.

The pitch was always likely to be the main problem but Bill had sensibly decided to put down an artificial surface rather than take potluck with nature and hope the soil would be kind to him. It is so much better for young cricketers to bat and bowl on a surface which has an even bounce. On a reliable surface, strokes can be learned and played with confidence while bowlers will understand the importance of control. The concrete pitch had been laid just before we arrived and Bill was positively purring over its smoothness. The following week the specially ordered coconut matting was scheduled to appear and then everything would be ready for the pupils of Aldwickbury.

At the far end of the ground to the house, Bill has managed to turn a building which, at first glance, looks as if it might once have been a large-ish sort of potting shed, but which turned out to have been an ancient beekeeper's operational base, into a most imaginative pavilion. He has touched it up and tweaked it here and there and, internally at any rate, it has become a pavilion which would be the pride and joy of any small cricket club. Outwardly, it still looks like an old Portuguese something or other. There are changing rooms and hot showers situated outside the pavilion which Bill is particularly pleased about. The problems of erecting hot showers outside cricket pavilions in the Algarve are obviously not to be sniffed at.

The central feature of the pavilion is the L-shaped Long Room, although it is long only in a Lilleputian sense, and it is there that I have to accuse Bill of being on a massive ego trip. His sporting heroes abound. Pride of place goes to photographs and posters of Graham Gooch who is a friend of Bill's and who has visited Orchard House. But I rather suspect that in Bill's mind Gooch ranks some way below Marilyn Monroe who, as far as we know, did not visit Orchard House but whose vibrant presence in particularly seductive poses also fills the odd square metre or two on the same wall.

Mohammed Ali is well represented and so too is Stanley Matthews, who has just sent a full back the wrong way before twinkling down the right wing. Then there is a photograph of Liverpool F.C. in their glory days with John Barnes well to the fore. Jack Russell, a particular favourite, looks perkily out from under his old washerwoman's hat and there is more besides. Russell is also strongly represented inside the main house as he had been painted by Sally, who is herself a considerable performer at the easel. In his travels, Bill had come across an antique Portuguese billiards table which is ready for action in the L-shaped bit. There is a dart board and, curiously, Bill's is surely the only Long Room in the world to provide a home for an electric organ – hardly an essential piece of cricket equipment. Outside again, but a respectable distance from the hot showers, I am glad to say, he has built a table tennis terrace. While Bitten and I were there, the new scoreboard arrived having been made with meticulous care by John Dale, a friend and neighbour. It was a good, honest, old fashioned scoreboard, some way up the ladder from the old tallywag on which so many of us, of my generation at any rate, cut our teeth, and yet comfortably short of the modern and almost totally indecipherable electronic jumble which now haunts so many contemporary grounds.

Cricket is far from unknown in Portugal. In Val de Lobo, which is on the Faro side of Vilamoura, there is a peculiarly English institution called Barrington's. I wanted to think it was named after Ken Barrington of Surrey and England, who, when manager of the England side, died of a heart attack in the middle of the Test Match in Barbados during the 1980/81 tour of the West Indies at the absurdly young age of fifty. No finer man ever played cricket for England than 'the Colonel', a nickname which stuck after he had appeared at the Christmas fancy dress party on a tour in a colonel's uniform.

Ken was the master of the *mal-à-prop*. When a bowler took a wicket with a ball which had the batsman in two minds as to whether he should play forward or back, Ken would cheerfully pronounce that he had had him 'in two-man's land'. The more places named after Ken Barrington, be they at Lord's, the Oval or Val de Lobo, the better for cricket. As I was later to discover, Barrington's was actually named after Jonah Barrington, who had performed great deeds for England in the squash court.

Barrington's has a few luxury suites, a competent dining room and an efficient bar but is really a multi-sporting oasis. It belongs to that most affable of expatriot Englishmen, Bob Oliphant. On the lower deck, the gyms and the keep-fit workrooms are so splendiferous that you can almost feel the pulled hamstring coming on. In the grounds outside, an Olympic-sized swimming pool, a golf driving range, a hockey field and a full-sized cricket ground battle for supremacy. When Bitten and I were there in the spring of 1997, the entire Middlesex squad of players, led by Mike Gatting, were shaking the winter's cobwebs out of their systems. They were presided over by the amiable and avuncular chairman of cricket, Bob Gale, and policed by the new chairman of the club, Alan Moss, who for long years had opened the bowling for Middlesex and on occasion had performed similar duties for England. Barrington's is the centre of cricket in the Algarve, but Orchard House will, no doubt, keep it on its toes. Of course, further north, the game has flourished and still does, within the port industry.

My computer was an important part of my baggage in Portugal. During the week we were there, momentous decisions of intent about the future structure of first-class cricket in England were being made at the Sheraton Hotel, Heathrow by the First-Class Forum, a body which sounds as if it might have been set up to investigate potential members of Mensa. The Forum is comprised mainly of representatives of the eighteen first-class counties and was now presided over by the chairman, David Morgan, a committee member of Glamorgan. Of course, Lord MacLaurin, the England and Wales Cricket Board (ECB) chairman, will also have made a significant contribution. Ever since MacLaurin had been elected as chairman of the Board after his retirement from the chairmanship of Tesco in 1996, there had been a continuing and vociferous debate about the form that county cricket should now take and he was the leading voice in favour of change.

There were those who had dug in their heels loudly proclaiming that what had been good enough for more than a hundred years, and had seen England win the odd Test Match, was good enough still. The fact that in the contemporary world it was palpably not good enough and that just about all the other countries had leapfrogged past England as they had turned professional themselves, had miraculously eluded them. This was the viewpoint generally taken by the older generation who are, perhaps understandably, not known for their eagerness to embrace change, and also those more anxious not to offend venerable opinions than to face up to the reality of the present day. In *Cakes and Bails*, I called them the old farts and I shall continue to do so.

The First-Class Forum was holed up in the Heathrow Sheraton for a couple of days. Each morning the cuttings from the various newspapers were faxed to me at Orchard House so that the avid readers of my website, blowers.co.uk, could be kept up to date. Sadly, I found that I was unable to send my pieces from Portugal because my computer had not been given the appropriate dialling code. After a number of highly fraught telephone calls, I was able to make the necessary adjustments, although I fear my interpretation of the deliberations at the Sheraton Hotel were a day or two too late.

The most remarkable thing about this meeting at Heathrow was that all those present apparently recognised the necessity to change the present system of county cricket and a vote to that effect was carried unanimously. In the build up to the meeting, the executives of a number of counties had been making distinctly audible over-my-dead-body sort of noises. One enlightened administrator had gone so far as to forecast 'the father and mother of all arguments'. Either someone had been playing the political game with considerable skill or unknown factors had come into the equation to deliver the vote.

There were rumours that the television contract for the next four years, then being negotiated between the ECB and what was thought to be a combination of BSkyB and the BBC, may have had something to do with it. Suggestions were made that the broadcasters concerned might only promise the Board the hoped for sums of money on the condition that certain changes were made to county cricket in order to try and make it a more competitive nursery for Test cricketers and therefore improve the standard of the England side. I am sure that this approach would have suited the Board, for if the television companies had indulged in a piece of gentle arm twisting, it would have had a bigger impact on those hostile to change than any ECB-inspired argument. Yet, while this may have been talked about as a potential threat, I do not believe the television people actually flexed their muscles in this way.

There was, I am sure, some crafty outmanoeuvring going on. When the delegates arrived at the Sheraton, they were divided up into groups of three to discuss all the possibilities open to county cricket before coming together for a final general discussion. Those who were known to disagree with the need for change (including, apparently, the MCC) and more specifically with the two-tier option for the County Championship which had emerged as the front runner, were put into groups with two other representatives known to favour change. Selective and efficient brainwashing followed, I would like to think.

This was never intended to be a meeting at which decisions were to be made. It was simply a get-together to discuss all the available options and the vote at the end signified the intent to change rather than an attempt to spell out anything more specific. The fact that the vote was unanimous indicated that the ECB had prepared their ground a great deal better than they had the year before, when the participants had voted 12–7 against changing the system of the County Championship. It was also clear evidence that a number of counties had had second thoughts. It really did look as though things were on the move although nothing had, as yet, been set in stone. That would be the job for the Forum the next time they met, in early December.

Hotels at Heathrow assumed an ever increasing importance for the world of cricket as the English autumn turned gradually into winter. Four weeks later, they were back in the news when one became the venue for the struggle following the West Indies players holding their Board to ransom over their first ever full tour to South Africa. But we are getting ahead of ourselves. By the time the First-Class Forum had had its say, Australia were already in action in Pakistan where they had not won a series since Richie Benaud was victorious in 1959. Pakistan cricket was in its usual state of disarray and even the Commander was hard put to disagree with this as he flitted around the world. They have just about the most talented players on earth but an ability to self-destruct that is also second to none.

We met the Commander, otherwise known as Arshed Gilani, in *Cakes and Bails*. He is a former Commander in the

Pakistan Navy who represents TransWorld International (TWI) in his part of the world, and blames me for his involvement with cricket. He is very close to cricketing officialdom all round the world and there is no Test series anywhere which is wholly safe from his attention. He plays a walk-on part in this book until he steals the show amid the tropical delights of Bedarra Island on the Great Barrier Reef, but all that is to come.

Now, Pakistan hit the self-destruct button again. Aamir Sohail is a restless character who has probably found it hard to live with his team mates, as he has openly accused some of them of being involved in match-fixing, allegations strongly denied. This will not have been a short cut to popularity in the dressing room, but nevertheless Sohail had been made captain for the three-Test series against Australia. It was, to say the least, a mildly surprising appointment and it was remarkable that it should have been ratified by the Board of Control. I wonder how the conversation went when the team gathered together under Sohail for pre-match discussions. To give Sohail credit, he had been a most engaging and aggressive opening batsman who had formed a wonderful all left-handed partnership with Saeed Anwar and never for a single moment were they dull. It had not been sensible of the selectors when they had split up this pairing a year or two earlier and this will not have helped Sohail who is rebellious by nature and convinced of his own righteousness. The Commander was once a great fan and it may, I suppose, have been his persuasiveness which convinced Sohail of his own rectitude.

Early in 1998 the Pakistan Board of Control had decided that the repeated allegations of bribery and match-fixing within Pakistan cricket needed to be fully investigated. This resulted in the setting up of a judicial commission in Lahore under the High Court Judge, Justice Malik Mohammad

Qayyum. A formidable list of players, both past and present, were called to give evidence to the commission, and further allegations were made. Salim Malik was the player who appeared to have the most to answer for. Betting in India and Pakistan is illegal, except on racecourses in India, but the illegal betting industry is enormous and organised with spectacular efficiency. Cricket is a particularly suitable game for the attention of both punters and bookies. It was bound to be nothing more than a matter of time before unscrupulous bookies tried to get involved with players and to shade the odds in their own favour.

It had always been seen as a problem peculiar to Subcontinental cricket. But in 1994, after touring Pakistan, three Australian players, Mark Waugh, Shane Warne and Tim May, alleged that Salim Malik, at that time the captain of Pakistan, had offered them considerable bribes to play badly in matches in Pakistan so that the locals would not lose. This story broke some time after the Australians had returned home and the Australian players involved were, by all accounts, most unhappy that it was made public. There was an inquiry into the allegations by the three Australians and Salim Malik was cleared by a judge who seemed to doubt the long range evidence of the Australians who had refused to come to Pakistan for the hearing. But even Imran Khan had spoken out saying that on one occasion in Sharjah he had heard rumours that some of his players were planning to lose a match. Whereupon, with great tactical skill, he let it be known within his side that he was going to bet the total amount of all their match fees and potential prize money on Pakistan who, not surprisingly, won the match.

At around the time Australia were starting their tour of Pakistan in 1998, Justice Qayyum was setting out his stall in Lahore to try and unravel all the allegations which had been reverberating through Pakistan's cricket for an indecently long time. The court room in Lahore became the scene for a soap opera that was to run and run. It provided a good deal of entertainment for those of us watching from afar although the Commander, whose peripatetic existence was based in Karachi, accused me of *lèse-majesté* when I spoke of the huge entertainment value it provided. But he also made a very important point that while it may have looked as if the ungodly were having their way, there was no concrete proof – surely a necessary requirement before anyone could be found guilty.

The nearest to positive proof were the accusations made by the three Australian players that Salim Malik had offered them $US200,000 to play deliberately badly in 1994. The judge was understandably anxious that the Australians should now appear in front of him. A compromise was arrived at whereby Mark Waugh and Mark Taylor would give evidence. Taylor was not personally involved, but was, as the Australian captain at the time, just about the first person to hear about the incident. To make sure his two players were fairly treated, Malcolm Speed, the Chief Executive of the Australian Cricket Board, flew to Pakistan to be with them when they travelled to Lahore to give their evidence. When the judge asked Waugh why he was making these very serious allegations against Salim Malik, Waugh had replied that all three of them had been shocked to know that a cricketer was willing to try and bribe players because they themselves played for the love of their country and not money. It was a remark which, in the light of events to come, was indeed a hostage to fortune. The judge later stressed the importance of Waugh's evidence.

The two Australians had gone to Lahore immediately after their side's victory by an innings and 99 runs in the First Test at Rawalpindi. Initially Pakistan had been held together by a most determined 145 from Saeed Anwar, but a first innings' total of 269 was never likely to be enough. Australia's leg spinner, Stuart MacGill, who was later to play a major role in the Ashes series in Australia, took five wickets in the innings. He was given his chance because Shane Warne was still recovering from the operation to his shoulder. MacGill had acquired the reputation of being something of a bad tempered larrikin, but he could certainly spin the ball as the Pakistanis discovered and the Englishmen were soon to find out. Hundreds from Michael Slater and Steve Waugh, together with healthy contributions from Darren Lehmann and Ian Healy, took Australia to 513. With MacGill taking four more wickets, Pakistan were bowled out a second time for 145.

Mark Taylor's session in the witness box must have done him a power of good for in the Second Test at Peshawar he batted for exactly twelve hours making 334 not out by the close of play on the second day. By this stage Australia were 599/4. Don Bradman had also made 334 against England although he had been dismissed. That innings, at Leeds in 1930, had until now stood alone as the highest score made by an Australian in a Test innings. It is now a matter of history that after a sleepless night and much thought, Taylor decided to declare so that his bowlers could have three full days to try and bowl out Pakistan twice. He made the memorable quote, 'I want to win a series on the Subcontinent, and this is the only way I can be bracketed with Bradman. I have equalled Sir Donald Bradman's record and that is enough for me.' Unhappily for him, the pitch was much too good and centuries by Saeed Anwar and Ijaz Ahmed, batting like a man with a clear conscience, and 97 from Inzamam-ul-Haq, whose favourite party trick seems to be to get out in the nineties, took Pakistan to 580/9 declared. In Australia's meaningless second innings, Taylor was out eight runs short of another hundred and the match was drawn. The Third Test at Karachi was also drawn after Aamir Sohail had made 133, Ijaz Ahmed 120 and Salim Malik a pair of spectacles. I wonder what the judge made of that. So, Australia had won their first series in Pakistan for forty years and returned home confident they would put the Englishmen in their place.

Australia's series in Pakistan had begun with the Greatest Living Yorkshireman back at the microphone for TWI, Mark McCormack's television arm, doing commentary in his usual admirably forthright manner. At the same time, no doubt, he was casting an eye over the room service arrangements in the local five-star hostelries, and tickling them up where they needed it. His absence from the microphone during the Second Test in Peshawar will undoubtedly have dismayed his army of admirers. Sadly for Mark Taylor, he was unable to make his 334 not out under the close scrutiny of the GLY because he was otherwise engaged in a perhaps more meaningful contest in the charming town of Grasse in the south of France. Just up the road from Nice, Grasse is more famous for lavender water and mountain trout than it is for abrasive Yorkshire opening batsmen.

Towards the end of 1997, Geoffrey Boycott had been found guilty by a French court, in his absence – he said he was in South Africa commentating on cricket at the time – of beating up a former girl friend, one Margaret Moore, in a highly exclusive hotel in the neighbourhood. While he vehemently protested his innocence, she had been able to produce photographs which had made her look as if she had come out substantially on the wrong end of fifteen rounds with Mohammed Ali. The GLY had generously claimed that he was saving her from herself after he had refused to agree to marry her and she had begun to throw his clothes out of their bedroom window. It was while he was trying to quieten her down, he claimed, that she had slipped and hit her face on an intolerably vindictive marble floor. One hears that there was even some doubt as to whether the floor was actually marbled or pile-carpeted. At this first hearing he had been fined the equivalent of five thousand pounds and given a three-month suspended prison sentence. While the GLY was full of outrageous indignation at the injustices of the French legal system, not all his employers appeared to be in complete agreement with him. Neither BSkyB nor the BBC had used him as a commentator on television or radio when England were in the West Indies early in 1998. He continued, though, to write his comments in the London *Sun.*

As he had been sentenced *in absentia,* it was his prerogative to demand a retrial which he promptly did. Meanwhile, the BBC did not use him as a commentator at the start of the series against South Africa in England in 1998. But as the summer wore on his lawyers pointed out – most forcibly one would imagine – to the BBC, that having opted for a retrial, his original sentence was null and void and the Great Man was going about his daily lot without a stain on his character. BBC television reinstated him, whether warmly and gratefully or through gritted teeth, it is not known.

The retrial was scheduled for October when the GLY would have been in Pakistan commentating on their Test series with Australia for TransWorld International who clearly take a pretty dim view of French justice or maybe just have a more lenient approach to the whole matter. In order to make sure that he was present in France at the second time of asking, he stood down from the team which covered the Second Test Match in Peshawar and returned to England and then travelled on to France. The GLY was presumably pretty confident that his defence was now watertight. On the eve of the retrial he arrived in France with a formidable phalanx of character witnesses, supporters, a psychiatrist, an expert in photography manipulation, doctors with great knowledge of facial injuries and ladies who had fallen on floors which had, one assumes, been made of marble, and had come up with a fullhouse of bruises without the assistance of human intervention. They were all presided over by that prince of publicists, Max Clifford.

Clifford had originally been approached by Mrs Moore in the hope that he would sell her story for no less than one million pounds, but had subsequently decided to change sides. The team photograph was a real joy. The GLY himself, stood in the middle of the front row with his inimitable Panama hat at a particularly jaunty, if not rakish, angle, but wearing a most uneasy smile. All around him were an assortment of ladies who, at first glance, looked as if they might be the surviving members of his grandfather's harem, while Max Clifford stood at the end of the front row looking not unlike Ron Knee, *Private Eye*'s famous manager of Neasden F.C. The whole troupe were staying nearby at a pretty good hotel and it was reckoned that the GLY's defence, including of course their participation, had cost him in excess of a quarter of a million pounds.

The scene was rounded off by the French judge, a most impeccably dressed lady, probably in her early forties, Dominique Haumant-Daumas. Unfortunately, the GLY became most upset during the hearing as it dragged on into the early hours of the next morning. He was distinctly unhappy that a French court had the temerity to conduct its proceedings in French, which is not one of his better languages. He also had it in for his lady interpreter to whom he complained with vigour that she was not doing her job to the high standard he expected, One wonders, considering his lack of linguistic agility, how he can have worked that out. One wonders too, if it ever occurred to the Great Man what an absurd figure he cut in the whole business and that he was not only making a complete fool of himself but setting himself up as the laughing stock of the year.

Before tripping off into her BMW and driving away into the night, the judge let it be known that she would consider her verdict and make it available in three weeks time. The GLY then returned to Pakistan to comment on the Third Test Match against Australia. The ways of a French court are different from those in England in addition to their unreasonable urge to conduct proceedings in their own language. The GLY came away upset that his character witnesses were not given as much of a hearing as he would have liked, and he was disappointed that his adversary – with whom he stood back-to-back in a pointed manner in court – had not been cross-examined. How different it all might have been if he had bothered to turn up at the first hearing.

The verdict, when it came, will have been disappointing for the GLY. He was found guilty as before and although his fine was nominally the same, current exchange rates meant that it would cost him an extra three hundred pounds. The suspended prison sentence stood. In her seven-page statement, the judge noted his rude interruptions in court and said that she did not consider that he had behaved like the perfect English gentleman that he had been at such pains to try and portray himself as. He was also ordered to pay Mrs Moore symbolic damages of one franc which the GLY will have seen as the final insult. That may be a debt his executors will one day have to settle on his behalf. This time the immediate reaction of the *Sun*, whose morals are all over the place, was to sack Boycott as its columnist, a decision which was received with contempt by its rival the *Mirror*. When, later in the year, the involvement four years ago of Shane Warne, the *Mirror*'s own cricket columnist, with illegal Indian bookmakers came to light, the *Mirror* sacked him on the spot. Oh dear.

Shortly after the retrial, there was a letter in the *Daily Telegraph* suggesting that the lady judge, Dominique Haumant-Daumas, should be elected as the first lady member of the MCC.

CHAPTER THREE

All Change from Lord's to Dhaka

No sooner had the first-class counties voted unanimously for change to the system of county cricket, than the cricket world in the United Kingdom was shaken to the core by the news that BBC television had lost the rights to broadcast the game. The new television contracts for the four years after the 1999 World Cup had been up for grabs and it was generally assumed that BSkyB, who had built their cricketing fame on the one-day game, would not waste the opportunity to get their foot in the Test Match door as well. It seemed likely that they would want to cover some of England's home Test Matches and the BBC would have the rest, presumably including the NatWest Trophy, the senior limited overs competition, which had always been theirs.

The England and Wales Cricket Board, headed by Lord MacLaurin, had succeeded during 1998 in convincing the Heritage Secretary, Chris Smith, that Test Matches in England should be taken off the list of the 'protected' events that had

to be shown on terrestrial television. The more than reasonable argument went that as financial support for cricket was
not forthcoming from the government, then it was hardly a
level playing field if cricket was not allowed to sell its crown
jewels, the home Test Matches, to the highest bidder,
especially now that lucrative tobacco sponsorship was soon
to disappear. The Heritage Secretary had agreed, provided that
the ECB honoured a commitment to make sure that a major
proportion of the home Tests would be seen on a terrestrial
channel.

Negotiations between the ECB, BSkyB and the BBC had
been in progress for a while, but the BBC had dug in its feet
well short of the point of generosity. About three weeks
before the eventual announcement was made, the ECB began
a conversation with Channel Four. In spite of talking enthu-
siastically for a time about the rights for the 1995/96 World
Cup, Channel Four had never before been involved in cricket.
But now they showed a strong, if rather late, interest. The
talks went well and, over the next week or two, promises were
made, agreements signed and the amount of money Channel
Four was prepared to come up with was in excess of the
figure at which the BBC had stuck.

The cricket authorities were badly in need of a new image
for the game and it is easy to see why Channel Four was so
attractive to them. They promised a new approach which
would have a particular appeal to the young and they were as
full of enthusiasm as they were of new ideas. Of course, the
BBC were highly indignant when they heard they had lost out,
but one did not get the impression that those at the top were
especially cricket minded. One wonders if they really gave it
their best shot because one hears that although Channel
Four's bid was bigger than the BBC's, there was not that much
in it. Perhaps the BBC were too arrogant.

BBC television had been covering cricket in England ever

since cameras had first been wheeled out at a cricket ground. This went back for more than forty years and because of the false sense of security that may have given them, they may have felt it was a God-given right that the BBC should always cover England's cricket at home. On the other hand, if you have been doing something for that long, it is difficult to refute the argument that it is time for a change.

Channel Four will do their best to reinvent television coverage of cricket and with Richie Benaud and Mark Nicholas heading their commentary team, they have guaranteed a certain continuity from the past. They have also brought on board Wasim Akram, the Pakistan captain, whose playing days will soon be over, whatever his government's reaction to all that Judge Qayyum comes up with in that courtroom in Lahore. It is a fair bet that BBC television will one day be given the chance to cover cricket again and if they accept, they will find that it has become something very different from the coverage they have now passed on to one of their rivals. In the meantime, I am sure that the signing up of Channel Four will be of great service to the game.

Having won the contract, Channel Four then had to employ a production company to make the pictures. The two who were far in front of the rest were TWI and Sunset and Vine, who now employ arguably the best director of all, Gary Franses. He had worked for TWI before being spirited away by Grand Slam, the production side of Alan Pascoe and Associates for whom he made the pictures of the 1995/96 World Cup in India, Pakistan and Sri Lanka. Franses was the executive producer then and it was widely acknowledged that he had done a brilliant job in extremely difficult circumstances. He is also the most charming and modest of men and I would be amazed if it was not the presence of Franses at Sunset and Vine which persuaded Channel Four to embrace them and not TWI.

The new contracts, which were worth a deafening £103 million to the game over four years, left BSkyB with all the International and domestic one-day cricket except the NatWest Trophy, and one Test Match besides. Channel Four has six of the seven Test Matches that will be played in England every year from 2000, in addition to the NatWest. They promised at an early stage that there will not be commercial breaks at the end of every over, but of course there will be a fair amount of commercial content for that is their life's blood and it won't take us that long to get used to it. Anyway, who would want to bet that by the time the BBC next shows cricket, that organisation will not have opened itself up to the advertisers?

October 1998 was a great month in England for iconoclasts. Colin Ingleby-Mackenzie's last move after being President of the MCC for almost two years, was to ensure that the club would open its doors to lady members. This had always been one of his objectives as President and at the vote taken in October 1998 the committee who had recommended that ladies be admitted to the membership were granted their wishes. The two-thirds majority, which was necessary before such a radical step could be taken, was forthcoming. This was an issue which had cost the club dear as a vote and a special meeting had already been held in the first year of Ingleby-Mackenzie's presidency and although that motion had been carried by a simple majority, it was less than the required two-thirds. There had for some time been rumblings about the political incorrectness of the MCC's men-only position. The illustrious Minister for Sport, Tony Banks, had had something to say about it and, because of it, the MCC had been refused lottery money to help with the cost of redeveloping Lord's.

The first vote had not been handled well, for the issue had not been properly explained to the doubting half of the membership who may have spent much of their lives in fear of the distaff side. For them the chance to escape occasionally to Lord's was a bit like having the opportunity to slip a fast one across the KGB. They were certainly not anxious to be hustled into anything and obviously had nightmares about armies of women descending on the place like so many platoons of militant suffragettes.

While Ingleby-Mackenzie may have to accept some of the blame for the first failure, it was his unflagging enthusiasm which has done so much to make Lord's a friendlier, more welcoming place, and also to ensure that the second vote was not wasted. Of course, some members will have felt, because of the proximity of the two meetings over this same issue, that it was being railroaded through. But the second time round the committee had done their homework and the out-going President had at last erected the monument he wanted to be remembered by. He had now done much to make MCC face the twenty-first century with confidence rather than with a sense of anachronistic suspicion.

The presence of ladies in the Lord's pavilion is unlikely to have quite the resounding impact that Marilyn Monroe had upon Bill Sykes's pavilion at Vilamoura. There is an eighteen-year waiting list for MCC members and although a handful of honoraries have been created, it will be quite a while before the constant ratatat-tat of high-heeled shoes will interfere with the post-prandial slumbers of those gently somnolent misogynists in the warm, afternoon sunshine. In time, I daresay that the presence of the lady members will smarten the rest of us up a peg or two. If ladies had been present, I wonder if those two splendid umpires, Dickie Bird and David Constant, would have been handled so roughly by the then distinctly insomnolent membership at the Centenary Test Match in 1980, when the umpires made the unpopular decision of bringing the players off for bad light. I can only think of one, hardly valid, reason for not admitting members to the MCC and that is that it will render obsolete one of the better Pavilion stories.

Going back most of the seven ages of man, it was been inconceivable that ladies should be allowed within the hallowed portals and those unfortunate disciples of political correctness surely found it difficult to point to a greater preserve of male chauvinist piggery in the country. There was one occasion each year, however, when the combined membership had to grit its collective teeth and make a vow to look the other way and say nothing. The Second Test Match was almost invariably the occasion of the annual Royal Visit to Lord's. After watching some play from the chairs in the Committee Room, the Monarch would meet both teams on the field at the end of a lengthened lunch interval or perhaps some other break would be arranged. One year, the Queen arrived and was watching from the Committee Room when an elderly member, who was unaware of the Royal Visit, came up the steps from the east side of the pavilion. As he walked past the open Committee Room window, he glanced inside and almost tripped up before making his way back to his seat. When he was sitting down. he lent over to his neighbour and said in a most audible voice, 'Good heavens! What's the place coming to? There's a woman in the Committee Room talking to Swanton.' I don't know why poor old Jim always seems to get it in the neck when it comes to these stories, but he might have rather enjoyed this one.

The White Conduit Club turned miraculously into the Marylebone Cricket Club in 1787 and so after a small matter of almost 213 years of all being boys together, the MCC membership will now have to put up with the ladies. At first, though, it will be the slightest of trickles who will all be observing a strict dress code which forbids the naked horror of bare shoulders. So it shouldn't be too bad for a while. The

MCC members can be a curmudgeonly lot. In 1999 as we shall see, the World Cup Final was held at Lord's, a ground which holds only 30,000 on a good day. There are just over 17,500 members of MCC and although there is not the slightest chance that they would all turn up on the same day, a significant proportion would not want to miss such an important game and would somehow have to be accommodated. This would inevitably restrict the number of seats available to the general public. If members had been admitted free, the receipts would not have been as healthy as the organisers would wish.

The number of seats for members had to be limited and the committee, presided over by Colin Ingleby-Mackenzie, did a deal with the ECB, the organising body. Members would be given the chance, on a first-come, first-serve basis, to buy a ticket for the final for £75, as opposed to £100, which was the price for everyone else. In two other games it was £45 as opposed to £60. These were decent concessions and yet even so, there were members who were still discontented enough to gang up together and call for a Special General Meeting in order to complain bitterly that they should have been asked to pay anything at all to go to the Final on their own ground.

MCC is an institution which sometimes invites the ridicule it so often receives, and I write as a member myself. After two Special General Meetings to discuss the admission of women, and now this, the dissenting members will soon be having to cope with a sizeable rise in their annual subscription to pay for these expensive junkets. Of course, their immediate reaction will be to call for another Special General Meeting to complain heartily about the new levels of subscription. Michael Parkinson has a point when he calls the MCC the Marylebone Clodpoles Club.

By the time it came to the second half of October, things were moving along nicely in that courtroom in Lahore. A number of distinguished players were being cross-examined in front of the High Court judge, and they all said that they were certain that match-fixing had been going on for some time. Salim Malik's name was mentioned by almost everyone and not far behind was Wasim Akram. Ijaz Ahmed was also in the frame and at one time or another a great many of the notable players who have represented Pakistan in the nineties had doubts cast upon them.

There was the direct evidence. Javed Miandad, one of the finest batsmen Pakistan has produced, said that Mushtaq Ahmed had warned him that 'the evil of match-fixing in the team is going on' and that once he was also involved. Aamir Sohail, one of the few not to be accused by anyone of taking part, said he had been approached and offered money by an Indian bookmaker in Australia and by a former player, Saleem Pervez, in Colombo. This was not the only accusation made by Sohail. Imran Khan said that fast bowler, Ata-ur-Rehman had told him that he had been paid money by Wasim Akram. Saleem Pervez, himself now the bookmakers' friend, said that most matches played by Pakistan are fixed and that he personally had paid Salim Malik and Mushtaq Ahmed US$100,000 for fixing a game in Sri Lanka. He also said that the team manager, Intikhab Alam, was involved.

The web became even more tangled when the court heard about the game in Colombo in 1994, when Pakistan lost to Australia after being 80/1 and needing only 167 to win. Intikhab Alam, the manager of that side, said that Basit Ali had confessed to match-fixing although Waqar Younis and Salim Malik had denied any involvement. Former captain, Rashid Latif, claimed that before a one-day match in New Zealand, in Christchurch, he had been called to Salim Malik's room and offered ten lakhs of rupees (£12,500) to play badly and he had refused the offer. Javed Burki, a cousin of Imran's and a former Test captain and chairman of the Board, told the court that when he handed over the reins to his successors, he strongly advised them that Salim Malik should never again be picked to play for Pakistan.

The more witnesses that were called, the murkier the story became. Fast bowler Ata-ur-Rehman said that when the Pakistan side returned from New Zealand in 1994, Wasim Akram gave him a hundred thousand rupees (£1,250) and promised him the balance whatever that may have been, if he continued to indulge in match-fixing. Basit Ali said it was nonsense that he had admitted match-fixing to Intikhab. Sarfraz Nawaz, the former fast bowler and one-time Sports Minister of Pakistan, who in a long and chequered career, has never failed to come up looking like the Archangel Gabriel, said that Salim Malik had been paid ten lakhs of rupees (£12,500) to lose a match for the Habib Bank against the National Bank of Pakistan. Sarfraz went on to say that he had written many times to the President and the Prime Minister, the Board of Control and anyone else concerned about match fixing, but he had never heard back from them. Also, he said that Javed Burki had disclosed that he had positive proof about match-fixing. As we have seen, important evidence came from Mark Waugh, the Australian, who told how he had been offered US$200,000 if he and some other Australians agreed to play badly in a one-day match at Rawalpindi in 1994/95.

There was also any amount of circumstantial evidence, which, of course, has to be treated with great care. Aamir Sohail told the court that in the World Cup in Delhi in 1995/96, after continually saying that he would be fit, Wasim Akram had pulled out of the match ten minutes before the start. On another occasion in Sharjah, Sohail had told Akram he would only be fit to play provided that he could bat down the order if Pakistan fielded first. Akram agreed but later insisted on his opening the innings and he was out straightaway. Majid Khan, a former captain and now Chief Executive of the Board, was dismayed that in Sharjah and South Africa, Wasim Akram sent in out-of-form batsmen at the top of the order. When Wasim was asked about this, he made the astonishing reply that he was not aware of who was in-form and who was out-of-form. Imran Khan also pointed a finger at former captain, Asif Iqbal, who, in a series against Pakistan in India in 1979/80, mysteriously declared Pakistan's innings behind India's first innings total.

Intikab Alam was another who was worried about Asif Iqbal. He told the court that Asif had flown from Washington in the US to Colombo after Pakistan had collapsed against Australia losing by eight runs although their target had been only 167 and they had been 80/1. Apparently, Asif's reason for coming to Colombo was that certain bookies had lost forty lakhs of rupees (£50,000) on that result and they wanted to recover their money. This makes it look as if there were warring groups of bookmakers who wanted different results – very difficult to organise.

At a Test Match in South Africa in 1994/95, Salim Malik had won the toss and, to the fury of some of the players, had fielded. After Pakistan had lost the match, Intikhab was rung up and told that seven or eight of his players were involved in match-fixing. Rashid Latif told the court that before the match he had insisted that all the players took an oath on the holy Koran in the name of Allah. Salim Malik went out to toss instead of taking the oath and, after putting South Africa in to bat, offered to take it on his return to the pavilion. Rashid told him it was too late. Both Rashid and Basit Ali retired 'due to the circumstances prevailing in the team' in the middle of the subsequent tour of Zimbabwe.

It was all the most colossal mess-up and it was not helped by the learned judge who took it upon himself to speak at random to the fourth estate, or, at least, within earshot of them. He gave his views as the case went on, saying that things did not look good for Wasim Akram and Salim Malik. He then commented on how important he considered Mark Waugh's evidence as it appeared to be the only clear-cut accusation, presumably because it was backed up by Shane Warne and Tim May, the other two Australians who were involved. Maybe he felt an Australian accusation carried more weight than a Pakistani one, for it seems to me that although several of the Pakistani cricketers told tales under cross-examination of money being offered and money changing hands and gave the names of the players involved, there was just never any corroborative evidence. Of course, the Pakistanis came from all angles and in a side where internal enmity is always a factor, this whole situation offered the perfect way of settling old scores. Some of the evidence seemed nothing if not contradictory, not to say untruthful.

If the charges and accusations had not been so serious, it would have been just like a Pakistani version of one of those lovely Whitehall farces which Brian Rix made famous. An expert script writer could have done almost anything with this particular courtroom scene. Imran Khan would have been pained and emotional and would have implored the judge with outstretched hands, a technique he used to perfection when winning the most remarkable Test Match of his career, in the High Court in London defending a libel action brought by Ian Botham and Allan Lamb.

Javed Burki, one of Pakistan's leading civil servants, would have spoken with a weighty authority and a deep, well modulated diction, but there would have been more innuendo and circumstantial evidence than hard fact. Javed Miandad, the epitome of the poacher turned gamekeeper, formerly something of a rascal in the side and then the respected Test team coach, would have enjoyed recommending to the judge that the culprits be punished severely and banned for life if need be. He would have spoken quietly with an artful smile not far away. Aamir Sohail who is highly strung, would have given his evidence with passion and a fair helping of injured innocence as he recounted his conversation with an Indian bookmaker who offered him money if he was out for less than ten, the night before the Australasia Cup Final in Sharjah in 1994. Majid Khan would have appeared scholarly, charming, precise and laid back all at the same time, tinged with that slight inflexion of curiosity and disapproval a guest might have who has suddenly been asked to do the washing up and doesn't want to be rude.

Intikhab Alam, big and cuddly, always looks and speaks like everyone's favourite uncle. He would have been genial and yet intense and his evidence would have made me feel that he might have been protesting his own innocence a shade too much. I wonder if he could have told us why, when he was the manager and kept hearing that his charges were behaving in such an ungodly manner, he didn't do anything about it. He would also have managed to get in a plug for his new book which shows that he is far from a commercial nincompoop. Saleem Pervez, the money carrier, would have known he was in at the deep end and would have been determined to make the most of it and duck as many other people as possible. Haroon Rashid, a big man with a friendly smile, a recent team manager and former batsman, would have been unsure of his ground, hesitant and charming with a story which fell some way short of setting the Indus on fire.

Ramiz Raja, a former captain and opening batsman and the most delightful man, would have been discreetly dressed, impeccably polite and would not have had much of a story to tell either, for if anyone was completely innocent it had to be him. There is as much chance of Ramiz Raja being a party to match-fixing as there is of Geoffrey Boycott taking his next summer holiday in the south of France. Sarfraz Nawaz would have spoken in the hushed and immensely plausible and highly confidential tones of a man who knows he has one over you because he is telling you something you have never heard before. There would have been a knowing look in his eye as he told the judge about the movements and adventures that Raj Bagri, the biggest bookmaker in India, got up to with the Pakistan team and how he used to live in the same room as Asif Iqbal and behave as if he was a member of the team.

The story which has been put about is that the redoubtable Sarfraz originally had plenty to say about match-fixing and anything and everything else if it comes to that, but the Pakistan Cricket Board fixed him up as a bowling coach in Islamabad at a salary of one lakh of rupees per month (£1250 – a sizeable sum in Pakistan). For the time being, his political career seems to have been put on hold. I once stayed with Sarfraz and his lovely film star wife in Lahore, although since then she has moved on and he has moved house.

Mark Waugh, for reasons that emerge later, would have been slightly flustered and apprehensive and would have spoken quickly from a well rehearsed agenda, grateful that he had not been asked any of the questions he feared. His open-faced honesty may have impressed the judge. Mark Taylor would have been charming and believable because he would have told the truth as he knew it.

All in all then, this was a cast with more than a touch of Fred Carno's Circus about it as it lurched frequently from the sublime to the ridiculous. The one aspect of it all which hit an outside observer in the face, even at this relatively early stage in the hearing, was the pains to which the Pakistan Board went to protect their players from something they knew was indefensible. They must have had a pretty good idea that something had been going on within the team for a long time and yet they appeared to turn their backs on it with a vengeance.

From a distance, it looks pretty obvious that the powers-that-be in Pakistan cricket over the last ten years have been keeping their fingers crossed in the hope that it would either all go away or that it would never come out. The evidence has been mounting over the years. Imran Khan made exactly this point in his testimony. 'In 1994 when allegations of match-fixing surfaced, I went to the Board which at that time was headed by Arif Abbasi [chief executive] and told him in the presence of Javed Burki [chairman], that stern action should be taken against the culprits. In my opinion, expediency came into the way of the administration in imposing some punishment, as at that time the Pakistan team was very strong and they did not want to disrupt it. Stern action must be taken against the culprits to save Pakistan cricket, including bans for life and fines.' In other words, the Board's reaction was hypocrisy of a high order.

Apparently Aamir Sohail rang up Arif Abbasi after that Pakistani defeat in South Africa when Salim Malik had somewhat strangely opted to field and told him all he knew about the situation. Abbasi is reported to have replied that either he or Javed Burki would be coming out to South Africa within a week. As it was, another Board member, Salim Altaf (Bobby to his friends) came and simply advised Sohail to forget everything and concentrate on the game. Also after that match there was the deafening silence from Intikhab Alam who, as manager, must be directly accountable to the Board. So, the inescapable conclusion must be that the Pakistani Board were, over the years, involved in a huge cover-up operation. This, of course, had a parallel in Australia, although at least the Australian Cricket Board took action against Mark Waugh and Shane Warne even if they did, most indefensibly, keep it to themselves.

*   *   *

October also saw the birth of another of those spurious one-day competitions which do so much to congest the fixture list and inevitably increase the wear and tear suffered by the top players. This one was known as the 'Mini-World Cup' and was held in Bangladesh under the auspices of the International Cricket Council (ICC). The competition was originally to have been held in Florida at DisneyWorld, which would have been an exciting adventure in more senses than one. The ICC and DisneyWorld had come to an agreement but politics now stepped in. The USA is an Associate member of the ICC and is represented by the USA Cricket Association. The USACA are represented in turn by Mascarenhas's WorldTel, a deal having been put in place by Billy Packer, a partner of the redoubtable Mascarenhas. The Association had received $200,000 from WorldTel and the contract said that they could not stage an international event like this without WorldTel being awarded the television rights.

The ICC, by its rules, had to have the competition sanctioned in the first place by the home governing body, the USACA who told both DisneyWorld and the ICC that they would have to get permission from WorldTel. This was apparently not forthcoming. In the final stages of the discussions, DisneyWorld, not surprisingly got cold feet and pulled out. It seemed utterly absurd that the President of the ICC, Jagmohan Dalmiya, should have been blocked in this deal by Mascarenhas, who has himself been Dalmiya's partner in various business enterprises. It was equally absurd that the ICC was thwarted by an associate member country taking a decision contrary to the best interests of the ICC as a whole. When you hear stories like this, it seems surprising that cricket is a game played by reasonably sane people, but then, maybe they are not sane after all. DisneyWorld and cricket probably deserve each other.

The competition was then going to be played in Sharjah

until Wills became the named sponsor and it was discovered that the governments in the UAE have outlawed tobacco advertising. It was then that a country less concerned about the condition of its collective lungs had to be found and Bangladesh came nobly to the rescue. The organisation in Dhaka was mainly in the hands of the Chief Executive of the Bangladesh Board of Control, Ashraful Haq. By all accounts it was beautifully organised and a great success in terms of the competition, which was won by South Africa, the conditions under which it was played and the amount of money that was raised.

There were big crowds of around 40,000, and the infrastructure, the hotels, the food, the transport and the arrangements generally, could not be faulted. The authorities in Dhaka had to cope, too, with the aftermath of record floods which had recently ravaged the country causing untold damage and loss of life. At one point, there was even talk of the competition being transferred to Calcutta, and to avoid this it may have been that resources organised for the relief of those affected by the floods had to be diverted.

However, over the years, the ICC had watched while one television entrepreneur after another had made a fortune out of televising cricket, especially to the huge audience in southeast Asia, which has an apparently insatiable appetite for watching one-day cricket especially, of course, if India and Pakistan are involved. They now wanted a share of the action for themselves to raise money so that they could help with the development of the game in the parts of the world where it still does not have much more than a toehold. Although it may have seemed yet another meaningless one-day competition, at least it was for the overall good of the game and not just for the financial benefit of entrepreneurial television moguls. Of course, television had to be involved if the appropriate money was to be realised. The two companies concerned were Doodarshan, India's state television company, who bought the domestic rights, and WorldTel for whom Mascarenhas had bought the external rights. In spite of the involvement of the ICC, neither television company will have lost money, you may be sure.

The problem is that the game does not need any more of these extra-marital jamborees driven by money alone. They put a considerable extra strain on the best players who now never seem to have more than about three short weekends a year to themselves and their families. Theirs is the eternal dichotomy because if they refuse to take part in these competitions so that they can have a much needed rest, they will not have the same number of doubloons and pieces-of-eight to put in the old oak chest. Nor can they be certain that the young hopefuls who take their places will not come through on a permanent basis. Another problem is that the international fixture list is already so congested that it has become increasingly difficult to find a slot for these competitions. Of course, as the Wills International Cup came with the official blessing of the ICC, that blessing will, no doubt, have been accompanied by a certain amount of arm twisting as far as the presence of the nine Test playing countries was concerned. More than that, the 'wish' went out that all countries should send their best sides. That raised an immediate problem.

The England party to play Australia in the Ashes series was going to Perth at about the same time to prepare for that particular battle. While the ICC did their best to demand Alec Stewart's presence in Dhaka, his main duty as captain clearly lay with the England side in Australia. Thankfully, the ECB refused to budge and Stewart flew with the side to Perth while Adam Hollioake captained England in Bangladesh. This was not as arduous a task as it might have been for they were knocked out in their first match, against South Africa. The only compromise was that England's official coach, David Lloyd, went to Dhaka and arrived late in Perth where the manager, Graham Gooch, had assumed the coach's role. There is one crucial question: which is more important, an Ashes series or a one-day junket even with the admirable intention of raising funds for the game as a whole? Happily, the right answer was just about arrived at.

Television tycoons, who are as obstinate and truculent a lot as you are ever likely to come across and consider that they have an inherent right not to be disagreed with, give not a fig for the game, or indeed for the lot of the players, whatever they may say. They are not going to shed many tears if the constant aeroplane journeys round the world cause the early arrival of human metal fatigue unless, of course, they have a vested interest in specific players or, I suppose, if the flight path of gold runs out. As far they are concerned, it is simply a numbers game which is why, although they generate the figures, their influence has not necessarily been for the good of cricket.

The Wills International Cup consisted of eight matches. After a qualifier in which New Zealand beat Zimbabwe to become the eighth side in the quarter-finals, there were the quarter and the semi-finals and the final in which South Africa, needing 248, won by four wickets. It was a game which will be remembered for some luminous hitting by the West Indian opener, Philo Wallace, who smashed five sixes and eleven fours in his 103 from 102 balls, and some fielding by Jonty Rhodes which was supernatural even when compared to his usual phenomenal standard. England and Australia were both knocked out in the first round but there, as we were shortly to discover, all similarities ended. But, meanwhile, the West Indies players had decided to become involved in some pretty successful arm twisting of their own.

CHAPTER FOUR

Storm Clouds Gather

It was an irony that the final in Dhaka should have been played between South Africa and the West Indies, an irony sensed possibly by the West Indians rather than the South Africans. Within the week, the West Indies should have been in Johannesburg preparing for the start of their inaugural Test series in South Africa. But some of the West Indies players might have known as they left the ground that day that plenty of excitement lay ahead before they arrived in South Africa and that there was even the chance that they might never make it.

The West Indies have always been the poor relations of international cricket because their Board is more or less permanently broke for the simple reason that they never make money from their home series. There are vast distances to be travelled between matches in what is an upmarket holiday area where living costs are high. In addition there is a low *per capita* income in this beautiful but impoverished part of the world, and there is a limit to what can be charged for admission. Local television is also fragmented and broke and produces a negligible amount of money, although with the help of TWI, they now have a more significant worldwide television income. But the Test grounds themselves are small. Three of them, Bourda in Georgetown, Kensington Oval in Barbados and the Recreation Ground in Antigua barely hold 10,000. So the West Indies Board has to make its money from overseas tours.

It is no surprise that the West Indies players answered with an enthusiastic unanimity the clarion call of Kerry Packer when he formed World Series Cricket in 1977. They were being paid peanuts. Of course, the Packer revolution considerably improved the lot of the best West Indies players. But by the late nineties they were beginning to lag behind once more in spite of the fact that they had been the best and most watchable of all the Test sides for getting on for fifteen years. As so often happens when everything is going well, those who ran West Indies cricket may have allowed the realisation that it could not go on this way forever to be pushed to the back of their minds. By the time 1998 had arrived, the West Indies were clearly no longer the world-beating side they had been under Clive Lloyd and Viv Richards, and there was a serious lack of good young players.

The older members of the side were doing their best to pin it up but after they had suffered the indignity of being beaten at home by Mark Taylor's Australian side in 1995, they began to lose with some regularity. Their cricket was now revolving more and more around one man, Brian Lara, whose genius for batting was undoubtedly flawed by character defects. The dramatic success he had had early in his career had gone to his head, he was a selfish man, both on and off the field, and he was obsessed with money. The president of the West Indies Board, Pat Rousseau, a Jamaican lawyer turned businessman who liked to surround himself with Jamaicans, had kept one, Courtney Walsh, in the captain's job as Richie Richardson's successor and once even overruled the selectors when they had chosen Lara as skipper ahead of Walsh.

England toured the Caribbean early in 1998 and before the series began, Rousseau found he could deny the claims of Lara no longer. The West Indies won that series 3–1, but were lucky to do so and Lara's brand of captaincy had been no help. It may have been that like many instinctive ball players, he really had no idea how he did it and just expected everyone else to do the same. It does not work that way and while Lara was no tactical genius, he was also not good at man management. He wanted the captaincy for his own reasons but had not been prepared to face up to the responsibilities which must go with it. His own form had not been good and this will have helped to make him feel isolated in the job. In turn, this will have affected his confidence within himself as a human being and this was then reflected in his captaincy. For all that, he was the greatest single asset in West Indies cricket and he knew it and so did the Board. Without him, the West Indies would sink further and, even more importantly, the aspirations of all those people in the Caribbean would sink with them. As a player, Lara's arrogance had set the Board against him on more than one occasion but no one realised his indispensability to the West Indies side better than Lara himself, who was appointed captain to take the team on their first official tour of South Africa.

First, as we have seen, the side, which was managed by Clive Lloyd, went to Bangladesh, but seven of the players who were to make the journey to South Africa were spared the one-day competition and would join their colleagues in Johannesburg. Walsh, Curtly Ambrose and Jimmy Adams were three of them. Walsh had been most unhappy when he had been replaced as captain by Lara just before the series against England, and it had taken him some time to make up his mind that he would be content to play under the new captain. Meanwhile, he had become the chairman of the West Indies Players' Association and perhaps had more time to cope with the grievances of West Indies cricketers.

The initial motivation for the rebellion which then occurred was an extraordinarily foolish act by the West Indies Board and presumably by Rousseau who, I imagine, takes all the decisions. The International Cricket Council had agreed with all its members that when teams travelled overseas, they should be put into Business Class and expenses for tours and tournaments were worked out on that basis. Accordingly, the treasurer for the Wills International Cup will have sent the West Indies Board the money so that their players could fly Business Class to Dhaka. The Board and Rousseau, in their infinite wisdom, thought they could make a quick bob or two by sending the players in the back of the aeroplane in Economy. One does not have to be Stephen Hawking to realise that this would be a severe punishment for the West Indies, as even without Ambrose and Walsh they are a great deal longer in the leg than any other side. It became a real bone of contention which probably grew out of proportion. But if you are a bunch of chaps who are already harbouring a quiver full of complaints, it was as good a place as any to start.

It is to some extent guesswork as to how it all was put together from then on. Clearly, Lara, as the captain in Bangladesh, will have got on the telephone to Walsh who will, anyway, have been unhappy about the payment and allowances for the tour of South Africa which were low enough to aggravate without actually rousing the players to action. But this mild piece of chicanery by their Board over the air tickets was the final straw. Walsh will undoubtedly have had Ambrose's ear and there may have been others who had some input. It did not take the assembled brainstrust long to realise they were in a cast iron position. The tour to South

Africa was being more keenly awaited than any before to that country. Lara's side would do wonders for the hopes and aspirations of the huge coloured community by showing them what was possible. Those, like Ali Bacher, who ran South African cricket, will have been confident that the presence of the coloured West Indies side was going to bring about a big increase in the interest shown in cricket by the coloured races in his country and make many of them much keener to have a go themselves. The political community, headed by President Nelson Mandela, was awaiting the tour no less eagerly than the cricket community. The West Indies cricketers would never have a better time to strike than this.

The official plans were that after the final in Dhaka, the West Indies side would fly to Johannesburg, meet up with those players who did not go to Bangladesh and, amid much publicity, the long awaited tour of South Africa would start. What actually happened was that in defiance of manager Lloyd's instructions, which were to proceed to Johannesburg, Lara and Carl Hooper, his vice-captain in South Africa (who had also taken a pretty lofty view of the Board's instructions over the years), boarded a flight in Dhaka which was bound for London. When they arrived, they took a taxi to the Excelsior Hotel near Heathrow where they joined forces with Walsh, Ambrose and the others who had not been in Bangladesh. Lloyd, meantime, looking more lugubrious and Paddington Bear-like than ever, guided his remaining troops to Johannesburg where they awaited developments. Lloyd was in the tricky situation of being an employee of the Board at the same time as almost certainly being sympathetic to the players' demands.

Presumably, Walsh, Lara and Company had a long meeting and then it all began. The players publicly voiced their disagreements and their needs. They wanted an assurance from the Board that players' fees would be improved on future tours and that the method of payment would change in that players would receive more money, the more Test matches they had played. Those were the general complaints which were obviously aimed at improving the lot of future West Indies players. The more immediate requirements were payment for the week-long training camp before the first match in South Africa on 10 November, (neither of which, of course, ever took place) and also increased meal allowances and guaranteed security in Johannesburg. Two Pakistan players had claimed the year before that they had been mugged in Johannesburg although that story had been found by the police to be a fabrication. They had apparently been unceremoniously booted out of a highly dubious nightclub for not paying their dues.

It was now over to the West Indies Board, for whom one must read Rousseau. Their offices are in Antigua where they are presided over by the luckless Chief Executive Steve Camacho, the one man who may have been able to settle this whole dispute without bloodletting on a major scale, but whom I suspect was given no chance. When Rousseau had taken over as President of the Board, he had deliberately dropped the word 'control' from the title because of its auto-cratic, not to say, colonial implications. This made his first panic call from Antigua faintly amusing. His *obiter dicta* boomed across the Atlantic to the Excelsior Hotel. Lara was sacked as captain and Hooper as vice-captain forthwith, and all the players holed up at Heathrow were to be fined for fail-ing to go to South Africa as instructed. This was followed by an indignant demand that Lara and Hooper catch an aero-plane to Antigua where they would enter the headmaster's study. Plenty of autocracy and colonialism in that little lot, I would have thought. One could not help but notice the relish in these words as Rousseau thought that he had at last cornered his prey.

While the Board was shadow boxing in Antigua, the cricketers at the Excelsior began to realise that they were in an even
stronger position than they had first thought. Ali Bacher was
like a cat on hot bricks and couldn't get to the Jan Smuts
Airport in Johannesburg quick enough. He flew to London,
bringing with him a letter for the West Indian players from no
less a person than Nelson Mandela, which emphasised the
importance of the political side of it all. Walsh kept Bacher
waiting for over an hour before he deigned to come down
from his room and even then approached him by a circuitous
route and then told him to be quick with whatever he had to
say. He must have felt that he had been made a present of a
South African gold mine when he got back upstairs and read
the contents. If he had known what was in the letter, Walsh
would have been waiting for Bacher in the road outside. No
Board was going to defy the wishes of Nelson Mandela and
from that moment the West Indies players knew beyond
doubt that they were going to collect. This was effectively
confirmed by the head of sport for the South African
Broadcasting Association when he said, 'We won't put up with
anything less than a full strength team. We owe it to our
sponsors, viewers and advertisers.'

While the West Indies Board might have felt that they had
right on their side at the start, that initial piece of invective
sent to London effectively cooked the Board's goose for it
made the West Indies players close ranks. Lloyd's contingent
in South Africa had by now flown back to London and the
players answered Rousseau's demand that Lara and Hooper
should come to Antigua with their own request that the
Board's representatives should come to London. They had no
option but to comply and I have no doubt that Bacher, at
least, had been on the telephone to Antigua or Jamaica or
wherever, telling them that this tour must go ahead and it
must be a full strength side. The Board may have hoped that

Bacher would help them out of their financial difficulties but he said that the United Cricket Board could not do this although this was little more than window dressing. Of course, a saviour was found, in the recently retired South African wicket-keeper, Dave Richardson, now a promoter, who announced that he had come up with a sponsor for the West Indies side. So an all too predictable way had been found of paying for all those little extras with which the West Indies Board now had to cope. I have heard, too, that Bacher's Board paid the West Indian players' hotel bill at Heathrow, which can hardly have been inconsiderable.

When Rousseau and Chris Dehring, who was in charge of the Board's marketing, came to London and eventually met the players, they will have been told in no uncertain terms what they had to do. The whole issue had been effectively decided. First, with Walsh's insistence, Lara and Hooper were reinstated as captain and vice-captain and the fines levied on the other players dropped. Afterwards, Rousseau gave his own 'peace in our time' speech to the press. He called it a 'misunderstanding', which was gold medal material as far as understatements go, and returned home with his tail between his legs. He also said that there were 'lessons to be heeded from the whole sorry episode.' I bet the players weren't half as sorry as he was. He may have been uncertain as to who now ran West Indies cricket, but one thing was absolutely sure: it was not him any more, even though he may stay as a rubber stamp for decisions made elsewhere. It would have been appropriate, I suppose, if he had travelled back to Jamaica in Economy Class. By the time he had arrived home, he might have had rather more understanding of why it had all gone wrong as his legs are not all that short, either.

Poor old Nicky Oppenheimer was left in the unfortunate position of having to dump a multitude of lobsters which he had organised for lunch at Randjesfontein for the West Indies' first match against his own Eleven. Lara's team arrived in South Africa on 10 November, the day the match should have been played but too late to make it. Lara made a public apology for his team's late arrival which said, 'We are sorry if we caused offence and we apologise to the people of South Africa for the delay. These things happen in sport. We hope that people will understand the situation.' It seemed a little less than heartfelt. There was, too, an irresistible postscript. Soon after the tour started, Rousseau visited South Africa and while he was in Johannesburg, he went with some West Indian friends one day to the township of Soweto to see the splendid cricket ground there and all the facilities. While they were looking at the pitch some locals arrived, held them up at gun-point, forced them to lie down and cleaned them out of money, credit cards, the lot. It transpired that all the West Indian players in South Africa had cast iron alibis and the police are still scratching their heads.

The England side set out for Australia in a mood of cheerful but guarded optimism after those two rather vexed victories over South Africa at Trent Bridge and Headingley. Nonetheless, whatever the reasons for their success, it will have done their morale no end of good to have won a series against a major cricketing power for the first time since Mike Gatting's side won in Australia in 1986/87. Whether it gave them a realistic chance of beating Mark Taylor's Australian side was another matter. Ian Chappell had been a visitor at the Oval for the final Test Match of the summer when England lost to Sri Lanka by ten wickets, and he was con-vinced that the Australians would find nothing to disturb them. Judges don't come shrewder than I. Chappell.

After England's rapid and mildly undignified exit from the tournament in Dhaka, it was not long before the party in Perth was up to full strength. But it soon became the mootest of points as to whether that strength was full enough. Victory in the first game at Lilac Hill in the Perth suburbs, by the slender margin of one run, was a muted start. This was a one-day pipe-opener with about as much significance as the one-day games the touring sides to England play against the Duke of Norfolk's XI at Arundel. There were legacies from that game, too, because Alec Stewart hurt his back and the prodigal Ben Hollioake who had been extremely lucky to be selected for the tour, badly injured a groin muscle.

Comprehensive defeat by Western Australia with a day to spare was next on the agenda, and those of us who are well versed in the horror story which the start of every England tour almost invariably becomes, were left shaking our heads in resigned and half-amused dismay. Mark Butcher had been hit a nasty blow in the face by Matthew Nicholson, an unknown fast bowler the Australians have a habit of producing, and had to be stitched up. Afterwards, the soothing words of Messrs Stewart, Gooch and Lloyd had a more than familiar ring. Defeat by South Australia in Adelaide was only prevented by Graham Thorpe and Mark Ramprakash batting through the whole of the last day while Butcher, who batted like a man who was not certain where he was, made two modest scores.

Victory against Queensland at Cairns was only achieved by one wicket when Robert Croft and Alan Mullally put on 36 for the last wicket. After this splendid partnership Mullally felt the urge to climb on his soap box and proclaim the importance of tailenders being able to make a contribution with the bat. We all felt he was made of the right stuff, but how he will have come to regret these boastful words! Atherton's back had again been a major problem. He did not play in Adelaide and did not stay in long enough in Cairns to determine whether it had mended or not. If England were to test Australia, so much depended on Atherton and Mark Butcher's opening partnership which had been such a help against South Africa. Butcher was no better in Cairns than he had been in Adelaide and England's much vaunted opening pair had become an object of ridicule. The party limped into Brisbane for the First Test Match in anything but a healthy frame of mind.

It is on occasions like these that passing straws are clutched at with feverish haste. I had just clocked in from London on the same aeroplane that had brought out Graeme Hick as a reinforcement in case Atherton's back should seize up permanently. We were soon reminding ourselves that when England had descended on Brisbane in 1986/87, the state of disarray was even more pronounced and yet, thanks to Ian Botham's last and most measured Test hundred, England had won by seven wickets. It was the match which was made even more jolly when, in the middle of it, Allan Lamb was discovered at some unheard of hour in a casino with Kerry Packer and his party. That such distant thoughts as these were the best we could do is a good illustration of the state we were in.

The Gabba was once one of those smallish, intimate grounds which had a great atmosphere and a charmingly disordered, higgledy-piggledy look to it. The stands were relatively small and sprawling and everything was pushed in where it would go. There was certainly no master plan to supervise its overall appearance. The Sir Gordon Chalk (whoever he was) Building propped up one corner, the Clem Jones (former Lord Mayor and one-time emergency curator at the Gabba) Stand stretched energetically across the Stanley Street end of the ground and the Hill and its lovely, grassy slopes was in the other corner on the same side. Then there was nothing very much until we got to the Don Tallon (wicket-keeper *par excellence*) Bar at the back of what was in those days the biggest of the stands, in one corner at the Vulture Street End. Then came the Queensland Cricketers

Club which served the best butterfly prawns in Australia. The players' pavilion was tucked away under the Cricketers Club and behind the sightscreen. The ground was ringed by a grey-hound track which on the evening the dogs ran has in days gone by dealt a mortal blow to the finances of many a half-pissed cricket supporter after the close of play.

It was even less built up than this when, in December 1960, little Jo Solomon pounced and, with Australia's last pair together, threw down Ian Meckiff's stumps when the scores were level and the First Test of the series between Australia and the West Indies had ended in the first ever tie in the history of Test cricket. The umpire at square leg was Col Hoy and I shall always remember his reply when I asked him some years later how far out of his crease Meckiff had been. 'I don't know, but he wasn't there,' he answered with a huge grin. Just imagine the dramas we would have had today with the third umpire and all those slow motion replays. Like the third umpire in Barbados in March 1998, he might, by mistake, have turned on the green light instead of the red.

The old Gabba produced a wonderful barracking story in the days when the Aussie barrackers had real humour and none of the obscene bitchiness which can ring out across the grounds today. In his first Test Match, in 1965/66, Dougie Walters made a small matter of 155 not out against Mike Smith's England side. During his innings, he smote some of Bob Barber's leg breaks to some mildly elusive parts of the ground to the noisy delight of almost everyone present. At the end of play, Walters was still not out and as the players were walking off, Barber was heard to say to a colleague something like, 'Well, he's only a bloody convict's son anyway.' The next morning's papers made much of this. In the first session, Barber was given another bowl and before long Walters dispatched him onto the upper reaches of the Hill. When the considerable noise had died down, a resonant Australian voice boomed out across the ground, 'You wait, Barber, till he's got his shackles off.'

Alas, the builders have now caught up with the Gabba, all in the name of progress. It is the home of the Brisbane Broncos, the Australian Rules Football Club who fill the Gabba between ten and twenty times a year. This produces the lolly that keeps the ground going and so, of course, the footie fans must have what they want. At the time we were there the ground closely resembled a building site. At the Vulture Street or pavilion end of the ground, a huge new stand had been about a quarter built. This will, in time, encircle the entire ground with the dead hand of doughnut-like conformity. The next quarter was in the process of being erected and in order to display their manliness and their vigour and, of course, their strength, the builders were giving it everything. There was crashing, banging, sparks, and revved engines and the yellow-hatted fraternity scurried about in the rafters and the scaffolding like so many demented spiders, turning in a command performance. But then it's not every day that builders play to a full house.

After an early morning radio chat at the ground which meant being there at 6.45 (only to discover that it should have been 7.45), I set off to climb to the BBC commentary box. This was in the Gods alright, but there was a most obliging lift which did much of the journey and only left the final ascent to be undertaken on foot. I had been sitting there for about twenty minutes when a particularly identifiable form of heavy breathing announced the imminent arrival of Peter Baxter, our intrepid and indefatigable producer who appeared looking a bit like Sherpa Tensing taking the final steps. He had that slightly strained appearance he likes to reserve for the first morning of a Test Match. He too, thanked God for the lift.

Over the last 120 years, Englishmen have had to concede that Australians often bat better, bowl better and field better, otherwise they would not have won more Test Matches than England. But why on earth they should be able to build better lifts at cricket grounds completely defeats me. At Lord's, the Oval and Trent Bridge, lifts have recently been installed in the pavilion of the first, and as an aid to ascension in the media centres of the other two. In the unlikely event of them not being broken down, they are the most reluctant lifts in the world. After being summoned, they arrive in their own time and when they set off, it is with extreme grumpiness and they go about their business with a painstaking and infuriating slowness. The Oval lift has got its eye on the record book but they all add an engaging element of uncertainty to the day.

The lift at the Gabba, like those in the Bradman Stand at the SCG and the Bradman Stand at the Adelaide Oval, was impressive in its response to your wishes. Without going so far as to say that any came close to breaking the speed limit, they seemed to appreciate the importance of delivering you to your destination approximately on time and without any of the jerkiness their Anglo-Saxon brethren take such a delight in providing. Sadly, the lift in the Lillee-Marsh Stand at the WACA ground in Perth has convict connections. It has good days and bad days and an endemic dislike of working at weekends.

Half past nine is plenty early to start any game of cricket, let alone a Test Match, but Jonathan Agnew would probably be sprightly and certainly hearty at 2.30 a.m., if need be. So I watched in grateful admiration as he coped with the first half an hour in his ebullient way. He also did six sessions of commentary a day for the ABC and, goodness knows how he did it all and managed to remain permanently cheerful. CMJ was already alerting the readership of the *Daily Telegraph* that Australia had won the toss and decided to bat and giving them some snappy stuff about the first few overs, so I succeeded Aggers. I was joined by just about my favourite Australian

Test cricketer of all time, Jeff Thomson, who, twenty-five years before, had been one half of one of the most feared fast bowling combinations in the history of cricket.

It was at the Gabba in 1974/75 that Dennis Lillee and Jeff Thomson came together for the first time, against Mike Denness's England side, and they made the decisive difference in a series which Australia won easily. England were even forced to fly out the soon to be forty-two year-old Colin Cowdrey as a reinforcement. When Cowdrey went out to bat in the Second Test in Perth and found himself at the non-striker's end, he turned to Thommo, stuck out his hand and said, 'I'm Colin Cowdrey. How do you do.' Thommo was less impressed then than he would have been today.

When Thommo burst upon the scene in 1974/75 he was depicted by Ian Wooldridge in the *Daily Mail*, perhaps unfairly but most amusingly, as Terror Tompkins, the moronic Australian fast bowler who did not have an 'H' to his name nor many of the social graces either, as well as a lively penchant for the 'F' word. Thommo's supposed reputation came from his immensely physical action which, with his hair flying all over the place, his obvious strength and his youthful belligerence, seemed to give a point to the phrase, 'brute force and ignorance'. I well remember watching that series in 1974/75 and as a much younger journalist, I was mildly apprehensive of Thommo who, at that time in his life, did not suffer fools gladly and any Pom came into that category automatically. That was a long time ago and Thommo has now become a qualified landscape gardener, a considerable fisherman and a man with a wonderful sense of humour and a gentleness you would have never have guessed at in a million years if you had watched him come into bowl like a prehistoric caveman who has got a whiff of his lunch and wants to get there first. I have never worked with a better comments man. He has a masterful way of unravelling complex events in the middle and reproducing them in an easily digestible form. He is an excellent companion, the most engaging of men and a man of many parts besides. When I was recuperating in Norfolk during the World Cup, Thommo took the trouble to ring me up to see how I was and to have a long chat.

In that 1974/75 series and afterwards I had more trouble with the other half of the act, Mr Dennis Lillee, who didn't much care for criticism. Not that he got much as far as his bowling was concerned because he was as good as anyone can ever have been and certainly the best I have ever seen. But he was full to the eyebrows with an assumed bombast which was both tiresome and petulant and we had to suffer some pretty ghastly behaviour out on the pitch. He loved to get involved in slanging matches with the opposing batsmen and, of course, the Australian crowds loved every moment of it. Once he and Javed Miandad had a run in of mega proportions in a Test Match against Pakistan in Perth. It ended when Javed was more or less pulled away by the umpire and fielders as he lifted his bat above his head as an executioner would have raised his axe. He was about to attempt to decapitate Lillee who had blocked him outrageously as he had tried to complete a run. On another occasion, against Mike Brearley's side in 1979/80, Lillee came out to bat in the Perth Test with an aluminium bat and, when Brearley objected to it, put on a pantomime that would have had Jack the Giantkiller and Captain Hook putting in for early retirement. Lillee went by the apparently strange nickname of 'Fot'. When Tony Lock, the famous left arm spinner who played for Surrey and England and later for Western Australia and Leicestershire, was captain of Western Australia, one of his charges was the young Dennis Lillee. In his restless search for epithet and metaphor, Lock hit upon the chance to call Lillee, sometimes fortissimo from the gully, a Fucking Old Tart.

*   *   *

The frustration which the England side was repeatedly to heap on the heads of its supporters as this series went on was clearly visible from the first at the Gabba. Taylor won the toss and batted and until shortly after tea, England bowled and fielded like a side which was indeed going to run Australia close in the coming weeks. They had half the side out for 161 but then it all fell apart. Suddenly bowlers whose control had been exemplary completely lost their way and Steve Waugh and Ian Healy, who need no encouragement whatever the situation, began to score runs as they pleased. The fielding went to pieces and two crucial catches were dropped when Angus Fraser put down Healy at third man off Darren Gough and Nasser Hussain could not hold on to Waugh low to his right at second slip, also off Gough. They both made hundreds and when, on the second day, the bowling was just as awful, Damien Fleming was allowed to make 71 not out and Australia went on to reach 485. It was inexplicable that a bunch of experienced cricketers could have shown such dreadful inconsistency. Why were the bowlers unable to go on doing what they had done so well at the start of the innings? Had they forgotten what to do or did they need telling? And how can one account for the dropped catches? It had been a transformation as extraordinary as it had been unaccountable and painful. And the batting was still to come.

In the first month of the tour Butcher had hardly located the middle of his bat, let alone lived up to his name. It was a real worry that that blow on the head in Perth had affected more than just his confidence. As we have already seen, Atherton's form was as worrying as the back trouble that came and went without rhyme or reason, while Graham Thorpe's back, even after that double century against South Australia, was still an unknown quantity. It was with something less than confidence that we watched Atherton and Butcher come out of the pavilion on the heels of the Australians.

It took Glenn McGrath, with his lovely rhythmical approach and high, smooth action, just three overs to re-establish his mastery over Atherton, whose wicket he had already taken seven times in twelve Test innings. This time, he was squared up by one which he played from the crease in that most unconvincing way of his, and was picked up low at second slip by Mark Waugh. He came off the field a rather forlorn, defenceless and strangely youthful looking figure as if he had just bumped into original sin where he least expected it and hadn't much enjoyed it. Butcher now showed what he is made of. He had less than any form behind him and fell back on guts and technique in equal part, spiced with an occasional slice of luck. When he came right forward and drove the ball back past the bowler, he timed the shot well and looked convincing. There was nothing wrong, either, with those strokes off his legs which he tucks away on either side of square and which bring him a good part of his income.

On that second evening, Nasser Hussain was, if anything, more impressive, particularly when he hooked both McGrath and Mike Kasprowicz for fours. Here were two Englishmen taking the battle to the bowlers who didn't like it. They went on the next day; the fifty stand came first, then the hundred and both batsmen were playing with a certainty which Australian supporters watched with just as great a sense of disbelief as the English contingent. In the field, the Australians were looking perplexed, but this is where Taylor is such a good captain. To start with, as he stands at first slip as comfortably tubby as his nickname suggests, he gives off exactly the same impression no matter whether the score is 28/6 or 240/0. His unflappability is immensely reassuring for Australia. His mind is never still as he endlessly explores the possibilities, now making a bowling change, now a subtle alteration in the field and then a leisurely trot up to the other end to have a word with his bowler in the middle of the over. Being human, the batsman can only wonder what it is all about and even that might cause his concentration to waver.

Stuart MacGill had his first bowl of the series but it was not impressive. He was obviously nervous and could not control the ball and Hussain and Butcher were ready for him. Butcher had a bit of a time with the edges which, luckily for him, went along the ground or avoided Taylor at slip. For all the propaganda, Australia had a fight on their hands. In the commentary box we were enjoying ourselves and Jeff Thomson was saying much nicer things about English batsmen than he had ever done when he was actively engaged in cutting them down. The strokes from Butcher and Hussain were high class, their defence was good, the running between the wickets was sharp and the only criticism was the inability or maybe the unwillingness to play for singles in order to rotate the strike. In retrospect, the sad aspect of this stand was that it was the last time that England's batting was truly competitive until the Ashes had been decided. The second wicket stand was worth 134 when, for no apparent reason, Hussain shuffled across his stumps to Kasprowicz, a former Essex colleague, and got an edge to one which cut back into him. Healy accepted the catch with all the assurance of a conjuror doing a favourite trick, and although the ensuing appeal was not very melodic, it was good enough for umpire Darrell Hair.

Alec Stewart strode out in that way of his which suggests that he is a minute or two late for an appointment, took guard, twirled his bat twice for good measure, looked round the field, twirled it again and took up his stance. The trial by spin which was to ruin his tour was about to begin. He had made four without much conviction when he pushed forward to MacGill and was dropped at forward short leg. MacGill jumped about like an electric shock and could not wait to get the ball back.

He then lost control of a leg break which, when it arrived at Stewart, was a juicy leg stump full toss. Stewart swotted at it without due care and attention and writhed in torment as Kasprowicz stood his ground at deep backward square leg and gratefully accepted the catch. Stewart departed as briskly as he had come, like a man walking to the gallows and anxious to get it over with.

After being bowled when he was 92 by a beauty from Kasprowicz which turned out to be a no-ball, Butcher, with a lovely cover drive for four off MacGill, became the fourth Englishman after Patsy Hendren, Eddie Paynter and Tony Greig to score a hundred in a Test Match in Brisbane. It had called for tremendous character to have come to the Gabba with his batting apparently in ruins and then to have been able to go out and play like this. He had made 116 when he came forward and drove a fraction too soon at an off break from Mark Waugh. Waugh stretched far to his right and held on one-handed. This was Taylor's wicket as much as Waugh's. Batsmen tend to relax a fraction when they reach a landmark and concentration can falter. Waugh is adept at breaking partnerships and his change of pace crucially deceived Butcher.

Still England fought on. Graham Thorpe, in that slightly humourless way of his, had already settled in and was square cutting with his usual gusto while Mark Ramprakash made the other end safe as if he was a reformed playboy who had at last decided to put it all behind him. He once crashed a short one from Waugh through the covers for four and then tried to pretend it had not happened. It was a self-denying ordinance we were to see again and again in Australia. The spectre of failure looms large over Ramprakash and as a result he may see hobgoblins where they don't exist. He had clearly decided that his best way of keeping his place in the England side was not to be in the least concerned about productivity bonuses.

The next morning, Thorpe pulled McGrath straight to square leg while Ramprakash simply soldiered on. He let his hair down when he square cut Fleming for four bringing up his fifty and later he hooked and pulled Kasprowicz for fours with a certainty which suggested that his vows of abstinence are counter-productive both for himself and for his side. Robert Croft apart, the tail subsided most ingloriously, especially Dominic Cork who deserved a spell in solitary confinement after his ludicrous attempt to pull McGrath. Cork's commitment in Australia was all over the place and such an experienced cricketer must surely have known that his job, as someone with some pretensions as a batsman, was to stay with Ramprakash for as long as could. Mullally's end was swift but not without enjoyment as he too decided that the way to go was to pull McGrath and go he did, first ball, leaving Ramprakash undefeated on 69.

Australia led by 110 and from England's point of view this was too much with a day and a half to go. The bowlers had now to keep it as tight as they could to force Australia to delay their declaration for as long as possible so that England would have less time to bat in the final innings to save the match. In the second over of the innings, in a clear signal of intent, Michael Slater drove Cork over extra cover for four. In the third over, bowled by Gough, a cover drive, a stroke off his legs and a square cut brought Slater three fours. When he clipped Mullally to mid on for four, his fifty had come in 56 balls. He found an excellent partner in Langer, who batted with a similar intent, and they put on 162 in 42 overs. Slater's hundred took him 129 balls and arrived with the help of a skimming off drive for six off Croft. England's bowling had disintegrated under the assault and the fielding was not much better. Taylor declared at 237/3 leaving England to make 348 to win and needing to survive seven overs that evening.

But Atherton set off at such a pace, driving and hooking,

that England were 26 for no wicket at the close and there were even cock-eyed optimists seriously contemplating an England victory, which was about as likely as bumping into Bill Clinton in a monastery. Nonetheless, this start will not have done England's morale any harm. The next day the openers continued to bat with the same spirit and Atherton kept hooking McGrath for four as if he had a point to prove. Alas, for England, it was McGrath who proved the point, for with the score on 46, he persuaded Atherton to play the stroke again to a ball going down the legside, and Fleming held the catch at fine leg. It's no good playing the stroke if you don't choose the right ball, which Atherton very often doesn't. Soon after that, Butcher made the mistake of padding up to a leg break which hit him on the back foot and was lbw, and Stewart's torture by spin ended quickly when he pushed the simplest of catches to silly point. Not many people had realised that Stewart's problems against spin were so serious.

So England were 108/3 at lunch and on the brink. The cavalry were badly needed but by now it was a fair bet that they would arrive, for already in the distance away to our right, behind the formidable Boggo Road Jail, a well-known Gabba landmark, the storm clouds were getting together. The experts, like Jeff Thomson, had been telling us that it was not a matter of whether or not but simply when. As the players came back after lunch, it was clear that the clouds were approaching but would they be in time for England? Thorpe pushed Mark Waugh straight to forward short leg and then Hussain, after batting for two and a half hours, was bowled off the bat handle cutting at a googly which surprised the hell out of him by turning viciously back into him. There now seemed to be a good chance that the weather would be considerably too late. Hussain departed looking as stunned as a man might do when he has trodden on a garden rake and the handle has sprung back and cracked him a nasty one on the forehead. When Ramprakash suddenly decided to go walk about and went rushing down the pitch to MacGill and was stumped by a mile, it was going to be a tight finish between Australia and the weather.

The Brisbane weather has had a dramatic effect on Test cricket over the years, never more so than in 1950/51 when, caught on a sticky dog, England declared their first innings at 64/8 and Australia their second at 32/7 in a match Australia won by 64 runs. Over the years, I have sat through some impressive displays of meteorological pyrotechnics at the Gabba and ear plugs are as essential a piece of equipment as a lightning conductor. One afternoon it will rain so hard that the ground will be flooded and it doesn't look as if play will be possible for a week at least, but the next day it almost invariably starts on time. When England lost their sixth wicket at 161, it was abundantly clear that a storm was approaching that could only have been dreamed up and orchestrated by Wagner. Cork and Croft hung on for dear life. After every ball eyes flashed to the right to see if it was getting darker and soon the only extraordinary part about it all was that it was not raining. The lightning was splitting the heavens in the middle distance ahead of us, and to our right the thunder was growling away and coming ever closer. Even now, there were one or two, of Aussie persuasion, of course, who said that a number of storms slip round the back and this might be one of them.

The umpires, Darrell Hair and 'K. T.' Francis from Sri Lanka, met at the end of almost every over for lengthy conversations, but kept returning to their positions. As they chatted, the batsmen met in mid wicket ready to race off the ground as soon as the invitation was forthcoming. One more wicket now and the rest could go like a card house in three or four overs. Mark Taylor brought back McGrath for another go from the Vulture Street end but Cork and Croft somehow hung on. Then a sudden clap of thunder exploded over the Boggo Road Jail and the light grew perceptively worse. The umpires met again, Taylor took off McGrath and now had two spinners operating. MacGill finished his over. They met again. This time surely they would be off. But no. Another over from Mark Waugh and they met again. And then it was back to MacGill. Perversely, the rain would not fall.

The black skies at the southern end of the Gabba were now being lit up every five seconds with cruel, jagged flashes of forked lightning. The lightning itself was becoming a danger to the Australian fielders who when they saw it, must have felt their eagerness to stay put wavering just a little. Then, finally, the umpires met again and after what seemed like an age, they offered the light to the batsmen. I have never seen an offer accepted more quickly. The Australians, understandably, walked more slowly back to the pavilion while the groundstaff scurried about nailing down the tarpaulins that covered the pitch. It grew darker but still there was no rain and the lightning continued to perform like some supernatural firework display. Surely it had now come too far to slip round the back.

I don't know how anyone could have had so little faith in those exceptional Brisbane clouds. Maybe, from time to time, they like to tease and now it was quite eerie. The wind was rising, it was darker than twilight and a few figures in yellow raincoats flicked here and there on the ground. But there was not a drop of water anywhere. Soon after bad light had stopped play, *TMS* had gone back to the studio in London and after a few minutes it was time for an update. The lights were on in the box and it was exactly like looking out at your garden in England at four o'clock on a very grey December afternoon. There were still snatches of spectators huddled together in different parts of the ground, but not many. Peter Baxter, at his most beguiling, spoke from the back of the box,

'Blowers,' he began, most unpromisingly for me, 'would you consider telling our listeners what's happening?' It was one of those questions that did not require an answer. I clambered down to the front of the box, past Vic Marks and into my chair next to Bill Frindall, who was positively itching to tell someone that the lightmeter had not shown such a low reading without it actually raining since Old Trafford in 1937. I put on my headphones and soon heard Simon Mann in London handing over to me.

I told listeners what was happening and then tried to describe the sense of eerie expectation which was gripping us all as the light grew even worse, the clouds, if there were more than one, even blacker, the lightning more frightening and ever closer and the thunder more reverberating. It was impossible to believe that it could be as dark as this without raining. Vic Marks and I tried hard to go through the day's events but it was rather like trying to make conversation with your neighbour as Frank Sinatra was just about to come on stage with the orchestra already warming up. But still the wretched rain would not start. Having finished the story of the day, Vic and I moved our thoughts to Perth where the Second Test began the following Friday, in under four days' time. Just as Vic was, as usual, making an immensely pertinent point, a clap of thunder to end all claps of thunder shook the stand and acted like a supernatural full stop to that particular conversation and back I rushed with considerable relish to the elements.

I don't suppose we came within a thousand miles of the feelings that round-the-world yachtsmen experience as they approach Cape Horn as nature is stepping on the gas. They fear for their lives and pray their equipment holds. At the Gabba that afternoon, there was nothing more than perhaps the excitement and the slightly nervous apprehension that we were about to experience for the first time a mild freak of nature. In our eyrie at the top of the stand, one was able to feel the frightening power of nature in the raw as the pyrotechnics continued unabated, and to realise that man was powerless to do anything except batten down the hatches as best he could. The dramatic impact of it all was tempered by the slight feeling of potential disappointment that perhaps after all this, it might just slip round the back and not only would the storm end in anti-climax but, horror of horrors, England might have to continue batting.

Then, suddenly it began. Clouds which had been mocking us now cleared their throats and handed their sweaters to the heavenly umpires. The tarpaulins which had been flapping in the wind now began to glisten. I swivelled to the right and I could see the rain sweeping in from the direction of the Boggo Road Jail, gently at first as if the impending storm had decided to have a bit of a warm-up. If so, it did not last for more than a moment and then the clouds rolled up their sleeves and let us have it. The rains swept in, blowing great drifts of spray across the ground and it began to look like a scene from one of those wartime movies, with a heavily oil-skinned Jack Hawkins playing the part of the captain on the bridge. The small groups of spectators who remained shrivelled as they huddled closer or, more sensibly, scampered to safety. The drops increased in size and smacked at an angle into the covers bouncing up again before they finally settled. There may have been some hail as well but it was mostly rain.

It was now completely dark as if all the lights except ours and those in the stand around us had suddenly been switched off. It was only just possible to make out the houses closest to the Gabba opposite us at the Stanley Street end. Even the lights of the jail had gone. The rain scudded across the ground with ever increasing intensity and already the drains were pleading for help. Surface water was appearing, first in small gleaming pools on the right and then, in the time it took to look round the ground and back, the small pools of water had created so many grassy archipelagos. All the time it grew darker. The surrounding suburb of Woolloongabba disappeared in a thickening misty spray and the clouds began to encroach into the Gabba itself. We were now in the clouds and the stands on the other side of the ground were invisible. The lights of the houses ahead of us and to the left and the right were unable to penetrate the gloom. Here we were at 3.30 in the afternoon when a Test Match should have been in progress, and it might have been midnight in the middle of a power cut. I have never seen anything like it and I wouldn't have missed it for the world.

Vic and I were still on the air although talk of the prospects for Perth was fighting a losing battle with awe at the elements and we were both spellbound by all that was happening outside. I did my best to describe the extraordinary forces of nature as they beat down upon us. The ground was now a lake with scarcely a blade of grass showing and still the rain sluiced down. The one thing which was beyond a doubt was that this First Test Match was over. Every now and then I made another valiant try to get back to the cricket but the 'Now Vic, let's get back to Perth', was scarcely out of my mouth before another flash of forked lightning, more vivid and closer than the last was followed by a crack of thunder of such proportions that it could not be ignored. Perth could not compete with fireworks on this scale and I would be off again.

Of course, it couldn't go on for ever. Gradually, it began to grow lighter and slowly visibility improved. The Clem Jones Stand reappeared, a few houses across Stanley Street were visible, we saw the lights of a car away to the right and the rain slackened to a downpour. The drainage at the Gabba is staggering: at one point the ground had been under water, but even before it had stopped raining, although there were obviously glistening patches of water lying around, the major part of the flood had disappeared. The tarpaulins had been shaken up in the wind as it occasionally rippled through underneath, but they had held. The winds now slackened, the lights in the surrounding suburbs glared, brightly and rather cheeringly at first, and the cars began to drive with greater confidence up and down those two neighbouring causeways to our right. When the Boggo Road Jail appeared, sturdy and, in the circumstances, greatly welcoming, one really felt that life was back on a recognisable plain.

It was wet in the road and we had to pick our way carefully to the car park. Even the diehard Queenslanders had been a little surprised by the ferocity of the storm although they tried awfully hard not to show it. The former Australian batsman, Peter Burge, now a match manager most definitely not to be trifled with, is an old friend and he offered to drive me back to the Sheraton. For this he deserved at least a medal as taxis were going to be at a premium for a long time to come. As we sloshed our way along he said smilingly, 'We get 'em like that, Blowers, you know.' Which, I suppose, helped put it all into perspective. I was rather disappointed. I had hoped it had been a first. Well, it had been for me anyway. An unforgettable first.

CHAPTER FIVE

The Back of Beyond

When the fixtures for this tour were planned, the eminently sensible decision had been made that instead of mixing up the Test Matches with the one-day games, they would all be played together in the first half of the tour. Then the arduous business of the eighteen one-day games for the Carlton & United Series would be fought out around the circumference of Australia. While it made great sense, this decision was forced on the ACB by the way in which the one-day game and Test cricket are divorcing themselves from one another. The Australians play an entirely different side for the one-day matches and while Mark Taylor was in charge of the Test side, Steve Waugh took over the reins for the shorter game. England had done this, too, when Mike Atherton captained the Test side and Adam Hollioake the one-day side and they had also played two very different teams. However, now that Taylor and Atherton had both given up the captaincy, Alec Stewart and Waugh were in charge of both the Test and the one-day sides.

Had both forms of the game been still intermingled during the Australian season, it would have meant that the England contingent would have been more than thirty strong and it would have been a bit like a race migration as they trekked around the country. Three days after a Test Match, the one-day side would have been in action, so the personnel for both types of cricket would have had to be there together and it would have been impossible to have kept them all in practice all the time. The cost of keeping so many people in Australia would have been extremely expensive, too. Therefore it made sense from every point of view to divide the summer into two halves.

The downside of this was that there were back-to-back Test Matches at the start of the series, in Brisbane and Perth, as well as the usual back-to-back Tests later in Melbourne and Sydney over Christmas and the New Year. When one match ends on the Monday and the next one starts on the Friday, it puts quite a strain on everyone. With the stopover in Melbourne, the flight from Brisbane to Perth takes six hours and this effectively rules out one of the intermediary days as far as cricket is concerned. The characteristics of the two pitches are even further apart than a six-hour aeroplane journey and there was virtually no time for the players to try and accustom themselves to the different conditions. The England players will have found it harder than the Australians who will all play at the WACA ground in Perth at least once a year. Some of the Englishmen have a go on it every four years if they are lucky. After gaining a huge psychological advantage at Brisbane and knowing what lay in store in Perth, the Australians will have had a much more enjoyable flight across the country.

Geographically, Perth is as remote a city as any in the world. Of course, jet aeroplanes have made a mockery of distance and isolation, but in the old days the big liners from England put into Fremantle, just up the road from Perth, as their first port of call. While some left the ship, those who were continuing their journey had time to find their land legs before rejoining the boat for the journey on through the Great Australian Bight to Adelaide and then to the eastern states. It was possible to make the journey by railway which was how those early cricket sides travelled, but the trek through the Nullarbor Plain and mile upon mile of arid, red desert brings home Perth's isolation even more.

Alan Bond, an English migrant from Ealing, probably did more than anyone for Perth's self-esteem and for its international identity by winning the America's Cup for the city. Ironically for a civic hero, he subsequently spent a longish while in prison for financial misdeeds. With the mining booms, Perth was a city of make-it-quick and lose-it-quick. Bond never really had it but was not rumbled for a surprisingly long time. Nevertheless, no one will ever be able to take away what he did for Perth, which went on to host the next America's Cup thereby extending the city's fame for a while longer. It did not matter that the defence of the Cup was unsuccessful for at last Bond had loosened the grip of the New York Yacht Club and in doing so had put Perth on the international map. Of course there is more to Perth than Alan Bond. The Western Australian vineyards flourish, especially around the Margaret River. The city has its opulent suburbs, a lovely setting with magnificent views of the Swan River, and the famous black swans. Then there are the riches from the mines. Test cricket came to Perth in the early seventies. The city itself is the usual Australian mixture of modern prosperous high rise buildings and old narrow streets where pubs once abounded and the six o'clock swill was a fact of life. In the final hour, between five and six o'clock when the pubs shut, the entire population would try and drink as much possible usually with disastrous or, at any rate, unattractive results.

Australia was perfectly defined by one of its most eminent historians, Geoffrey Blainey in his book, *The Tyranny of Distance*. The title tells the story and nowhere in Australia can have been much worse affected by the tyranny of distance than Perth, which was isolated both from the rest of the world and from the rest of its own country. This creates a great togetherness among the people who live there and a slightly cussed, 'We'll show you' attitude, which is the prerogative of those who are always made to feel the poor relation, whether rightly or not. When I paid a brief visit the following March to Invercargill, the most southern city of the world, which sits at the foot of the South Island of New Zealand, one comes across something of the same attitude. Like Perth, Invercargill is the friendliest city one could hope to find. Everyone pulls together in the ever-present urge and anxiety to find a greater level of acceptance and self-identity.

When you land at Perth Airport you disembark by walking down the steps of the aeroplane onto the tarmac apron and into the airport building, which doesn't happen that often at international airports these days. It starts one thinking that it's all just a little bit different. When we arrived this time from Brisbane, we were waiting near the appropriate baggage carousel when a woman who worked for security arrived with the most delightful beagle on the end of a long lead and encouraged it to sniff at all our bags. For a moment I wondered which of my colleagues was most likely to be involved in the world of drug trafficking, when I realised that what the beagle was sniffing for was vegetable produce. At most airports in Australia there are big notices telling passengers that if they have vegetable matter with them, they must leave it the bins provided. This is to prevent agricultural diseases being brought from one state to another. This little beagle was a splendid chap and thought it was the best game he had ever played.

There was one middle-aged lady who, like the rest of us, was waiting with an empty trolley for her case, when the beagle sniffed her hand luggage, pointed at it and barked clearly thinking that she had most of her garden inside. Very politely, the dog's handler went through the bag she was carrying and discovered two apples which were confiscated. I hope the beagle, who looked as chuffed as anything, was given an extra biscuit. The woman, who I would not have earmarked as a natural apple smuggler, looked suitably embarrassed and that was the end of it. The next time I saw this happen was in Auckland when I flew in from England in the middle of the following March, the day before the Second Test Match in Christchurch between New Zealand and South Africa. This time, there was a golden retriever and a beagle and maybe while the beagle was also after vegetable matter, the labrador may have been in search of bigger game, but both drew a blank. The pair of them had a pretty thorough sniff at my computer but, I am glad to say, gave it a clean bill of health.

There is, however, one extremely irritating and unnecessary diversion at Australian airports. When you have retrieved all your bits and pieces, the chances are that you will need a trolley to push it all to a taxi. There are long lines of trolleys within easy reach but in order to get hold of one, you need a two dollar coin to put into a machine which then releases the trolley. Of course, the two dollar coin is the hardest to come by in Australia and you almost invariably forget to change a five dollar note when paying the hotel bill that morning and so it becomes necessary to change a note when you already have one hand on the trolley. There is never anywhere to change money that is less than a route march away and what can you do with your luggage while you go off and get a two dollar coin? It's infuriating and I cannot believe this generates enough money to make any difference to anything. It's simply bossy, bureaucratic nonsense which leaves many people with short tempers before they have even left the airport. This happened to me in Perth and so I tried to hump all my bags at once over to the taxi stand and it was a wonder I didn't lose half of it and also that I didn't pull a significant muscle.

My hotel room offered the most spectacular view of Perth Water, although on a grey and rather windy evening there was only one small sail to be seen. I was hardly through the door when the telephone rang and it was none other than Bill Sykes. He had driven from Vilamoura to London where he had boarded an aeroplane bound for Perth which had landed that afternoon. He is an indomitable follower of cricket and he had promised, when Bitten and I were staying at Orchard House, that he would be all present and correct in Perth and he was as good as his word. He was staying in the same hotel as the players which was on the other side of the river and told me that he was about to walk round to my hotel. I told him it was rather a long way but it didn't appear put him off.

Forty minutes later, when I was working flat out for blowers.co.uk, the telephone rang again and there he was downstairs in the foyer. We got to work on a bottle of excellent Chardonnay, did a *post mortem* on Brisbane and Bill ticked me off for being so gloomy about the prospects for the Perth Test. He also gave me a copy of the video we had made when I was staying with him in Portugal in order that the prep school boys who came to Orchard House should not miss the finer points of Miss Marilyn Monroe in the pavilion. He told me that the visit of Aldwickbury House had been an unqualified success. We made plans for the rest of the week and then he walked back to his hotel leaving me to feel that I had become an indispensable piece of equipment for a health club.

*   *   *

England left Brisbane almost certainly regretting they had not played seven batsmen in the First Test and it was likely that this was what they would do for the Second in Perth. It looked as if Crawley or Hick, probably Crawley who was a member of the original party, would come into the side for one of the bowlers. The next and most pertinent question was how best to adapt the bowling for the fast pitch at the WACA. The evidence of the First Test showed that for all his hard work and success for England of over the last year, Angus Fraser was most unlikely to be such a significant bowler in Australia. In the West Indies at the start of 1998, Fraser had been the scourge of the Spread Betting industry. Every wicket after the twelfth that he had taken in that series had cost my friends at Sporting Index £3,000 and he ended up with twenty-seven. It was quite a while before Compton Hellyer and Lindsay McNeile, who mastermind that particular operation, were able to move on from a rather tired looking platter of yesterday's sandwiches for today's lunch. For this series a good many punters decided that Fraser was again the goods and every wicket he took after his first eleven would have cost Sporting Index £4,000. There was the chance that yesterday's sandwiches might have been swiftly followed by sackcloth and ashes, to say nothing of the Official Receiver.

But at the Gabba, Fraser had managed only one wicket in each innings and Sporting Index gave a considerable collective sigh of relief when the selectors gave him the heave-ho for the Perth Test. When they did not bring him back for Adelaide, fevered brows were again all the rage at Gateway House, the home of Compton and his cohorts. Of course, the punters were not going to collect on Fraser, but unless he played in one of the last two Tests, the bets on Fraser's wickets would become null and void and sandwiches would continue to be the order of the day. But that is to come. For now, Fraser was out of the side.

Apart from his initial spell on the first day, Dominic Cork had also been a big disappointment in Brisbane, but his ability with the bat was probably going to keep him in the side. The fastest bowler in the party was undoubtedly Alex Tudor who was only twenty-one and had been brought to Australia to gain experience rather than to have a role to play in this Ashes series. Since arriving in Australia he had made an excellent impression with everyone. He had worked extremely hard at his game and, unlike some of his colleagues, was prepared not only to listen to advice but also to act upon it. He played in the match against South Australia at the Adelaide Oval, a notorious fast bowler's graveyard, and although it will have broken his heart, he came through the match well enough. The pitch at the WACA had recovered much of the pace it had in the sixties when it was presided over by Roy Abbott, the best of curators as the Australians like to call their groundsmen. If Tudor was to have a use as a member of the side on this tour, Perth was going to give him his best chance.

If this Second Test had been played in England, I would have offered long odds against Tudor being picked by an essentially defensive minded bunch of selectors. They would have talked about him for a long time and then, with knowing shakes of the head, they would have pulled a has-been out of the cupboard who would have been unlikely to have made any impression. Now, in Australia, their choice was limited and although Graham Gooch, Alec Stewart and David Lloyd are the very essence of conservatism, Nasser Hussain, the vice-captain, was also on the panel and he may have brought some much needed positive thinking to their meetings. I have no idea how the conversation went or who wanted whom, but Tudor took Fraser's place which had to make sense. Cork predictably kept out Dean Headley which, in the light of things to come, was not an inspired selection. On the batting front,

Crawley and Hick both found their way in because shortly before the match Graham Thorpe's back went on him again. Croft, whose off spin had been such a disappointment in Brisbane and would be irrelevant now, was dropped.

The Australians made two changes, one of which was a surprise. Although he had had a good match in Brisbane, Stuart MacGill, the leg spinner, was left out for Perth on what their selectors described as a 'horses for courses' policy. They brought in seamer-cum-off spinner Colin Miller from Tasmania who, at the age of thirty-four, had won his first Test cap on Australia's recent tour to Pakistan. The England batsmen will have been delighted as this will have meant a rest from the torturous business of trying to sort out and play a leg spinner. But when they saw the way the pitch was going to play, they will have realised that it made not the slightest difference. The selectors had said that MacGill would be back for Adelaide, for although Shane Warne had begun to make a tentative comeback for Victoria, he was nowhere near ready for Test cricket. The other change saw Jason Gillespie, the best fast bowler in Australia after McGrath, take the place of Mike Kasprowicz who is never going to do much more than hang on at this level.

The key to an extraordinary match which was over well inside three days, was the pitch, which was fiendishly difficult for batting. It had an extravagant bounce and there was enough grass to allow the seam bowlers disconcerting movement. Stewart again called 'heads' and Mark Taylor put England in. It was not an unfair reflection of the pitch that the score at lunch stood at 76/6. They were all out soon afterwards for 112 and McGrath, Fleming and Gillespie were near enough to being unplayable. It was hardly surprising that England's batsmen were made to seem wholly inadequate. Some of the strokes which were played seemed avoidable, but that is always the way when the odds are stacked so heavily in favour of the bowlers. No batsman in the history of the game would have enjoyed playing on such a difficult surface.

Of course, Butcher should have moved his front foot further across when driving at Fleming and Atherton should not have played at McGrath outside the off stump. Stewart, after a few heroic strokes, was bowled between bat and pad; Crawley flapped firm footed at Gillespie and Hick waved his bat as if to say goodbye which he was, in a manner of speaking, but neither made any attempt to get behind the line of the ball. It is the nature of high class fast bowling in helpful conditions to take wickets like this. In the best of all worlds, none of these batsmen would have got out as they did but the relentless barrage England received that day created great pressure and inevitably distorted both nerve and technique. Mark Ramprakash, who has the best technique of all, was as composed as anyone before he was undone by a brute of a lifter and even with him it had been just a question of time. Only the greatest of batsmen make runs in these conditions and even they will need a good slice of luck. Another batsman to make the job look possible was, most surprisingly, Tudor. His defence was collected and well-organised and he stood up and drove Fleming and steered McGrath wide of the slips with great composure to make 18 not out. Inevitably, the innings ended with another Mullally extravaganza when he had a prehistoric slog at a short one and was caught behind.

The difficulty of batting on this pitch was there for all to see when Australia had their turn. If England had not had another severe attack of butter fingers, which caused them to drop no less than four catches in Australia's first innings, the lead could have been kept to about fifty which might have been manageable. The Australians continually played and missed, particularly against Mullally who bowled superbly, but without any luck at all. He was miserably ill-served to pick up only one wicket. The problems of the pitch were made starkly apparent by the Waugh twins who both reached the thirties and made invaluable contributions, but played and missed more than anyone for over after over.

Tudor had a spell on the first evening when nerves seemed to get the better of him and he was expensive. The next day he was an altogether different proposition. Now, he did not strive for extra pace but ran in rhythmically finding a lot of power in his delivery stride from his strong shoulders. And he was quick. He did not make the common mistake of bowling too short on a pitch which has plenty of bounce and, for the most part, kept the ball well up to the bat and made the batsman play. Bowling at the two Waughs will have been a great experience for him and he was not in the least unsettled. Far from it, it inspired him to produce his best and when Steve went back to force him through the covers, he was bowled between bat and pad as the ball nipped back off the seam.

Not a bad first Test wicket and five runs later he did it again. Mark Waugh now came forward to drive one which left him and he was caught by Mark Butcher low at third slip. It had been a fairytale start for Tudor and one which was richly deserved. In these few overs he had given a wonderfully mature display and it was as if he had remembered all the advice he had been given and was putting it into practice with telling effect. He clearly has an excellent temperament which is as important for a bowler as it is for a batsman. Before he had finished, he had Ricky Ponting caught behind and Glenn McGrath in the gully, taking 4/21 in the spell and making the sort of a start to a career we had all despaired of seeing again from a young England fast bowler.

England's second innings was a rerun of the first. More splendid bowling by the Australian seam bowlers exploited the same old cracks in technique and, at 67/5, an innings defeat looked likely. But at this point a rather desperate Graeme Hick strode to the crease and went for his strokes in an innings which had the look of being the last wish of a condemned man. An early piece of luck saw a hook fly off the top edge and just over Healy's upstretched finger tips. Then, when Gillespie pitched short, a fierce pull cleared the mid wicket boundary and this was followed by a thumping square cut for four and another robust pull for six later in the same over. On the second evening, England were 126/5, still two runs adrift. Another top edged hook and a cover drive took Hick to 50 the next morning, but when he had made 68, he drove at Gillespie off the back foot without too much footwork and was caught at third slip.

It had been a cheering innings both for England and for Hick but being the enigma he is, one could only wonder what sort of frame of mind it had left him in. Was it a declaration of intent for the future or would he now lapse back into his bad old habits as he allowed a mind that is riddled with doubts to take over again? Once more, Ramprakash soldiered on until he had run out of partners and the innings ended most ingloriously but with great amusement when Mullally stepped so far away from his wicket that he was unable to reach the slowest of full tosses from Gillespie, which hit the stumps with Mullally doing the splits somewhere over towards the square leg umpire.

Australia needed only 64 to win but they were made to fight for them. First, Mullally's effort to hold onto a simple return catch from Slater was on a par with that ludicrous effort at the end of England's second innings. He recovered himself, though, to find the edge of Taylor's defensive push and after Gough had made no mistake with a simple caught and bowled from Slater, Tudor found the edge of Langer's bat before the Waugh twins restored order and saw Australia home in the twenty-third over. If Australia had needed to score around

150, it could have been so different. As it was, the Waugh twins were admirable in their devotion to duty. They are as different in style as they are in appearance, so much so that at times it is hard to remember that they are even brothers, let alone twins. Their characters, too, are as different as their appearances. Steve could no more have become involved with an illegal Indian bookmaker, a story which now lay only just round the corner, than Mark could have played the innings that Steve put together in Brisbane and later in Melbourne. But, my goodness, I would like to have them both on my side.

I arrived in Adelaide a week before the start of the Third Test because I had been asked by the former Australian wicket keeper, Barry Jarman, who had been the match referee for England's series in the West Indies at the start of the year, to spend a few days on his houseboat in the Murray River. John Reid, the former New Zealand captain who was the match referee for the Ashes series, was also coming with his wife, Norleigh, and there would be some other friends of BJ's. He had promised this invitation when we had been in the West Indies and he had spelled out the details during the Brisbane Test when he had come up for a dinner for all the surviving Australian Test captains. BJ had captained Australia once at Headingley in 1968 when Bill Lawry was unfit.

He picked me up from my billet on North Terrace after an early breakfast and then the Reids from their hotel in Hindley Street, in the middle of a rather disappointing red light district. We then set off for Lyrup where he kept the boat, which was about a three-hour drive towards the middle of South Australia. The houseboat, *Gooda's Gold*, was named after Tony Gooda who achieved both fame and notoriety as one half of the Gooda-Walker syndicate that lost many people a great deal of money when the insurance world of Lloyds of London went bottom up. BJ had met Tony Gooda at the

Cricketers Club in Blandford Street in West London when it had first been opened by Frank and Sheila Russell in 1964. Gooda's sister, Jane, was the club secretary, and her brother often used it for lunch. He and BJ became good friends. He went on several occasions to stay with the Goodas at their house in Coolham, near Billingshurst in Sussex. The house had originally been called Kummer Cottage but in the mid-eighties, Gooda had renamed it Jarmans. BJ had bought his houseboat in 1982 when it was most unromantically called *Number Ten,* being the tenth member of its original fleet. Tony Gooda then paid a visit to Adelaide and BJ got back onto level terms when, at a suitable ceremony, his boat was relaunched as *Gooda's Gold.*

BJ's nautical instincts came from his father who was born and bred at Wellington on the mouth of the Murray. He was a professional fisherman and they had moved to Adelaide when BJ was eighteen but it was not until 1981 that he forsook life as a landlubber. At Easter that year, he had hired a houseboat for the family and some friends and they had all enjoyed it so much that they took it a second time. But when they wanted it yet again, BJ found that it was already booked. The owner told him that he should build a boat of his own. It was then that he bought *Number Ten* and over the years he has almost completely rebuilt it, mostly with his own hands, and it now has four double cabins, all mod cons, an excellent kitchen and plenty of room for all the wine we had brought with us.

We left Adelaide in two cars. I went with BJ in the first and the Reids followed with Doug Sanders, a friend of BJ's who was coming with us. The journey was interesting in that it gave one a good impression of the outback of Australia. Once we had moved away from the coastal strip and left the river, we drove down interminably straight roads which more or less disappeared over the horizon, with barren scrubland stretching away on both sides as far as one could see. It was all a colossal emptiness, inhabited only by an assortment of desiccated gum trees. Occasionally we would go past a group of three or four dusty old wooden houses with rickety wooden awnings that looked as if they had just popped out of a Nevil Shute novel. There was the odd crossroads too, where usually there were a few houses, perhaps a small all-purpose shop and maybe a pub. At these little settlements there was often a group of small children engaged in energetic games and, on the other side of the road, two or three old men would be passing the time of day, which looked to be a lengthy process. They stopped talking and stared at us as we went by. Every now and then we would pass the entrance to a private road which ran deep into the country and led to a farm. Once or twice BJ pulled out to pass a piece of farm machinery making slow progress usually near the middle of the road. Generally, the pace of life lay somewhere between dead slow and stop.

We drove past one memorable game of makeshift cricket. At the moment we arrived, an elderly spectator decided to give chase to a legside hit and after a stuttering start had taken him about four paces, he lost his footing and as he capsized, he disappeared into a huge cloud of dust. The two batsmen were still running when the game disappeared from view. We drove for mile after mile, sorry, kilometre after kilometre (Australia has become aggressively metric), without seeing another car. BJ enlivened the journey with some stories of how he and his joint owners had made killings at a couple of country race-courses we passed.

BJ was a member of a distinguished cricketing syndicate which was composed of Ray Steele, a onetime chairman of the Australian Cricket Board who managed a number of Australian sides overseas, Richie Benaud and Norman O'Neill. They had owned a horse which was deceptively called

Sleepwalker and was trained by Colin Hayes who operated in South Australia and is one of the great figures in Australian racing. Sleepwalker was entered for a five furlong sprint at the old Tailem Bend racecourse. Tailem Bend is a small township named after the bend in the Murray River on which it sits. The syndicate were convinced that Sleepwalker was going to win. BJ arrived at the course with a suitcase full of money which he distributed to half a dozen of his friends who went round the bookies placing the bets. The race could hardly have been more agonising and the wait afterwards, too, before the official verdict came that Sleepwalker had won by a short half head. The last word belongs to BJ's father who had gone round all twenty-seven bookies in the ring putting a pound on Sleepwalker with each. BJ asked him what on earth he was doing and he replied, 'It has always been my ambition to take money off every bookmaker on the racecourse.' Although he didn't tell me, I imagine BJ had to hot foot it to Tailem Bend's luggage store to buy another suitcase or two so that he could take the money home.

The other coup which had been a more modest affair, had taken place at Mindarie Halidon which again fell some way short of being a great metropolis. This time the horse was called Hit The Seam and was owned by BJ and Steele and a few of his Adelaide friends, and it had won a more convincing victory than Sleepwalker. Their wallets had been big enough to hold the loot on this occasion and, rather disappointingly, the suitcase had been left at home. Hit The Seam's offspring was called Pick The Seam although I would not have thought that such a highly respected match referee would have wanted it put about that he had anything to do with an animal of that name.

We were twenty or thirty kilometres from Loxton when suddenly the country around us changed dramatically. The barren, dusty scrubland became green and fertile, there were animals grazing on lush grass and then after a few miles, the road burst into a huge, rich wine growing area. Now, row upon row of neat and succulently green vines stretched away to the right and the left. Once again, we were within reach of the Murray River and of course the irrigation had transformed the countryside. Then we were in Loxton, a modern town with marvellous amenities which, in their gleaming newness, had an almost clinical appearance. There were schools, endless sporting facilities, a hospital, a cricket ground where a number of touring sides have played against Country Elevens, a couple of small hotels, some new factories and shopping centres and of course a cinema or two, some roundabouts and enough cars to justify several sets of traffic lights. It was a thriving centre and is the hub of life for all those who live in this part of the world.

A few kilometres further on and we came to Berri which was much the same but on a smaller scale. BJ stopped across the road from a big bakery and I helped ferry to the car the order he had telephoned through from Adelaide that morning. The delicious smell of freshly baked bread was as enticing as ever and I could hardly keep myself from tearing into one of the huge brown loaves I carried across the road. Once the goodies were in the car, we set off on the last lap to Lyrup. We turned right off the main road which was going on to Renmark, and in a few hundred yards reached the ferry which would take us across to the other bank of the Murray where *Gooda's Gold* was moored. We could just see her in a narrow cut on the other side, a short distance downstream. We waited for the ferry, which had only just set off for the opposite bank, to get rid of its cargo and return to take us across. A car parked beside the boat announced that the Jacksons from Port Augusta, who completed our complement, had beaten us to it.

Before we boarded *Gooda's Gold,* we drove to the local store to get some more provisions and John Reid had to send a fax to his masters, the ICC at Lord's, and I had to let my website know that I was about to take to the river. The owner of the store looks after the boat when BJ is not there. He services it after each trip and generally keeps an eye on it. Back at the boat, Captain Jarman showed us to our cabins and we took our luggage on board. He quickly explained how the bathrooms and the loos worked before getting on with the business of opening the first bottle, which showed that there was nothing much wrong with his priorities. The engines were then started and slowly we backed our way out into the river and set off downstream principally because we had to put in to Berri and stock up the cellar. We found a strategically placed drive-in bottle store so close to the river that it was almost a sail-in bottle store.

For years, BJ had run a sports shop in Adelaide, but having sold it, he is now able to concentrate on his houseboat, which has become part hobby and part business. He takes groups of tourists down the river and also parties of business men who come to Riverland to play golf in the day and to sample BJ's cooking in the evening. *Gooda's Gold* takes a maximum of nine people, eight in the four cabins and BJ himself sleeps on a camp bed in the dining area. I can confidently say that no Test Match wicket keeper has ever attained the culinary heights that he has scaled. The cooking is done on an old-fashioned Weber and watching our host scurrying from saucepan to saucepan adding a bit of this here and a bit of that there, was worth the journey on its own. It was good, plain fare of lamb chops, gammon steaks, salads in abundance, the odd sauce or two and the tour de force came on the last night when he cooked to perfection a fillet steak which he had most skilfully marinated for the past twenty-four hours.

Our three days were delightfully uneventful and we discovered that when not wearing his chef's hat, BJ is an aspiring

Master Mariner. The Murray River is huge and although it glistened most amiably under a succession of cloudless skies, there was something a little frightening about its power as it raced downstream. It clearly needed to be treated with respect. There was almost no traffic and the nearest we came to a disturbance was when we were buzzed on the second day by a series of yuppie waterskiers. Just occasionally we came across a car which had parked on one of the banks just back from the river and belonged to people who had driven out, perhaps from Adelaide, for a picnic. The river, which is getting on for a quarter of a mile across, is hemmed in by trees on either side and again I was continually amazed by the vast emptiness of it all. The huge river, miles from anywhere, bores its way through the continent and can carry boats as far as the northern point of New South Wales. Just occasionally, civilisation had a toehold on one of the banks. Berri was, I suppose, more of a footprint than a toehold.

On our second day, we came to Lock Four. There are thirteen locks on the Murray and negotiating the fourth of these was child's play to BJ. The Lock Keeper, a moustachioed man in his late thirties with heavily bronzed skin and rippling muscles, kept an eye on us but he needn't have bothered. His companion was a delightful little terrier which was more Jack Russell than anything. It ran busily up and down the edge of the lock and seemed about to jump into the houseboat. Stan, the keeper, told us that this was done more in the hope of persuading passengers to part with food rather than as a prelude to a dashing display of aerobatics. As a young dog it often fell over the side into the water but without suffering any ill effects. Middle age had taught it discretion. Stan's job must have been one of the world's loneliest and Kelly, the dog, will have been a much needed and spoiled companion. When the lock had fallen the few feet that was necessary and we had edged our way out to continue downstream, Kelly sat on the end of the lock and barked a resonant farewell. It was well after lunch and Stan told us we were the first people through that day. I can only say that he must have been one of the most conscientious of lock keepers for the whole area was kept in tip top order. We warned him we would be back the next morning and he took the news on the chin.

The first night, we hove to not far beyond Berri and put the world to rights sitting in the back of the boat, our glasses full of another of BJ's famous reds while he himself took up the cudgels and bent in businesslike fashion over the Weber. Inevitably, the conversation stayed within reach of cricket which will not have surprised or phased Norleigh Reid although Pat may, I am afraid, have found it harder going. BJ and John Reid are both forthright match referees and it was interesting to hear their views on the modern game which were heavily tinged with the urgent need to improve standards of behaviour. They both had some good stories to tell but I was sworn to silence otherwise their employers at Lord's might have a word or two to say. I heard how, at the Gabba, during the First Test of the present series, one of England's young players, with his way to make, had gone out with the drinks wearing a shirt with a forbidden logo on it. When this was pointed out to him, he apparently could not have cared less. The management enlisted the match referee's help to try to make the miscreant realise the seriousness of what he had done. The referee himself had not noticed the logo but he will have left the player in no doubt as to the error of his ways. It is a story which demonstrates an appalling arrogance by the player concerned and reflects the way of a world where authority no longer has too much going for it.

One mind boggling incident which came out on *Gooda's Gold* I shall repeat because it was the worst of its sort I have ever heard. During New Zealand's tour of South Africa in 1994/95, they played a one-day game against Nicky

Oppenheimer's Eleven in Kimberley and while they were there, they were shown round the famous diamond mining museum. At one point, they were shown trays of fabulous stones and when none of the staff were looking, two of the party grabbed handfuls of diamonds and shoved them into their pockets. They had not noticed the security cameras. Later, the tour management were told that if all the stones had not been returned by a certain time the next day, there would be a police prosecution. All the stones were returned and, quite staggeringly, the two players concerned continued to play for New Zealand as if nothing had happened, and one still does. I can't think of a worse story than that.

We chugged on downstream propelled by two state-of-the-art outboard motors and spent the second night under the stars somewhere between Lock Four and Loxton. BJ won his second Chef's Hat award and the next morning we began the return journey to Lyrup, going rather more slowly upstream. After stopping in Berri for the day's papers, we anchored in the home cut in late afternoon in plenty of time for our host to get to work on his marinated fillet steak. It was the perfect end to the sort of rest cure one is badly in need of in the middle of every cricket tour. It was back to reality the next day with the long, straight, dusty drive back to Adelaide. I went with Doug who, soon after we started, bravely surrendered the controls of his car to me and we had a lovely drive coming into Adelaide through the gently picturesque Mount Lofty Ranges. For me, it was then the airport and time for three days in Melbourne where England were engaged in a somewhat bloodless contest against a Victorian side shorn of its best players.

CHAPTER SIX

The Beauty of Adelaide Betrayed

While I was travelling from Perth to keep my appointment with Barry Jarman on the Murray River, great deeds were being enacted in the offices of the ICC at Lord's. On the afternoon of Wednesday, 2 December, the members of the First-Class Forum met at the start of their two-day meeting to decide upon the future structure of first-class cricket in England. As we have already seen in the second chapter, the representatives had agreed at their exploratory meeting in October that there was a need for radical change. When the process of change had first been explored twelve months earlier, there had been considerable opposition to it and the MCC and the counties who belong to the Forum threw it out by twelve votes to seven. The situation had now changed. The ECB had prepared the ground much more thoroughly and their PR had greatly improved. Also, England's performances, even allowing for that lucky victory over South Africa, were hardly an argument for retaining the *status quo.* So there had been a unanimous vote for change in October.

At the meeting in early December it was decided by a big majority that from 2000 onwards the County Championship would be split into two divisions of nine sides each, with promotion for three sides each year and relegation for three more. The initial make-up of the two divisions would be dictated by the final table at the end of the 1999 season. The sop offered to persuade those still wavering was the promise that the central handout from the ECB each year would continue to be the same for all counties, whether they were bottom of the second division or top of the first. This will have given those counties certain that they are destined for the lower division a guarantee of financial stability. They may have been thinking that if they were condemned to an eternal place in the lower division, bankruptcy would not be long in following. Ironically, this is probably the main reason why the two-tier system as it now stands is unlikely to provide the hoped-for answers to England's cricketing malaise.

There will be a grave danger that with a satisfactory amount of money coming through into the lower division, a contented and happy travelling club will develop there just as it has in the middle and lower reaches of the current Championship. It will become the sort of comfortable existence that soon blunts ambition. It is desperately important that from hereon in the First Division sides are better rewarded than those in the Second. The urge to succeed from below must be stimulated and a hunger must be created that will only be satisfied by collective or individual performances that gain entry to the top level. The desire to better oneself is basic human nature and is the best incentive of all. It must be harnessed to help improve England's cricket.

As soon as players realise that whether they bust a gut or not, their reward will be the same, the other side of human nature will ensure that a great many of them will happily settle for an easy life, especially the older players. This, in turn, has a deadening effect on youthful enthusiasm and is one of the reasons why many talented youngsters have been lost to English cricket in the last few years. Their eagerness to play and to succeed is suffocated by the attitudes of the old pros, who are playing out their careers mostly in county Second Elevens. There is no doubt that England's young cricketers are as good as any in the world at the Under-19 stage but four years later, the Under-23s are much nearer the bottom of the ladder.

Of course, promotion and relegation will keep the excitement of the county season going for more sides for much longer than now happens. This will eliminate so many of those pointless matches at the end of the season between sides who are out of contention for anything, where the players often do little more than go through the motions. One of the main jobs the lower division has to perform is to act as a feeder league for the top division, not only through the promotion of its three best sides, but also by producing young and talented cricketers who will then gravitate to the top division and help the concentration of excellence there. This will lead to cricketers being better prepared when it comes to Test cricket. To facilitate their upward passage, an acceptable transfer system must be created. Ideally, it would be better to have a top division of only six sides so that the standard could be refined even more, but with nine sides it is crucial that they contain all the best players so that competition between them is as sharp as it can be.

So, while the first and largest step has been taken, a great deal still remains to be done. The old farts have not been completely routed yet, although they are in a state of some disarray. No sooner had I arrived at the Adelaide Test Match than I found myself locked in head-to-head combat with the redoubtable and implacable Robin Marlar who takes up a World War Three stance on this subject. After two years as chairman of Sussex in which he led the county from the front, he has handed the job over to Don Trangmar, who has recently retired as a main board director of Marks & Spencer (who, judging from their results, may soon want him back). Trangmar is also in charge of the ECB committee that is looking into the vexed question of whether the best players in the land should be contracted to the ECB or their own counties, or both. Under his leadership, Sussex may have been more willing to toe the ECB line when it came to voting for change.

Having told me that I had got it all wrong in *Cakes and Bails* where I argued strongly in favour of the two-tier system, Robin confidently forecast the end of county cricket as we know it and the disappearance of a few counties within the next two years. He was coming nicely to the boil and I feared a major disagreement, when the Archangel Gabriel appeared in the person of Peter Roebuck who, I am delighted to say, raised a verbal eyebrow at some of Robin's more forthright utterances. We went on our way beaming smiles of guarded neutrality. There is no one I know who is better at getting an argument off the floor than Robin, as well-practised readers of the *Sunday Times* will appreciate. I encountered the perfect antidote to Robin later in the match in one of the corporate hospitality boxes in the Bradman Stand where I bumped into Bernie Coleman, one of the game's unsung administrative heroes. He was a member of the Surrey committee for years, he had a good spell on the old Test & County Cricket Board, and I am sure he has had a most helpful influence on the footballing fortunes of Wimbledon and Crystal Palace. But he has always disliked appearing in the headlines. He has approached every issue with a clear and modest common sense, one of his main attributes as an extremely successful businessman.

No cricket ground in the world could, in spirit, be further removed than the Adelaide Oval from the turmoil of controversy which seems increasingly to wrap itself around the game of cricket. Ironically, it was at Adelaide in 1932/33 that the infamous Bodyline tour came to the height of its fever when Harold Larwood hit both Bill Woodfull and Bertie Oldfield. Angry telegrams flew between the Australian Cricket Board and Lord's and at the sacred Oval, rows of spectators, mostly wearing three-piece suits in spite of the extreme heat and packed in like sardines, came within a whisker of jumping the fence and joining the battle. Relations between the two countries fell to an all-time low. The current teams were gathered in Adelaide now to practise for the Third Test when shattering news broke. As a result of lengthy, persistent and brilliant investigative journalism by Malcolm Conn, the chief cricket writer on *The Australian,* we learnt about the financial involvement of Mark Waugh and Shane Warne, some five years before, with illegal Indian bookies, news of which had been scandalously suppressed by those who ran the Australian Cricket Board at the time.

I awoke to the news in Melbourne two days after I had stepped ashore for the last time from *Gooda's Gold.* The story had been broken the day before by the former Australian batsman, David Hookes, who has a radio programme in Melbourne and had been tipped off by one of those whom Conn had spoken to on the telephone in his attempt to cross all the 'T's before the story was printed in the following day's paper. He was unlucky that it had been passed onto Hookes. During the Australian tour of Sri Lanka in 1994, both Waugh and Warne, neither of whom are averse to having a bet themselves, were approached at different times by an illegal Indian bookmaker who offered them money for providing information about the weather and the likely state of the pitch for the next match. This was information which he could just as well have got from the papers, the radio or by casual enquiries at the ground. Waugh had apparently been contacted on several occasions and had been given US$6,000 while Warne had received US$5,000.

As we have already seen, after the Sri Lankan leg of the tour, the Australians went on to Pakistan and when they returned home after that, three of the players, Mark Waugh, Warne and Tim May told the Australian Cricket Board that they had been approached by the then Pakistan captain, Salim Malik, who had offered them US$200,000 to play badly and that they had refused. The very next day, the Australian batsman, Dean Jones, revealed that he had refused an offer of US$50,000 to give information to the Indian bookies on their tour of Sri Lanka in 1992/93. The chairman of the ACB at that time, Alan Crompton, and the chief executive, Graham Halbish, naturally wondered if any other players had been involved and if so, had any of them accepted the money.

Halbish rang Ian McDonald, a full-time employee of the ACB and a former journalist, who was the team manager and was with the side then in New Zealand. He instructed McDonald to start an immediate inquiry with the players. The situation within the party may already have been tense as the players who had been approached by Salim Malik were most unhappy that, in spite of the ACB's efforts to keep it quiet, the story had been broken in the Melbourne *Age* and the *Sydney Morning Herald*. McDonald spoke to all the players individually and asked them if they had ever been involved with bookies insofar as cricket was concerned. Of course, the moment the first player had been spoken to, the news of the inquisition will have spread like wildfire through the rest who were waiting to be interviewed. It is easy to imagine a hurried and horrified conversation taking place between Mark Waugh and Warne. Something they must have prayed had gone away, had now resurrected itself. They already knew that the story of Salim Malik's approach had been in the papers and they will have been fearful that the ACB had collected the details of what had gone on in Colombo as well. The best thing, therefore, was to come clean. If the ACB were already in possession of the facts and they both denied it, they could be in big trouble. They told McDonald the full story.

One attempted cover-up now led to another. At the end of the short tour of New Zealand, the team returned to Sydney for one night at an airport hotel before flying out the next day to the West Indies. Crompton, Halbish and McDonald met with the two culprits at the airport hotel. Crompton and Halbish took the decision to fine Waugh A$11,000 and Warne A$9,000, there and then, and to leave the events in Colombo as an in-house matter. The players, who are almost certainly both millionaires, paid their fines at once. But Crompton and Halbish did not leave the matter completely in-house. By a strange coincidence, the two leading figures of the International Cricket Council, the president, Sir Clyde Walcott, and his chief executive, David Richards, happened to be passing through Sydney. They were told, in the strictest of confidence, exactly what had happened.

It was not until after the team had left for the Caribbean the next day that the rest of the ACB were informed of Crompton and Halbish's decision. It may be an unfair suggestion or the aircraft may have left extremely early in the morning, but one cannot escape the feeling that this may have been done deliberately to make it more difficult for the Board members, if they disagreed with the original decision, to ban the players. To have pulled them out of the tour once they had reached the Caribbean was surely unthinkable. Some members undoubtedly had reservations about the action that had been taken, but nonetheless the decision was ratified. More damningly, it was subsequently discovered that the minutes of this meeting did not include any mention of the affair.

The procedure which enabled the ACB to cover up this entire episode had effectively been set up by McDonald quite a while before. He had organised a system whereby players who stepped out of line were fined in-house as a private method of maintaining discipline. Crompton and Halbish had apparently decided that the information the two players had given them concerned an isolated and self-contained occurrence with no effect on anyone else. They must have felt that there was no harm in following the established pattern of punishment. In truth, it is hard to believe that they could have been so naïve as not to make a connection between what the ACB had been told by Waugh, Warne and May about Salim Malik's efforts to bribe them, and the paying of Waugh and Warne tidy sums for information which could so easily have been picked up elsewhere without payment. May's inclusion at this second stage without him apparently having been given the earlier sweetener, is strange, unless those who may have been behind it all felt, belatedly, that it was crucial, if they were to get the result they wanted, to nobble both spinners on a turning pitch. Or, I suppose, May might have been sharing a room with one of the other two and his inclusion became unavoidable.

I find it hard to believe that these two at the head of the ACB, and Crompton is himself a lawyer, can have failed to see the bigger picture. Did they never ask themselves why Indian bookmakers would have wanted to throw away not inconsiderable sums of money on getting information from the players that they could find out for themselves for free? The only sensible answer to that question is that this was the first stage in the process of sucking these two players into the illegal world of Subcontinental bookmaking. The questions Waugh and Warne had been asked in Colombo were irrelevant; it was the subsequent ones which were going to carry weight and surely they must have realised that there was more than a good chance that Salim Malik's intervention in Pakistan was the next stage in the process. Once you enlarge the picture like this, it becomes abundantly clear that what Crompton and Halbish had been told by these two players was of the greatest importance to the rest of the cricket world. If Waugh and Warne had been earmarked in this way by the Indian bookmaking fraternity, was it not likely that other countries' cricketers had been similarly approached? The immediate revelation of this story could only help with the process of international policing. If Crompton and Halbish did see it in this light but still chose not to act, it is also interesting.

However much those involved may have protested to the contrary, when all this became public knowledge the concerted efforts of those running the ACB to hush it all up also had a funny smell about it. Halbish, who succeeded David Richards as the chief executive of the ACB when the latter became the chief executive of the ICC, is a slightly shadowy figure in all of this. He appears to have had a considerable influence on all that went on and yet in 1997 when Denis Rogers had taken over from Crompton as chairman of the ACB, Halbish was sacked by Rogers for unspecified reasons. One cannot help but wonder what else had been covered up by the ACB and, indeed, if the stated reasons for the cover-up were the real reasons. It would be nice to think that the present Board will do what they can to get to the bottom of it all. Although Denis Rogers was not the chairman in 1995 nor Malcolm Speed the chief executive, there is no way they can escape blame for not coming clean about the events in Colombo to the Pakistan Board before Waugh and Mark Taylor were interrogated by the Commission in Lahore in late 1998 about the Australian accusations against Salim Malik.

As we have seen, Waugh and Taylor gave evidence about Salim Malik's attempt to bribe the three Australians to play badly in a one-day game in Rawalpindi and a Test Match in Karachi. The accusations made by the Australians were considered to be a most important piece of evidence by Judge Qayyum and one of the few bits which was corroborated. In view of what they knew about Waugh and Warne's earlier involvement with the bookies, the ACB must have been reluctant to agree to the cross examination of their men. But as the ACB had, for a long time, been exhorting the Pakistanis to clear up all the many bribery and match-fixing claims, counter claims and rumours which had been part of their cricket for too long, it would have been hypocritical in the extreme if they were seen to be preventing valuable evidence from being given. The upshot was that Speed flew to Pakistan as well in order to be with the two players in Lahore and also to have his own talks with the Pakistan officials. It would be interesting to know the course they took, though, of course, no mention was made by Speed of Waugh and Warne's transgressions in Colombo. Speed can only have been working to an agreed agenda.

It beggars belief that the Australian Board could have acted in such a crass way. Small wonder that in doing so, it led to the logical suspicion that they were themselves involved in covering up something else as well. My own feelings were not so much that they were trying to conceal something specific, but that they had been caught with their pants down by an issue which they had hoped had gone away. They were now terrified that it was going to turn out to be even more far-reaching than they had thought when Waugh and Warne's accusations against Salim Malik were first exposed by the Australian papers. They must have been desperately worried that there were other Australian players, past and present, who had been involved.

The role of the ICC in all of this must now be called seriously into question. Walcott and Richards had been told because they were passing through Sydney when it all came to light. If they had not been there, it must have been highly unlikely that they would ever have been made aware of what had happened. They had been given the information in confidence which they had respected. Australia is one of nine full members of the ICC, all of whom are as important as each other. Pakistan is another. The ICC will, of course, have kept an eye on what was going on in that court room in Lahore. They will have known that the ACB had given permission for Waugh and Taylor to testify. In my view, it was the clear duty of Richards as chief executive of the ICC to have spoken to Speed and told him that, while he had until then been prepared to respect the original confidentiality of the story, now that Waugh and Taylor were going as witnesses to the court in Lahore, he had no alternative but to pass on the details to the Pakistan Board. Richards himself was in a particularly vulnerable position in view of him being an Australian. All nine full member countries of the ICC must surely be equal, but was Richards not guilty of showing that, in his mind at any rate, Australia was more equal than some of the others?

Personally, I don't believe that being an Australian had anything to do with his silence. I feel that it had much more to do with his gut reaction, which was to sweep things under the carpet if he could and to keep them there if at all possible. This may either come from a belief that in doing so he is protecting the game of cricket, or from a natural inclination to push it all into the folder marked, 'Too Difficult'. The name, International Cricket Council, may make it sound as though it is an immensely powerful body, but the reality is that it is largely toothless and ineffectual because the member countries have never been prepared to give it any real power. The individual countries have never wanted to surrender control of their own domestic game for reasons of self-interest. This, though, was a situation where the ICC could have acted properly and legitimately by passing on information it had been given by one country which had wrongly thought fit to keep it secret. The ICC shirked their responsibility and by doing so, further damaged their credibility.

When the news broke a couple of days before the start of the Adelaide Test Match, the ACB had no option but reluctantly to confirm that Waugh and Warne had accepted money for giving information, on more than one occasion, to illegal Indian bookmakers. The ACB then immediately engaged in a major damage limitation exercise. The day before the Test Match, Waugh and Warne both took part in stage-managed Press Conference at the Adelaide Oval at which they both looked at best uncomfortable and at worst as guilty as hell. They read prepared statements in which they claimed they had been naïve, denied they had ever been involved in match-fixing and said they were deeply sorry. The statements added nothing to the debate, although the fact that neither player stayed to answer questions from the assembled press was a matter of some surprise. On the first day of the Test Match, Denis Rogers came to the Press hospitality room to answer questions. He was accompanied by Malcolm Speed, who managed to look urbane and on edge at the same time. Rogers did the best he could at trying to second guess the reasons why Crompton and Halbish had wanted to hush up the original story and tried to defend what was presumably his own decision not to pass on the information to the Pakistan Board before Waugh and Taylor said their bit in Lahore. I asked him if he was confident that no other Australian players were involved. His hesitant answer amounted to, 'I have not the slightest idea, but I am keeping my fingers crossed.' It was abundantly clear that this was a story which was going to run and run.

In Pakistan, the story caused outrage, both feigned and real. Salim Malik saw it as a life-line from heaven and expostulated against the two Australians, saying that he was going to sue them but without saying where or on what grounds. But it deflected attention from him for which he will have been grateful, for the net appeared to be closing around him. He and his lawyers obviously wanted to release as big a smoke-screen as possible although, of course, the fact that the two Australians had been paid money by an illegal Indian book-maker for answering questions about a series in Sri Lanka between Sri Lanka and Australia, could hardly deflect more than immediate attention from the more serious accusations which had been levelled at him for his alleged activities in other parts of the cricket-playing world. What it did mean, though, whether rightly or wrongly, was that the strength of the argument mounted by Waugh and Taylor in Lahore the month before was watered down. Basically, it made them appear as much less convincing witnesses. Malik's reaction was predictable enough and so too was the reaction of the Pakistan Board of Control who had every right to have expected that the ACB would have brought this whole affair out into the open before Waugh and Taylor came to Lahore.

Once again, the waters had been muddied irretrievably and the people responsible were the ACB and the ICC. Once they had decided to go down the path of secrecy, one can only wonder what on earth persuaded Crompton and Halbish to tell Walcott and Richards in the first place even if they had been having a drink in the next door room. This was not the least barmy aspect of the whole business.

It was hardly the ideal build up for the Adelaide Test Match which is usually such a glorious feature of the Australian summer and a splendid social occasion in its own right. I watched the match from the balcony in front of the media refreshment room along with three television cameras, a mildly irascible Pat Murphy from BBC's Radio Five Live, and the delightfully urbane Eddie Bevan. Eddie was working for BBC Wales and for two Test Matches had been having his work cut out to bring Glamorgan's Robert Croft into each and every broadcast for the simple reason that he had not been selected. It was no good him complaining that Croft should have been playing in place of Peter Such, for Such took five wickets in the match and bowled well. Our doughty producer, Peter Baxter, took over from me on *Test Match Special,* just as he had done from Chris Martin-Jenkins in Perth where Peter's considerable fan club had felt justifiably short-changed by a two-and-half day Test Match.

The top of the new Bradman Stand provides a wonderful view but, far from living up to the setting and the occasion, England's cricket was a disgrace. They had not had a good build up either with a poor game against that weak Victorian side and then they had seen Graham Thorpe return to England with a recurrence of his back trouble. The Victoria match had been sad from another point of view because there had been hopes at the outset that this tour would see Ben Hollioake establish himself in the side as that rare commodity, an allrounder, who would bat at seven and bowl his seamers. His groin injury at the start of the tour in Perth had been a blow but now that he had recovered, one could only question the effort he put into his cricket. He was awful against Victoria and, unhappily, he did not give the impression that he was in the least bit concerned by his form, or lack of it. If he could have shown that he was ready to take his place in the side in Adelaide, it would have given the team an important boost. His apparent lack of effort was shameful.

Mark Taylor won his third toss of the series and batted first. Thanks to Justin Langer, who made an excellent 179 not out in his neat and largely unobtrusive left-handed way, and with useful help from Taylor himself and Steve Waugh, Australia made 391. The pitch took plenty of spin from the start and saw Such and Ramprakash bowling their off breaks in tandem on the first day. Mark Waugh's appearance was eagerly awaited because it was going to be interesting to see how the public would react to him after the recent revelations. He strode to the wicket pursued by as many boos as cheers. He looked distinctly uneasy and was beaten in the air and caught and bowled by Such for seven. He and Warne had received a severe roasting in the Australian newspapers which will surely not have surprised them.

For once, Mike Atherton looked in command at the start of England's innings but still that big score eluded him. He had made 41 when he shuffled across his crease in characteristic manner and pushed defensively at a leg break from Stuart MacGill. The ball flew low towards Mark Taylor at slip who reached forward and scooped the ball up with both hands low in front of him and claimed a catch. Atherton's head had spun round the moment he had made contact and he stood his ground, certain that Taylor had not made a clean catch. The umpires met and the decision was referred to the third umpire and the television replays. This important role was filled by Paul Angley who had adjudicated in a mere three first-class matches. None of the replays, which we all saw on our monitors, was conclusive. It was impossible to be certain that the ball had not bounced before reaching Taylor. One or two were quick to accuse Australia's captain of being a cheat on the basis that he must have known the ball had hit the ground. I do not personally believe Taylor has it in him to cheat, for in everything I have ever seen him do, he has been an honourable man and his deportment has always been admirable. He said later he did not know whether or not he had made the catch although he claimed it at the time in the heat of the battle. I have not the slightest doubt that if, as it should have done, the third umpire's decision had gone against him, Taylor would have accepted it without a murmur.

The third umpire, probably feeling under considerable pressure to make a decision as soon as possible, made up his mind much too quickly without appearing to have had a second look at all the replays. He turned on the red light and Atherton was out. He walked slowly off looking far from gruntled. It was a decision which could only have been given as a result of apprehensive guesswork and it flew in the face of the Laws of the game which state unequivocally that if there is the tiniest shred of doubt, the benefit must always be given to the batsman. It is absurd that such an important position, as the third umpire has now become, should be entrusted to someone who has had such frighteningly little experience. It is the duty of the ICC to make sure that the umpires who are appointed to fill this role should be officials who have enough experience to be able to cope with the problems that come their way and are not still wet behind the ears at this level of the game.

Stewart's disturbing weakness against spin was again ruthlessly and rapidly exposed by Colin Miller's off spin before a good partnership developed between Nasser Hussain and Mark Ramprakash. Just before the end of the second day, a fine cover drive off McGrath took Hussain to 50 and their stand was worth 76 by the close. Ramprakash reached his 50 early the next day but when they had put on 103, he nibbled outside the off stump at McGrath and at second slip, Mark Waugh, as always, made the catch look easy. England were then 187/4 and fourteen overs later they were all out for 227 with MacGill taking three more wickets with his leg breaks.

Hussain was marooned on 89 not out at the end of another horrendous collapse which had, of late, been such a feature of England's cricket. Mullally entertained in his customary manner, driving extravagantly across the line at Fleming for his fourth successive duck. When Australia batted again, Michael Slater made 100 in 68 overs while Langer and Mark Waugh (more cheers and less boos this time) made good 50s. Taylor's declaration left England to score 443 to win, but they got no further than 236, with the last five wickets falling for only fifteen runs. As always, Ramprakash resisted stoutly and Stewart fought bravely, if a trifle fortunately against the spin and was left not out with 63. How much better it would be if he came in first where he always has had the ability to dominate rather than barely to survive. Yet again a main batsman was left high and dry underlining the pathetic nature of England's lower order batting, although this time Mullally dug deep and encountered riches, snicking a four to the third man boundary before succumbing to Fleming for the second time in the match.

Two mornings later, we all awoke to the headline, 'England Bloody Awful' and reading on will have discovered that these were among the refreshing thoughts of none other than Mr Raymond Illingworth. Which made us all sit up sharpish. Mr Illingworth has taken the art of 'I told you so' politics to new and braver frontiers. His own managership of England had been, for an assortment of reasons he had found unaccountable at the time, less than the dizzy success he had anticipated. At least he now welcomed the proposed two-division County Championship although he was unable to resist the temptation to add, 'I proposed two divisions in 1976.'

In the same paper, perhaps predictably, Tim Lamb, the Chief Executive of the ECB, who merits a place in the premier league for finding silver linings, stressed that at the junior level, 'great strides were being made.' Thank heavens, it was nothing like as bad as we had all thought. How silly of us for jumping to the wrong conclusion. A page further back in this particular paper produced the news that the former Australian allrounder, Tony Dodemaide, was to join the MCC at Lord's as its Head of Cricket. I don't know about anyone else, but it all made me feel much more at peace with the world as I rolled over to negotiate my early morning cup of tea. At a time when all Englishmen were beginning to feel a bit doubtful about Australians in Australia, let alone anywhere else, we had now been ambushed by the news that they were taking over at Lord's as well.

After only three Test Matches, the Ashes were still in Australia's safe-keeping. The series had been as one-sided as the most pessimistic had feared and if it had not been for that famous storm at the Gabba, England would have been three matches down. The best Alec Stewart's side could do now was to draw the series which, as Australia already held the Ashes, would not be enough. The Australian public were owed an apology by English cricket. Even they were growing tired of seeing England thrashed like this. Of course, they wanted to win but victory is best appreciated when it comes after a good fight. For three Test Matches, England had simply capitulated. It is no good their apologists saying that there was not all that much between the two sides and that if only the catches had stuck and Stewart had not had such bad luck with the toss … If only Graham Thorpe had not had to fly home with a recurrence of his back trouble and if only the Perth pitch had been a trifle more sympathetic to English batsmen … The fact was that England had been thoroughly outplayed. Sides that deserve to win do not drop their catches and are able to compensate for losing the toss, while injuries are a permanent part of cricket just as a fast bouncy pitch is what one should expect in Perth. England had had their chances but were not good enough to take them and when the going was tough, Australia had consistently played the better cricket.

They were, too, masterminded by an outstanding captain as we have already seen. England were captained by a man who, as a cricketer, is nothing short of a phenomenon, but his career has been bugged by England's perennial shortage of allrounders since Ian Botham called it a day. Six batsmen, four bowlers and a wicket keeper has left the attack dangerously exposed and, according to the way in which the game has moved on, the spinner has almost inevitably been the man to have been left out of the twelve when the selectors have plumped for only four bowlers. Stewart's wicket keeping, which had begun as a makeshift affair used in order to fit another batsman into Surrey's one-day side, had become the only available option for the selectors if they were going to give the England side a more balanced look. To start with, he was not close to being the best keeper in England and every so often, after important chances had gone begging, common sense made the selectors jettison Stewart's keeping and turn to Jack Russell, who was generally supposed to be the best wicket keeper in the country, although that, too, was a debatable point.

Every time this happened, the six batsmen seemed to fail England and so back Stewart came behind the stumps so that a seventh batsman could be accommodated. But when England went to the West Indies at the start of 1998, Russell was chosen and Stewart was not going to have his batting compromised by the wicket keeping job. Of course, Sod's Law now took a hand and Russell had a shocking tour. So when South Africa came to England in 1998, Stewart was not only back wearing the gloves but he was also captain, as

Michael Atherton had fallen on his sword after losing to the West Indies in a series in which he should never have been captain in the first place.

Stewart's brand of leadership was outwardly more positive than Atherton's. He understood the importance of body language, which had never interested his predecessor. There was something mildly inspiring and impressive about Stewart striding onto the field at the head of his side or with a bat in his hand. Every entry he made should have been accompanied by martial music of the Colonel Bogey variety. Here was a man whose every gesture showed that he could not wait to get at the opposition. How different from some of the others whose obvious distaste for the battle ahead hardly made edifying viewing. Some would clearly loved nothing more than to be still waiting in the pavilion. But Stewart led his men from the front and it was only when he reached the middle and began to deploy them, that his limitations became apparent. For five years he had been in charge of a Surrey side which had had the ability to have won any of the county competitions and more than once at that, and yet had conspicuously failed to win any except the Sunday league in 1996, which was his last year in charge. Stewart is a thoroughly modern cricketer in outlook and approach. He is deeply suspicious of spin and uses it only as a last resort and he does not understand field placings for spinners. He worships at the shrine of seam bowling for he feels that that way he can maintain control for longer. At the same time he is disappointingly unadventurous. He is too prepared to let the game drift in the field, hoping that something will turn up and that a wicket will fall without doing anything positive to try and make it happen.

Successful captains are blessed with a certain amount of flair and also the natural inclination to take a calculated risk. A good captain is able to read the way a game is likely to develop; he watches the opposing batsmen carefully and objectively notes their strengths as well as their weaknesses. When two opposing batsmen settle in, he does not allow the game to get into a groove, but instead tries to unsettle the batsmen, to make them think that he has something up his sleeve, or that he has seen something they have not. In Australia there was a marked gulf between Stewart and Taylor, who had a much more agile grip on the game. I have no doubt that if Taylor had been in charge of England, he would have got more out of his players. For example, he would have made greater use of Mark Ramprakash as an off spinner and would have given him the confidence to believe in his own bowling. As it was, Ramprakash could not have failed to pick up the message that came through loud and clear from his captain, which was that Stewart does not believe he can bowl. If he had changed sides, I wonder how Stewart would have viewed Mark Waugh's off spin which Taylor used to such telling effect. Stewart's lack of imagination over Ramprakash cost England what might have become an important bowling option. I daresay, too, that the brainstrust of Gooch and Lloyd in the pavilion were as unimaginative in their approach off the field as the captain was on it. When a side is up against a better team as England were now, a captain has to be that much more mentally nimble to try to create opportunities and then to take advantage of them. He has to try and do something to upset the natural course of events which Stewart, to England's cost, was unwilling or unable to do.

I never thought I would be glad to get away from Adelaide. Maybe it was just that I needed a break from England's cricketers. I arrived in Sydney in the evening on the day Australia had held on to the Ashes and I had written a piece on the aeroplane for *The Australian* wondering if I would live to see the day when England would regain the Ashes, which shows how depressed I was by it all. I was going to have a week away from the cricket, thank goodness, while England went to Canberra for a one-day game against the Prime Minister's Eleven and then on to Hobart for a more strenuous contest against what amounted to the Australian Second Eleven. My purpose in going to Sydney was fourfold. I wanted to spend a few free days in one of my favourite cities in the world as well as meet up with some old friends. Also I was going to do the rounds of radio and television stations to promote the predecessor to this book, *Cakes and Bails*. Lastly, I was going to meet up and have a lot of fun with the best concierge in the world, Tony Facciolo. Facci hails from Venice and has made his life in Sydney, first at the Sheraton Wentworth Hotel and now at the Sheraton-on-the-Park. He is the president of the worldwide concierges' association, '*Le Clef d'Or*', and his range of influence is remarkable. Ring him from London and tell him you want a room in Timbuctoo and he will be back to you within the hour with all the details. There will also be a free car at the airport to meet you and an upgrade to a suite if one becomes available, thrown in for good measure. He will send a message of greeting to the General Manager, who will be an ally from the past, and when you arrive you will find that the red carpet has been unrolled with something of a flourish and your room rate is less demanding than you will have feared.

Facci, who is of medium height and rather more comfortably upholstered than he once was, is a gem. He is a mine of information on just about everything; he is the best source of gossip I know. He knows everyone of any importance. I have seen Bob Hawke, when he was Prime Minister of Australia, make a detour to call in at the old Sheraton Wentworth to pass the time of day with him. Gough Whitlam, Malcolm Fraser and probably John Howard will all have trodden the same path. Royalty, statesmen, film stars, top businessmen and high society all know Facci and, in one way or another, he will have improved the lot of them all. We had first met in the late fifties in England when he worked at the Savoy in London. I would not dare to go to Australia without nipping in to see him and up to the neighbouring Taffersall's bar in Elizabeth Street to ward off dehydration with him. When I say he is the greatest Mr Fixit of all time and the truest of friends, I cannot pay him a higher compliment.

Copies of *Cakes and Bails* had been flown out from England and Simon & Schuster in Sydney had arranged all sorts of interviews and signing sessions for me. Having worked each southern summer for several years doing an alternative cricket commentary for Radio 2UE, who were the top rating station in Sydney, I knew that particular world quite well. Our commentary had been rather more lively than the traditional offerings from the Australian Broadcasting Commission and I had joined forces with Dennis Cometti, a lively commentator both on cricket and Australian Rules Football, and good friend from Perth, Ray 'Slug' Jordan, a former Victorian wicket keeper whose broad Australian accent was not often confused with my own. Also there was Bill Jacobs, known as 'Fagan', who had managed a number of Australian sides, and whom I had once filmed on video when he was riding a donkey with a frightening lack of skill on a beach in Grenada in the West Indies. We had also been helped by various members of the Channel Nine television team. Richie Benaud, Ian Chappell, Tony Greig, Bill Lawry and for a short time, Rod Marsh all did stints with us although Marsh was fired by Kerry Packer himself when he had the temerity to say that he thought Test cricket was far superior to one-day cricket, which had been such a feature of the Packer-inspired revolution of 1977. We had all had the greatest possible fun but after the sudden death of Brian White, who was General Manager of 2UE and had been the driving force behind the start of our commentary and the formation of the team as well as a personal friend, the others in charge at UE and the sister stations became less keen and in the early nineties the plug was pulled.

Sydney is exciting wherever you look. It has an infectious bustle at street level, the views of the Harbour are eternally brilliant and the people are friendly and on the go. The bars are full and vibrant, the restaurants have got better and better and the wine is as good as you want it to be. The Harbour Bridge and the Opera House are both wonders of the modern world; it has a fantastic cricket ground and a fish market which is mind-boggling. I must also recommend Doyle's fish restaurants, especially the one at Watson's Bay. Sydney also has a great many other things which I shall keep wishing I had not forgotten to mention as I read through these pages. One minor irritation is the taxi drivers who seem to be foreigners almost to a man and it is an incredible piece of luck if any of them have even the faintest idea of where you want to go. They don't all read their maps as well as they might, either, let alone speak English, which can lead to conversations that grow increasingly fraught as the journey gets underway. One's original request is nothing more than a pretty flimsy base for geographical negotiation.

My days in Sydney began on the twenty-somethingth floor of my hotel where I would have a delicious breakfast surrounded by the sort of views that glossy magazines regard as obligatory but which seldom happen in real life. The huge windows looked out over Hyde Park and the Cathedral and then on towards Woolloomoolo and the Harbour, which I think is marginally even more spectacular than that of Rio de Janeiro. I had gone there as assistant manager on a Derrick Robins tour to South America early in 1980. It was on that tour that the Robins Eleven bowled out Brazil for something like 27 and Derek was beside himself because of the four byes which he had felt had grossly and unforgivably enlarged their total. Robins, a most successful businessman, owned Banbury Buildings and also Coventry City Football Club which, with considerable help from Jimmy Hill, he put firmly on the footballing map. He was a hard taskmaster and fierce competitor.

As I breakfasted in Sydney, I could just make out the Heads in the far distance with the high-rise blocks of Manley away a fraction to the left. It was a scene which never palled. Every morning when I looked out at it, I saw something different and, of course, in the foreground was the famous Opera House, once so memorably described by actor Robert Morley as looking like 'A lot of nuns in a rugger scrum.' From my impressive vantage point I could also just see the floodlight pylons at the Sydney Cricket Ground away to the right.

Elizabeth Street nudges Hyde Park on one side and the Sheraton on the other, and is a main artery, even if the painfully slow and apparently unsynchronised traffic lights bring one all too frequently to a grinding halt. Go out down the stairs to the small back entrance of the hotel and you come into an old fashioned, narrow street where young and old sit alongside each other. This is Castlereagh Street where the narrow pavements are always full and the usually stationary cars jammed bumper to bumper to an orchestration of much tuneless horn blowing. The small shops are doing a good trade, the newspaper sellers on the corners are making their presence felt and it is an invigorating bustle. Those narrow streets were not laid out for the convenience of modern traffic or, indeed, for the size of the modern population. Pitt Street, which is Castlereagh's parallel neighbour, has solved the problem by allowing itself to have been turned into a slightly overemphasised pedestrian precinct. David Jones, the department store where one zooms all over the place on the most up-to-date moving staircases, is in Castlereagh Street while Grace Brothers hold court in

Pitt Street, even though both look as if they could do with a tiny bit more elbow room. A short walk tells you that all is thriving and the cash tills are working overtime.

A week's rest and recuperation, in the evenings visiting Lucios in Paddington or Pruniers in Woollhara or other equally splendid restaurants, with a constant flow of interviews promoting *Cakes and Bails* during the day, put me in a better state of mind for the Fourth Test Match in Melbourne. Unhappily, the chances of it being anything other than a repetition of the first three seemed so remote as not to be worth considering.

One memorable adventure came two days before I left for Melbourne. I was picked up at eight o'clock in the morning and taken for breakfast to Sydney's fish market in Pyrmont, which was a wonderful experience. There is something irresistible and satisfying about row upon row of gleaming dead fish expertly and appetisingly arranged on their huge refrigerated stalls by the assembled company of fishmongers. It made me think that as this was done on a daily basis, the fish population must, generally speaking, be alive and flourishing. Their lugubrious faces and unseeing, rather soulless eyes, seemed to speak of the resigned inevitability of ending up on a dining room plate. There was, too, I have to admit, a mild look of rebuke in their faces, as if to say, 'It's all very well you having such a good time but if one of my bones ends up sticking somewhere down your throat, don't come to me for sympathy.' John Dory, Whiting, Bream, Cod, Swordfish or whatever, their eyes seemed to follow me wherever I went.

The oyster openers were operating feverishly as if engaged in permanent combat to see who could open the most in the next ten minutes. I suppose it's just like riding a bicycle: impossible if you don't know how to do it, but once learned never forgotten. Pick up the oyster in the left hand, fiddle away for just a moment with the pointed knife, the oyster opener's tool, to find that place where the shells are joined, one more fiddle and, hey presto, the shell opens. Some of them were clearly showing off for they would keep on opening the oysters without even looking down at them and, just to rub it in, would carry on a conversation with a fellow opener whom, I suppose, they may have been trying to put off. It was fascinating to watch and there was, too, that lovely smell of salty water which comes out of a newly-opened oyster. We bought a couple of dozen, some rolls, which were so fresh they were still hot, and some coffee, and then sat in the sun on a neighbouring jetty and devoured just about the best breakfast I have ever eaten. The only improvement would have been a bottle of champagne and I was told later that I could have had that, too, if I had known where to look. It would have been the ideal accompaniment unless, of course, you happen to be a fan of Black Velvet, a mixture of Guinness and Champagne. But, even without either, it was still almost too good to be true.

CHAPTER SEVEN

Catches Win Matches – Victory for England at the Melbourne Test

I flew down to Melbourne three days before Christmas with a strong sense of anticipation which was, I am afraid, accompanied by a hollow foreboding at what would be in store for England's cricketers at the Melbourne Cricket Ground on Boxing Day and thereafter. But first, I was staying for two nights with Jeremy and Jennifer Oliver in Hawthorn and as Jeremy is one of Australia's leading wine writers, it is not hard to understand why I was travelling with a keen sense of expectation. He met me at Tullamarine, Melbourne's airport which is situated such a long way from the city that it might almost be someone else's. It is, of course, very close to Sunbury, once the home of Sir William Clarke whose statue one passes on the lovely walk through the Fitzroy Gardens each day on the way down to the MCG. It was at Sunbury in 1883 that The Honorable Ivo Bligh, who was captaining England, was presented with the famous urn containing the ashes of a bail or maybe a ball. The idea of the

Ashes had come into being when Australia had beaten England at the Oval by seven runs the previous year and a mock death notice written by a journalist, Reginald Shirley Brooks, had been put in the *Sporting Times* the following day. It read:

> In affectionate remembrance of English cricket which died at the Oval, 29th August, 1882. Deeply lamented by a large circle of sorrowing friends and acquaintances. RIP. N.B. The body will be cremated and the Ashes taken to Australia.

Ivo Bligh's side won the subsequent series in Australia and during the tour they played a game at Sunbury where a group of ladies had the idea of making the Ashes a reality. These they then personally presented to the England captain. Bligh became the first England captain, therefore, to regain the Ashes. In time, Ivo Bligh succeeded his father as the Earl of Darnley and kept the urn at Cobham Hall, the family seat in Kent. The story has been handed down that an over-zealous housemaid, while dusting the mantelpiece where the urn was kept, had knocked it onto the floor and it had opened spilling its contents. Whereupon, the butler, a veritable Jeeves, realised what had happened and put back a dollop of ash from the huge fireplace before returning the urn to the mantelpiece. No one can be sure, therefore, what is actually inside the urn which, in 1927, when Lord Darnley died, was given by his widow to the MCC. It has remained, unopened, at Lord's ever since, apart from making one state visit to Australia for the country's Bicentenary in 1988. Most appropriately, the urn travelled there and back on the same aeroplane as Prince Charles.

I had first met Jeremy Oliver in Melbourne just before Christmas in 1983 when I was covering a series against the

West Indies. I was staying, as we always did in those days, at the Windsor Hotel, which was the traditional home for cricket teams in Melbourne. With the festivities looming, I needed to stock up with wine and I found myself in a wine store in Chapel Street in Prahran where I was helped by a young assistant who clearly knew a great deal more about the subject than I did. Talk also turned to cricket and it became fairly clear that he knew a good deal about that, too. When I had gathered together all the boxes I had bought they were rather more than an armful and it was going to be quite a business to get it all back to the hotel by taxi. The assistant had introduced himself as Jeremy Oliver and told me that he was studying agriculture at University and was earning some much needed pocket money at the wine store over Christmas. He now offered to cart all the wine round in his own car when he knocked off that evening. I promised him we would drink a bottle of his own choice when he arrived. Jeremy turned up with the wine and I'm not sure we didn't drink two bottles. He told me that he was writing a beginner's wine guide but he had not yet been able to come up with a title. I suggested 'Thirst for Knowledge' which was what it ended up as, and at the age of twenty-one he was and still is, the youngest writer ever to have published a book on wine. He has more than lived up to this promising start, aided and abetted by his most attractive wife, Jenny, whose palate is also pretty nimble.

We had an unashamedly thirsty two days. They live in a charming house in Hawthorn which they have more or less completely rebuilt, and one of the principal features is the cellar, which is Jeremy's own invention. After moving one or two things out of the way, a circular part of the highly polished sitting room floor lifts up revealing a ladder leading down to a most impressive array of bottles stacked against the circular walls. It was full to the brim and he was already scratching his head about the need for an extension. We began with a glass of Chardonnay and I soon lost track of the number of times the trap door was raised and lowered, but I do know that not a single indifferent bottle came back up the ladder. The 1992 Giaconda chardonnay and the 1994 Bass Phillip pinot noir were to die for. He told me all about his life, for it had been a year or two since we had last met. His frenetic activity seemed to me bound to lead to an early demise but people in the wine trade are past masters at the art of spitting and not swallowing when they are tasting wine. I have tried awfully hard to pick this up but I am afraid it still eludes me.

When Jeremy is not teaching at his wine school, making an after dinner speech or a wine presentation, he is hunched over his lap-top writing pieces for magazines or another book about it all. If all else fails, he rushes to his tasting room and starts on the bottles he has to taste for his annual Australian wine guide, in which he is splendidly forthright and is not afraid to ruffle one or two pretty conservative feathers. There are more than nine thousand wines in the *Onwine Australian Wine Annual* which he publishes himself. On the blurb at the back of the latest edition and probably all the others as well, he confesses that his ambition is to commentate on cricket for the BBC. The next time I see him, I shall try and arrange a mutually advantageous swop, which will have to include at least the bottom half of that redoubtable cellar.

The day before Christmas Eve, Jeremy had arranged a lunch at a tiny Italian BYO restaurant by the Melbourne Market called Maria's. The Australians seem to have been the inventors of Bring-Your-Own restaurants. These are such an excellent idea because you can bring much better wine with you than you will ever be able to afford from the usual restaurant wine list where the mark-up is colossal. You can bring what you want and at the right price. The *dramatis personae* at Maria's included James Hird, the captain of the formidable Australian Rules Football team of Essendon, of which Jeremy is a passionate supporter. James was in his mid-twenties, extremely good looking in a tallish, open-faced, fairish sort of way and was full of charm. He was reckoned to be just about the best in the business and I shudder to think how much money he was earning. But there was not the slightest side or arrogance about him. None of that awful the-world-owes-me-a-living bombast and strutting that so many lesser sportsmen parade so unattractively and with absolutely no justification. He is, too, a considerable expert on wine and not just the Australian variety, which probably means that he has spent too much time with Jeremy. His knowledge was most impressive and after lunch it was at his insistence that we visited a hugely upmarket wine bar in that exciting new development around the Casino just across the Yarra. There we drank a bottle of French burgundy at a supersonic price in order to compare it with the 1994 Bass Phillip pinot noir we had drunk again at lunch and which undoubtedly came off the better of the two.

Another Essendon devotee who came to lunch was a powerful businessman of Greek origin, Alex Epis, who had much to do with the running and, I daresay, the financing, of the club and who, in his spare time, produced some lovely Epis Chardonnay which kept on appearing in half bottles. It was awfully chablis-like and a delight. The other member of the party was Danny Corcoran who had been James's personal coach at Essendon. He had just jumped ship and gone to the Melbourne club who play at the MCG. Everyone still seemed to be great friends and I suppose he had struck a better deal. During lunch football took a back seat to wine and it became abundantly clear that I knew much less about the subject than anyone else. As I listened to them all talking about Alex's plans to produce more Chardonnay – when Alex was at a party, it was never that easy to listen to anyone else for he made the rest of us sound like unadventurous monosyllabics – I could not help but wonder how the conversation might be going if we had been in, say, London or Manchester and the principals had been Alex Ferguson, David Beckham and his private coach who, I suppose, might have been Posh Spice. After two days with Jeremy and Jenny, I was glad to be able to report that the Australian wine industry was in mid season form.

The England cricketers had arrived back in Melbourne considerably chastened, for on the last day in Hobart they had left the Australian Eleven to score 375, a target they reached for the loss of one wicket in only 228 minutes off 55.2 overs. Once again Greg Blewett was the chief destroyer, making 213 not out to add to the 169 he had made in the first innnings. By all accounts, Graham Gooch, the team manager, had quivered and bristled and had been apoplectic with rage. It was someway short of the ideal build up to a Test Match which, with the Ashes already decided, it was feared might test the loyalty even of the Melbourne public in spite of their ingrained habit of trooping along to the MCG in bulk on Boxing Day.

It was made to seem all the more forlorn when Boxing Day dawned grey and wet. On the walk through the Fitzroy Gardens, we passed Captain Cook's Cottage, which was involved in trying to cope with a major invasion of Japanese tourists who seemed to possess not less than three cameras each. I was glad of the ebullient company of Robin Marlar and Stephen Fay who was covering the tour for the *Independent on Sunday*. Robin had flown in from Sydney that morning and was as sprightly as ever. When we arrived at the MCG we found that the doubters need not have worried. The ground was bustling and already more than half full. Just before play was called off for the day without a ball being bowled, the announcement had been made that 61,580 people had come to the ground. To me, this indicates that a great many Melbournians must have been dropped on their heads when babies, or else that the city's sadistic inclinations when it comes to beating the Poms have become somewhat exaggerated. The Australian Cricket Board will not have enjoyed having to give the spectators their money back. The rain let up for just long enough before the official starting time of eleven o'clock, to enable Mark Taylor to win his fourth successive toss and, in the delicate terminology of cricket, to invite England to bat. It then began to rain again and in terms of the small print at the bottom of the ticket which settles these things, the toss on its own does not constitute positive action and the money had to be returned.

In keeping with the Laws of the game, the two captains had exchanged teams before the toss had been made and this meant, therefore, that they could not be changed. Whatever conditions applied when the match began, the captains were stuck with their original selections. The disturbing news as far as England was concerned, was that Alex Tudor who, but for those pusillanimous selectors, would have played in Adelaide, and had surely been a certainty in Melbourne, had suffered a light injury to one of his hips while playing football with his team mates on Christmas Day, and would not be able to play. Apparently, it was nothing more than a slight flesh wound of which some players would have made light. Tudor has acquired something of a reputation of being hard to get onto the field and in three years he has only played twenty odd games for Surrey. With all their troubles, the last thing England now needed was a reluctant starter, especially one as talented as Tudor. Perhaps if he had played in Adelaide, his bubbling enthusiasm for Test cricket might have altered his thinking and so maybe the selectors had got what they deserved. Angus Fraser had taken his place and the team could not be changed even when Tudor recovered in time for the delayed start.

This news made Sporting Index sit up and when Fraser took only two wickets at the MCG and did not then make the cut for the Fifth Test in Sydney, the management hired a bus and took off like Michael Schumacher for the Savoy Grill and tucked in like nobody's business. They had won back the money they had lost in the Caribbean and at the time of going to print, no charges had been laid against their man in the dressing room for nobbling Alex Tudor on Christmas Day although, I daresay, investigations are continuing. Their clients got their own back, however, when they took leg spinner Stuart MacGill to their hearts and the nineteen wickets he came up with in the last two Tests cost Compton and his lot £3,000 apiece. Needless to say, he took it on the chin. Just occasionally the muscles on his weather-beaten face crack into a watery smile as a knock on his office door at 12.45 heralded the arrival of the sandwich tray and with it, a brimming glass of water. It's a foolish man who feels sorry for bookies and I have it on good authority that overall Sporting Index had an excellent series and that Compton and Lindsay are back on the luncheon trail in earnest.

The second piece of news for England, that Stewart was going to open the batting and Warren Hegg, the reserve keeper, take over behind the stumps, produced strong and opposed reactions. There were those who felt it was crazy to disrupt a side in order to accommodate one player. Stewart would now open with Atherton, which meant that Mark Butcher, who had scored two centuries as an opener in his last six Test Matches, would now have to drop down to number three. Consequently Hussain and Ramprakash, who had established themselves through the series at three and four, would each have to move down one place in the order.

The argument which I subscribe to is that Stewart's greatest use to England is as an opening batsmen where he naturally dominates. It is no good tucking him away in the middle order where he is immediately exposed to spin, which he plays so badly. It is no good, either, compromising his batting by making him keep wicket. Throughout the series, England had been seriously short of runs in the first innings and this is usually where Test Matches are lost in Australia. Atherton had been shot to pieces by Glenn McGrath and he and Butcher had been unable to give them the sort of start they had managed against South Africa in England. If Hegg had to play in place of a seventh batsman, so be it. He was unlikely to be significantly less productive than John Crawley whom he would replace. But, if the tour selectors had seen this scenario arising, they would surely have plumped for Leicestershire's Paul Nixon as the reserve wicket keeper for he is a better batsman than Hegg. If England had been holding their own in this series it would have been wrong to mess the side around for Stewart, but if that had been the situation, the thought would never have occurred in the first place. In the circumstances of a tour which had become an embarrassment, I believe the right decision was now made over Stewart. I know he had fiddled around for hours for his 63 not out against the spinners in Adelaide, but he showed then that in the middle order he is at best a match saver while as an opener, he is a match winner.

On the four remaining days, play was now scheduled to begin half an hour early, at 10.30, and finish half an hour later, at 6.30, so that as much as possible of the lost first day could be made up. This is an excellent initiative by the ICC although it ran into trouble on the third day which also turned out to be the last when the final session continued for more than four hours, which was too long for everyone. When Stewart and Atherton emerged from the pavilion the day after Boxing Day, their progress to the wicket was an eye-opener. Stewart strode out like a man who did not want to waste a second before starting to have a go at the new ball. Alongside him, Atherton's down-at-heel shuffle made me think more than anything of a turtle who is having a dreadful time trying to decide whether to stick its head out or not. In order to keep pace with Stewart, it had to be a rather quicker shuffle than usual. Having reassembled himself at the crease at the business end, Atherton pushed half forward to McGrath's fifth ball which was wide of the off stump. There was a loud noise and Atherton stood shocked as a huge appeal rang round the ground and the Jamaican umpire, Steve Bucknor, who usually likes to take his time about these things, put his finger up with almost indecent haste. Atherton shuffled off whence he had come, a figure of dejection. When I met him in the street the day after the match, he told me that his bat had hit his pad and although he did not know whether he had hit the ball, there had been such a tremendous noise that he knew there would be no reprieve.

With his brother-in-law, Mark Butcher, now at the other end, Stewart drove, airily and in hope, at Fleming's first ball and edged it through the slips for four. English nerves had hardly settled after that when Butcher played half forward to McGrath and hit the ball in the middle of the bat only for Justin Langer to hold a brilliant diving right-handed catch at forward short leg. England were 4/2 and safety, let alone prosperity, seemed as far away as ever. Stewart's next scoring stroke also went for four, this time off the inside edge as he played forward to Fleming. The agony of the first few overs cannot have helped the cause of the assembled company of insomniacs in the UK who had decided to tune in to *TMS* for a few moments before dropping off into a dreamless sleep. After that, they will have needed more sleeping pills than ever.

English supporters were cheered up a little when Nasser Hussain began with a couple of rasping strokes off the front foot and this obviously encouraged Stewart, who began to drive and square cut as only he can. The Australians had brought into the team fast bowler Matthew Nicholson, who had caused havoc when England had played Western Australia at the start of the tour. Jason Gillespie and Mike Kasprowicz were unfit which gave him his chance. First night nerves got the better of him now when Taylor brought him on for McGrath. He is tall with a gangling run up and nothing was particularly coordinated, especially the end product, and 26 came from his first three overs. When Stuart MacGill came on to bowl the twentieth over, Stewart came charging down the pitch and drove him over wide mid on for four. His transformation against spin was extraordinary. For the first time in the series, except that for that brief flurry in England's first innings in the Perth Test, he felt the ball coming off the middle of the bat, and by the time Taylor turned to spin, his confidence was probably higher than it had been at any other time so far on the tour. If ever justification was needed for promoting him in the order and telling him to leave his wicket-keeping gloves in his bag, this was it. In MacGill's next over he straight drove him for a no-nonsense four which brought him to 50 from 66 balls with eight fours.

His uncomplicated strokeplay and his decisiveness did English nerves a power of good. But only two more runs had been scored, taking the total to 81, when Hussain thrust forward at a wide one from Nicholson at which he should never have played and, to universal delight, Ian Healy made sure of his 350th catch in Test cricket. Hussain departed like a man who was utterly mystified by the unfairness of life, although he had only himself to blame for a stroke that was probably caused by a moment of lost concentration. For such a good player, Hussain makes too many misjudgements or has too many lapses in concentration. The admirable Ramprakash took his place and was soon showing off that splendid technique. Because of his innate fear of the darker side of life which, as far as cricket is concerned, means getting out cheaply, his inclination is to shelter behind his technique in defence rather than put it to more profitable use. He had been impressively consistent in Australia although when he did not run out of partners he had continually been getting himself out in the fifties or sixties. It was undoubtedly a blemish on his overall performance that he had been unable to translate any of these splendid pieces of batting into the hundreds that he should have been scoring with some regularity.

Now, at last, he began to bat as if had exorcised that particular ghost, and for nearly thirty overs he and Stewart dominated in a way no two Englishmen had managed since Butcher and Hussain had played so well in England's first innings in Brisbane. They were not checked either by the return of MacGill. A square cut for an all-run four off the leg spinner took Stewart to his first hundred in a Test Match against Australia and, after that slightly edgy start, what a handsome and dominant innings it had been. Sadly for England, he may have allowed his mental celebrations to continue for too long, for when he had scored only four more, he swept at MacGill without taking the precaution of moving his front foot across into the line of the ball and was bowled behind his legs. It was not a good stroke, but as Stewart walked off to ringing applause, he must have felt that he had made his point with some emphasis. It was another major blow when, two runs later, Ramprakash also seemed to lose concentration and unaccountably drove Steve Waugh to mid on. He was deceived by Waugh's gentle pace and once again Ramprakash had been undone when he should been concentrating on his hundred. Graeme Hick was the only batsman to hold up Australia after that and he played some fine strokes. But after swinging MacGill away to mid wicket for a huge six, he tried to repeat the stroke later in the over and holed out most unnecessarily to deep mid on. The final total of 276 did not seem as if it would be enough.

It was made to look a little better when Darren Gough removed both the Australian openers in his first spell. Michael Slater, who only seems to make runs in the second innings, was lbw to one which nipped back on him, and when Taylor dabbed outside the off stump, Hick came up with a good catch low to his right at second slip. No one in the England side tried harder than Gough in this series and several times, most particularly in the First Test at Brisbane, he had been dreadfully unlucky. Yet for all his zest and enthusiasm, it is not often that he knocks over, say, four of the first five in the order. It is true that he did so now but he was helped by a couple of wild strokes the next morning and he did not ruffle the batting side in the way that Glenn McGrath or Allan Donald would have done, or indeed as Fleming had done in England's second innings in Perth. Is it bad luck or does he have shortcomings as a fast bowler of which this is a reflection? Australia had reached 59/2 at the end of a wonderful day's cricket.

It was no less compelling the next day when, although wickets fell regularly, Steve Waugh held Australia together and fashioned a magnificent hundred in an innings of rare quality. Langer and Mark Waugh had got away to a good start and the score had reached 98 when Waugh was lbw trying to play Fraser to mid wicket. Steve Waugh's first ball had lifted on him and he played it away uppishly to fine leg, but this was the nearest he came to making a mistake and he recovered himself almost at once with a glorious on drive for four off Fraser. Langer had reached 44 when he drove at Gough and was well caught by Hussain in front of his face in the gully and, at 151, after two flashing offside strokes, Darren Lehmann cut wildly at Gough and was caught behind. This brought in Healy who is always a feared opponent as far as England are concerned, and he at once started to pick up runs in that busy way of his. He is a delight to watch as he plays those cheeky improvisations and runs furiously between the wickets. The 50 stand arrived and Waugh reached his own 50 in nearly two and a half hours. But one run later Healy pulled at Fraser and Dean Headley held the catch at fine leg. Neither Fleming nor Nicholson lasted long and Australia's eighth wicket went down at 252 when Gough felled Nicholson with a scorching yorker. England were in the market for a slender first innings lead. For three and a half hours, Waugh's defence had been impeccable and at the same time he had never wasted the chance to put a loose ball away for runs. It had been the careful and watchful innings of a great technician who is no mean tactician either. There is something commendably relentless about Steve Waugh's batting.

During the tea interval, the tactician took over and he came back onto the ground with a restless intent to play his strokes regardless. He threw his bat around, slashing Gough for four, slogging him over mid wicket for another, and in moments England were once again involved in a damage limitation exercise. The bowlers went to pieces and appeared to have no idea what to do next. The greatness of Waugh as a batsman has never been better displayed than it was now, for he was suddenly able to dominate an attack which he had for a long time simply been content to hold at bay. Not many players can transform themselves as he did now. He was lucky to find such an admirable partner in MacGill who is far from being a mug with the bat and he too hit the ball extremely hard. A hook for two brought Waugh to his hundred from 156 balls and the attack disintegrated. When MacGill was caught behind cutting at Mullally, they had put on 88 in just over an hour and a half and ensured that Australia would have a significant lead. It turned out to be 70 when McGrath was out before another run had been scored and Waugh was left with 122 after having faced 197 balls and been at the wicket for 315 minutes.

I don't think I was the only person there to feel that in the 98 minutes of Waugh and MacGill's partnership England had effectively lost the match. This feeling was confirmed when, in the second over of England's second innings, Atherton was trapped on the crease by a ball from Fleming which pitched on the middle and leg stumps and hit the off. During our street corner conversation two days later, Atherton told me he should have played forward rather than being caught in no-man's land. With his helmet in his hand, Atherton shuffled off to the pavilion to reflect upon his first 'pair' in Test cricket. He was shaking his head and managed a watery smile. I suppose in those situations, gallows humour is a legitimate last resort. The brothers-in-law, Stewart and Butcher, were heroically undeterred by this nasty setback and they produced some stirring strokes which let the Australians know that they still had a fight on their hands. The score had reached 61 in double quick time when MacGill ran in again with all that twinkling and beguiling enthusiasm which seems to be the prerogative of leg spinners. Butcher swept off the middle of the bat and Langer at forward short took hurried evasive action and to his and everyone else's amazement the ball hit him amidships and stuck. Butcher will not have been good company that evening.

Dean Headley, the nightwatchman, did not hold things up for long the next morning and neither did Stewart. Soon after reaching 50, he stretched forward to MacGill and was caught off bat and pad at silly point. With four wickets down, England led by only eight runs. A useful stand now developed between Hussain and Ramprakash and both played some fine strokes, especially Hussain. They had put on 49 and it began to look as if they might set Australia something worthwhile when Ramprakash was, for once, let down by his technique as he pushed forward to Nicholson and was bowled between bat and pad when the ball nipped back into him. You could sense his disappointment and maybe his anger as he walked off looking like a man who would not easily see the funny side of things. Hick took his place and was more at ease with himself than he often is. He calmly began to pick up the runs on offer without doing anything extravagant and saw Hussain to his 50. Hussain celebrated by cutting Nicholson with fearsome power and the ball made a noise off the bat like a shot out of a gun, but the smile froze on Hussain's face as Slater took the catch in front of his knees at cover. Had it been a yard either side of him … Hegg enjoyed slashing Nicholson over the top for four but it went to his head and he tried to do it again without realising that there was now a fly-slip in attendance. At the other end, Hick moved up a gear and began to go for his strokes. Then, at 221, Gough pushed MacGill to silly point and in the next over Hick unaccountably drove all round Fleming and was bowled.

England were 221/9, 151 runs ahead and even the most optimistic of Englishmen, if one such still existed, can only have given them the faintest chance of victory. Our old friend Mullally who, as we have seen, only carries a bat because someone once told him he should, and had five ducks to his name in the series so far (although his batting had contributed greatly to the general entertainment value), now entered the arena. The Australians will have viewed his arrival with something less than apprehension. McGrath who is slightly taller than Mullally and much fuller of menace, does not take prisoners and was clearly in no mood for charity now. His straight, fluent run up to the wicket was full of deadly intent and when Mullally, with a good old fashioned heave, dispatched him back over his head for four, McGrath stood there looking for all the world as though Cinderella had pulled a gun on him. He walked back to his mark with smoke coming from his ears and when he hitched up his trousers before setting off again, it was a gesture which seemed to carry a message. But dear old Mullally was having the time of his life and when McGrath let go of the next ball, he swung his bat with impudent defiance and this time the ball disappeared over long on for four. There was a little bit of chatter from both participants and McGrath's manner suggested that the Archangel Gabriel had turned up with an AK47 in his hands. Of course, it couldn't go on and when Mullally swung again, the ball steepled up on the legside and McGrath charged after it failing to notice that Michael Slater from short leg was also hovering underneath it. But this was one McGrath had to have himself and he trampled Slater into the ground when he took the catch. By then, Mullally had scored the most memorable sixteen runs of his life, had put on 23 with Angus Fraser and, as the afternoon wore on, the importance of these runs became ever more significant. Australia needed 175 to win and there was not an Englishman in the ground who was not busy remembering what a hash Australia had made of it at the Oval in 1997 when they had been left to score a mere 124 to win and had been bowled out for 104.

England's second innings had ended just after 3.10, within half an hour of the official tea interval at 3.40. In accordance with the Laws, tea was therefore taken between the innings with the result that the final session of the day stretched on for just over four hours. First, the extra half an hour which had been tacked on to the end of each day after the first had been lost to rain, had to be added on. Then, there was the half an hour which is available at the end of any of the first four days if the umpires consider a result is possible, and which the Australians wanted to claim. Then, there was the chance, as happened, that all this time would elongated still further by a slow over rate. Four-hour sessions are too long for everyone, players and spectators, and the ICC need to make provision to prevent this happening again.

It seemed imperative that if England were to have any

chance of a remarkable victory, they had to take at least a couple of wickets early in the Australian innings, but it did not work out that way. Taylor and Slater gave the innings a work-manlike start and had taken the score to 31 when Slater played back to Headley and was lbw to one that kept a little low. Ten runs later, Taylor seized on a short one from Mullally and Headley judged the catch well at fine leg. Before another run had been scored, Langer played back and felt for Mullally outside the off stump and, although Hick's catching had improved noticeably and he got both hands to this one low to his right at second slip, he could not hold on. Langer and Mark Waugh now put their heads down and runs came in what for England was a steady and discouraging trickle. Waugh was as quick as only he can be on anything loose while, in his less demonstrative left-handed way, Langer gleaned runs on either side of the pitch.

At 100/2, it had surely to be all over, especially as Steve Waugh was still waiting to come in. Then, at 103, when Australia needed 72 more, there came one of those extraordinary incidents that completely change the course of a match. Mullally bowled a short one to Langer who swivelled and hooked powerfully and the ball flew away to square leg about two feet off the ground. Mark Ramprakash was fielding there and his initial movement was to his left before he realised the ball was going the other way. He managed to change direction and dived as far to his right as he could, judging it perfectly with the ball hitting his hand in the right place. He held on as he hit the ground. It was a staggering catch which must have shaken Australia just as it inspired the Englishmen. Steve Waugh now joined his twin brother. Australians must find his presence wonderfully reassuring. He is as unflappable as he is unemotional and gives off an aura of dependability. His arrival should have soothed Australian nerves. When he took guard, it will not have occurred to many that Australia could still lose the match.

The brethren had put on 27 without undue alarm when Mark, the flashier twin, played back to Headley, and in trying to work the ball to leg, played a fraction too soon and Hick took the catch in both hands diving to his left at second slip. So far in the match, Headley had been largely unnoticed. He had taken 0/86 in Australia's first innings and he had been a distinctly forgettable nightwatchman, but now in the final innings he had hung on to Taylor and removed Slater and Mark Waugh. Suddenly he became a larger-than-life figure as he ran in to bowl with rhythm and ferocity, the products of a confidence which had come flooding back. He was now a bowler who could not wait to get his hands on the ball. It was as if he knew he would succeed.

Darren Lehmann thumped one straight back past him for four but when he drove again, the ball flicked the edge and Hegg gratefully accepted the catch. England will not have particularly enjoyed watching Ian Healy make his way to the crease, so often has he made important contributions against them with the bat. Most recently, in the First Test of the series, he had made a hundred as had his partner, Steve Waugh, who was now at the non-striker's end. They need not have worried. The score was still 140 when Healy played forward to Headley and Hick again held on at second slip, this time falling to his right. As Healy left the ground, English supporters really felt for the first time that this was a story which might after all have a happy ending. This feeling was underlined later in the over when Damien Fleming floundered half forward, was hit on the pad and, after a long pause, was sent on his way by umpire Bucknor. The scoreboard now showed that Australia were 140/7, 35 runs from victory. But Steve Waugh was still there.

At this point, he found a most resolute partner in Matthew Nicholson and together they inched the total towards the target of 175. Once it was in the 160s Australia were again the favourites. The day's allotted number of overs had now been completed and Stewart and the England side set off for the pavilion. But Waugh spoke to Bucknor and, feigning great surprise not to say astonishment, Stewart and co. were forced to return. Waugh had wanted to continue against an attack which must have been feeling pretty exhausted. On the other hand, the light was now awkward because at one end the bowler ran in in bright sunlight but bowled in dark shadow, while at the other, he approached the wicket in the dark before being brilliantly lit up in his delivery stride. Headley raced in again summoning up every last ounce of energy. Nicholson groped and there was Hegg, who never put a foot wrong, throwing up the catch.

With fourteen needed to win, Steve Waugh faced Gough with MacGill at the non-striker's end and McGrath padded up in the pavilion. Waugh played Gough's first ball to fine leg and without any second thoughts about trying to protect MacGill from the strike, ran through for the single. After the leg-spinner's efforts in the first innings, Waugh may have thought that MacGill could look after himself. Gough thought otherwise and now produced the perfect yorker, which made a dreadful mess of MacGill's stumps. With thirteen needed, McGrath must have been having dark thoughts as he stalked out to bat about those fours Mullally had hit. He took guard and peered round the field before failing to make contact with his first ball, which was outside the off stump and he probably didn't see. He did not locate the second either which hit him a crushing blow on the boot and umpire Harper agreed with Gough and the rest of the England players that it would also have rearranged the stumps. England had won by twelve runs. Steve Waugh, who had made a total of 152 runs in the match without being out, walked ruminatively back to the pavilion. He will have been telling himself that Australia should not have lost. Maybe it occurred to him that he might have done a little more at the end to try to make sure they did not.

It had been a wonderful cricket match, completed in three extended days in which an extraordinary level of tension and excitement had been created and maintained. It was a game which this Ashes series had desperately needed. It was irrelevant that if the Ashes had still been an issue, Australia would probably have won by about six wickets just as they would surely have made those 124 two years before at the Oval if the old urn had still been up for grabs. During the first three Test Matches of this series such notable critics as Ian Chappell had publicly doubted that England were any longer worth a five-match series. After Adelaide, it had been difficult not to agree with him. There had been rumours, too, from New Zealand, that their representatives were going to raise this very issue at the meeting of the ICC in Christchurch in early January. Momentarily it looked as if there was a chance that the oldest and most traditional series of all might be downgraded because of the pathetic state of England's cricket.

But this Test in Melbourne had grabbed the imagination of the Australian public and suddenly interest in the series rose from not very far above zero to the top of the scale. If reports which we, on *TMS*, had received from London were anything to go by, the same was true in England. It had been a real red-blooded contest and it prompted the chairmen of the two Boards of Control, Denis Rogers and Lord MacLaurin, to get together and work out a plan of action if anyone in Christchurch now dared to suggest that future Ashes series should consist of only three Test Matches. This Fourth Test also put one-day cricket in its place, something which needs to be done from time to time. When a two-innings match fluctuates as this one had done at the MCG, there is nothing much finer in the whole sporting spectrum.

After a last walk back through the Fitzroy Gardens and past Captain Cook's Cottage, where even the Japanese tourists had given up in the twilight, I had to write a piece or two for the next day's papers. So it was not until just after ten o'clock that I was able to catch a taxi to Hawthorn for a final go at Jeremy Oliver's cellar. I had alerted him that I would be very late and he had most nobly arranged for a little to be left in every bottle so that I would not miss out entirely. Jenny had also produced a delicious steak, but as I tucked in, I was unable to avoid another monumental ear-bashing from Alex Epis who had brought along some more half bottles of his own Chardonnay. Eight different wines were poured and by the time I got back to where I was staying in Collins Street, I hardly knew what day it was, let alone the result of the Test Match. It was the perfect way to unwind and thank goodness Jeremy sent me a list of the wines we drank otherwise their names would never have survived Alex's garbled soliloquy which, by the time I left – in mid-sentence – had become a candidate for the *Guinness Book of Records*.

It had been a happy evening. So too, was lunchtime the following day although it was also tinged heavily with sadness. One of my oldest friends in Australia is Peter McFarline who, in the seventies and early eighties, had been the distinguished cricket correspondent of the Melbourne *Age*. In 1981/82, he was in New Zealand covering the tour by Greg Chappell's Australian side when he was taken ill and the doctors eventually discovered that he had contracted an extremely rare illness called Syringomyelia, which affects the central nervous system. It was started by a cyst on Peter's spine which the doctors were unable to remove. It is impossible to imagine the effect this dreadful diagnosis would have on you. Peter took it on the chin from the start and with his extraordinary spirit and his wonderful, ebullient and waspish sense of humour, he kept going as long as he could. He was very good for Australian cricket because he was a writer who could not stand bullshit and those who purveyed it and he was never afraid to expose them. He made many telling journalistic contributions at the time of the founding of Kerry Packer's World Series Cricket, which emerged from the depths of an uncomfortable secrecy in 1977. I know of no one who has had a better network of contacts, and even when reporting the dullest and most insignificant of cricket matches, he was always well worth reading partly because of his trenchant views and partly because he had the rare ability to spot things in the play others would miss.

Gradually, the wretched disease took hold of him and early in 1990 he was condemned to a wheel chair, not that it had the least effect on him, outwardly at any rate. He was still as cheerful as ever in his buoyantly extrovert way and carried on with life regardless, but at what inner cost, one can only guess. The last Test series he watched was when the Australians toured South Africa in 1993/94 and this was only possible because of the fantastic support he had and still has from his wife, Del, who has been every bit as brave and cheerful about it all as Peter has himself. The catalogue of horrors continued. In July 1995 he had a respiratory arrest followed by pneumonia, and during the treatment his vocal chords were damaged and he has been unable to speak since, although his brain has remained as agile as ever. All he can do now is to mouth his words which can be lip read. Since the end of 1995, he has been on a ventilator and since then he has not been able to use his nose to breath or his mouth to eat and drink and he is fed through tubes which disappear straight into his stomach. His lunch was poured in by a nurse when I was there.

Del picked me up in the city and we drove the fifteen miles to the hospital where Peter lives. He had not been warned of my visit and was sitting in his wheel chair with tubes going everywhere and a sizeable ventilator whirring away alongside him keeping him on the straight and narrow. When I stepped in front of him, his infectious smile, which was the Peter of old, did me good. I must have been with him for more than an hour and there was not a single word of complaint. I was staggered, too, to find how well informed he is. Better so, I suspect, than many members of the Press Box. He has a constant flow of visitors who keep him up to date on everything that is going on. He had a stand in front of him on which rested that morning's copy of *The Age*, although he is unable to move his hands and the pages have to be turned for him. He was full of chatter and though Del had to interpret some of it, the longer I was with him, the better I became at lip reading. We had a far from one-sided conversation. He hears everything and is always keen to have a laugh. He is not totally anchored to the hospital, either, and on one day of England's game against Victoria he was taken to the MCG where he enjoyed seeing many of his old friends. There was the thought while I was there that the two of them might fly up to Sydney for a few days. If Peter thinks there's a good chance of it being alright, he is prepared to give these things a try, which speaks volumes for his spirit.

The best news of all is that he is still able to write a couple of pieces a week for *The Age*. He had had his say when the story broke about Mark Waugh and Shane Warne's involvement with the illegal Indian bookmaking fraternity. I have no doubt that he knew more about this story than I did and he assured me that there was still plenty more of it to come. He is extremely good, too, at comparing the contemporary game with the game as it was when he was writing about it on a daily basis. He comes up with some splendid stuff from his trips down memory lane. He mouths these pieces to Del who writes them out for him to correct. Having seen his circumstances, I came away staggered by his sheer guts and bravery.

Most of us, if faced by his problems, would have given up years ago. He is an object lesson to us all and I would love nothing more than to be able to hold him up to the world of moaners who are all around us, to show them how thoroughly ashamed of themselves they should be. If a man in Peter's condition can see that life has a funny side to it and is well worth living, I think we should all be ashamed. No wonder when I asked Del how she was bearing up, she had said happily, 'It's wonderful, he's such an inspiration to me.' By the time I left Peter, I had seen for myself. Almost his final words to me (and I was able to lip-read them) were, 'I can still enjoy a glass of whisky too, even though they pour it straight into my tummy. The effects are good.' And he grinned, fit to bust. As I walked out of the sunny, corridor-like room in which he was sitting, he asked for the newspaper to be put back in front of him and I expect he felt another piece coming on. What an example Peter is for all of us.

It was the end of December when I saw him. By the time the English summer had come round I had had those three operations and gained a new appreciation of Peter's inspirational strength and guts. In time, I recovered; he never did and never will and yet is still able and eager to laugh as loud, as long and as often as any of us.

CHAPTER EIGHT

Spin Rules Supreme in Sydney

Staying up until all hours, drinking far too much and trying to remember the elusive words of 'Auld Lang Syne' all seem to be an inescapable part of life on 31 December. Anyone who decides to go quietly to bed on the basis that the 1 January will be much the same as any other day, is considered to be more than something of a spoilsport. It is all greatly overdone and these words are being written in fear and trepidation at the excesses that will be indulged in on the evening of the 31 December, 1999. In 1998 Bitten arrived in Sydney at the crack of dawn on New Year's Eve and although I reached the airport ten minutes before she did, I managed to position myself at the wrong gate. So instead of gaining a few important brownie points, I lost a whole lot more. If she had remembered the name of the hotel in which we were staying and gone off on her own, it might have taken me half the morning to locate her.

We failed to secure a couple of berths on a boat that would

have allowed us to watch the extravagant firework display from an excellent vantage point on the Harbour. Nevertheless, the evening went off a great deal better than I had expected. Those friends of mine who got on the Harbour trip seemed generally to have had a night of more or less unmitigated disaster. One was decanted at the final mooring point on the north shore and, being unable to find any sort of transport, was forced to undertake an immensely long walk back across the Bridge and from there to the Eastern Suburbs – not the best way of greeting 1999 or any other year, come to that. The main trouble with boats is that it is absurdly easy to find oneself cornered by the biggest bore within a five hundred mile radius and the only conceivable escape is to jump over the side, which is seldom rewarding. Bitten and I kept both feet firmly on dry land and had an excellent dinner at the Sheraton after which we joined the General Manager and his wife, Peter and Marie-Louise Thompson's party at the next door table and welcomed the New Year in with them. We drank some more wine, sang 'Auld Lang Syne' with hesitant gusto, made a token appearance on the dance floor, narrowly avoided taking part in a conga and then made our escape and the happy discovery that our bed was as comfortable in 1999 as it had been in 1998. A great relief.

The next week brought back some happy schoolboy cricketing memories from Norfolk. After living in Sydney for nearly forty years working for Swires, those megabuck traders who are based in Hong Kong, Edward Scott, an old friend and one-time fast bowler, had returned to England where he had taken over as chairman of the company. We had played together for Eton. In 1956 Walter Robins, who had captained both Middlesex and England, brought down to play the school a Forty Club side consisting of eleven former Test cricketers. We not only beat them but Edward took no less than five wickets including those of the former Australian opener, Arthur Morris, and that of Denis Compton himself, who was starting the most tentative of comebacks having had a kneecap removed. He played almost exclusively on one leg and yet went on to make 94 against Australia in the Fifth Test at the Oval later that summer.

Edward's uncle, Archie Scott, the first Old Etonian bookie, lived at Runcton near King's Lynn and every year the Scotts organised a boys' cricket match in the summer holidays on the Runcton ground, which is now used from time to time by Norfolk for a Minor County match. I first met Edward Scott as a ten year-old playing in one of these needle contests, in which, as far as I can remember, the mums became a great deal more vociferous and competitive than the participants. It must have been in about 1950 or '51. One keen observer at some of these games was none other than the old Australian leg spinner, Arthur Mailey, who will then have been in his sixties and who was brilliant at coping with small boys. My mother always told me that one day he took off his coat and bowled me a few balls. Sadly, I can't remember it.

Arthur Mailey was a great friend of the Scotts and whenever he was in England he loved to come down to Runcton. He was a brilliant cartoonist, not least of his cricketing colleagues, and an extremely funny man besides. In 1956, he sent me a signed copy of a small booklet entitled *Cricket Humour* that he had written and illustrated. On the front was a delightful drawing of a bowler, dripping with sweat, handing a five pound note to the umpire who seemed to be making sure that no one was looking before he pocketed it. Just before this book was printed, I bought a delightful self-portrait of Mailey, which is shown here among the photographs. Also, not long ago, I was lucky enough to buy at an auction in Melbourne a menu from the dinner given at The Savage Club in London in honour of the 1934 Australians. Mailey was covering the tour as a journalist and on the menu he had drawn some splendid cartoons of some of those at the dinner. There is one of that literary giant, A. P. Herbert, who had signed his name under the cartoon. Mailey had made much of his nose.

The menu came from the collection of Ben Barnett whose name is written in pencil at the top of the menu. He was the great Bertie Oldfield's deputy behind the stumps on that tour and later settled in England and went on to captain and keep wicket for Buckinghamshire in the Minor County Championship. I can well remember him in action against Norfolk at Lakenham and I was entranced by his loud Australian appeal and also by the baggy dark green cap which he always wore. Dinner that night in 1934 at The Savage had consisted of consomme brunoise, cold Scotch salmon and cucumber, strawberries and cream followed by coffee – solid inter-war British fare. I wonder what they drank because the menu refrains from mentioning it.

Edward Scott was in Sydney for Christmas and the New Year together with his wife Angela, who narrowly failed to become the first lady member of the Australian Jockey Club and is a considerable horsewoman herself. On the second evening of the Fifth Test Match, we rousingly celebrated Edward's sixtieth birthday in the upper room at the Belview Hotel in Paddington. On New Year's Day, we spent the afternoon with them racing at Randwick where we were given what I can only describe as Royal Box treatment. When he was in Australia, Edward had owned quite a number of highly successful horses although I am afraid that the one called Blowers justified none of the minuscule amount of confidence bestowed upon it by the punters. Randwick is an excellent racecourse where everything is easily accessible. Racing in Australia is nothing like as expensive as it is in England and there is little of the attendant snobbery. But there was one glaring similarity to English racing.

The winners were just as difficult to pick.

I have made the journey to Sydney Cricket Ground by taxi on countless occasions over the years but it had never been as difficult as it was on the first morning of the Fifth Test. It took well over an hour for a journey which should have taken hardly more than ten minutes. I had to walk the last half mile and when I arrived at the top of the Bradman Stand, I was not the only person who was hot and bothered. The cramped eyrie which had been allotted to *TMS* did not make any of us feel any better.

It was an important toss to win but Sod's Law, which had been having rather a time of it, dictated that Mark Taylor, in what turned out to be his last Test Match, would become the first captain of Australia to win all five tosses in a Test series in Australia. There were no prizes for guessing that he chose to bat. These days the pitch at the SCG invariably turns from the start and does so increasingly through the five days during which the bounce also becomes lower. Australia had at last decided to bring back Shane Warne who had, by all accounts, just bowled well for Victoria against New South Wales at the SCG, and with Stuart MacGill in the side, Colin Miller made the third spinner. There were rumours that England were going to pick Ashley Giles, the left arm spinner who was practising at Brisbane with the others who had flown in for the forthcoming one-day competition, the Carlton & United series. In the end, they did not select him, which made sense for in the one Test Match he had played, against South Africa at Old Trafford in 1998, he had not looked up to it at this level. Therefore Peter Such was England's only spinner and it was an indictment of his form in Australia that Robert Croft was not chosen as well. In the late seventies, John Emburey and Geoff Miller won a Test Match at Sydney with their off breaks and in the sixties, two more off spinners, Fred Titmus and David Allen, had fared none too badly.

It was a vibrant first day played in front of a full-house crowd lured by the dramas of Melbourne. Australia lost three early wickets before being saved by a fourth wicket stand of 190 between the Waugh twins. Steve carried on from Melbourne, unsmiling, determined, supremely efficient and giving the bowlers nothing. On the other hand, Mark was, as usual, more flamboyant and gave the impression that he was enjoying himself while his twin brother was engaged relentlessly on a self-denying ordinance. It came as a great surprise when Steve got himself out when he was four runs short of his hundred. He suddenly came charging down the pitch to Such, drove across the line and the ball hit his off stump. It was strangely out of character. Mark had reached 121 when he was caught behind playing half forward to Dean Headley, and Darren Lehmann was the next highest scorer with 32. There was a terrible clatter of wickets at the end of the innings as Darren Gough completed a spectacular hat-trick. Healy was caught behind cutting and then two splendid yorkers burst through the tentative defences of MacGill and Miller, neither of whom seemed entirely sure of what had happened. It was the first hat-trick for England against Australia for a hundred years, since J. T. Hearne's at Headingley in 1899. Australia were now all out for 322 and their innings had accounted for the whole of the first day.

For the first two days of this last Test Match we had Bobby Simpson, the former Australian captain, in the commentary box with us. When his playing days had ended, he became one of the most successful coaches in the history of the game. He orchestrated the transformation of Australia's cricket under Allan Border's captaincy in the late eighties and early nineties. When Simpson took over as coach of Australia for the series against England in 1986/87, their cricket had reached rock bottom and Mike Gatting's side won that series. He proceeded to gather together youthful talent where he perceived it and systematically to take that talent to pieces and to reassemble it. It required skill and patience. Simpson has always been a man who has roused strong feelings, both for him and against him, but he is the most lucid thinker about the game and understands it as well as anyone can ever have done.

Listening to him now making his observations while England were in the field on the first day, made me wonder yet again about the direction the England players received from within the dressing room. He made some telling points. In this first innings, Steve Waugh was facing the off spin of Peter Such with Dean Headley on the boundary at deep backward square leg, presumably waiting for the sweep. Yet when Waugh plays that stroke, he goes down on one knee and fetches it from outside the off stump, hitting with the spin, and the ball goes away to deep and rather straight midwicket. He played one such stroke for six against Such at Adelaide and some others along the ground. When Such came on now, Headley went straight to backward square leg and that was that. If he had been sent to a straight deep midwicket, Waugh would either have had to take the risk of being caught or he would have had to have forgotten about that particular stroke and compensate elsewhere. This would have set Waugh a problem that might have played on his mind for a time and, who knows, might have upset his concentration. It is situations like this which make the whole process of cricket so fascinating and is one of the reasons why coaches who can sit back and see things in a different perspective can be so useful to their captains. Of course, Waugh now swept Such to deep mid wicket with impunity and England and Alec Stewart missed a trick, and so apparently did David Lloyd in the England dressing room.

It was Simpson's opinion that while the Waughs were together, the seam bowlers should never have had three men in front of square on the offside saving one – a cover point, extra cover and mid off. The Waughs are brilliant at picking up singles and there was often a huge gap at mid wicket into which they were able to push the ball repeatedly for the singles that kept rotating the strike. One of those three fielders on the offside should have gone over to midwicket with mid off moving a yard or two wider and cover a fraction straighter. A third fielder would not be have been needed there unless half volleys were going to be served up, but they are bad balls and a captain must never set a field for bad bowling. Stewart's field placings did not make life as hard for the Waughs as they might have done. Why couldn't someone in the English camp see these things?

It was comments like these which illustrated the meticulous manner in which Simpson had approached his job of coach. They spoke volumes for his knowledge of the game, but he does not have a monopoly in this and surely the England dressing room could have come to similar conclusions. There seems to be a feeling within the England camp that if a cricketer is good enough to play for his country, he does not need to be told what to do. Simpson always saw it as his job to shape talent and to advise players how to make the most of their ability, not only for themselves, but also for their teams. Having played for Australia while Simpson was coach, I have no doubt that the current coach Geoff Marsh, although more understated than Simpson, carries on his good work. It would be interesting to know what sort of equivalent conversations the management orchestrates within the England dressing room.

Losing the toss made this an almost impossibly difficult match for England. But it was still a disappointing second day. Alec Stewart soon edged McGrath to third slip where Warne juggled and held on. After that all the batsmen played themselves in but none went on to make more than John Crawley's 44, which was, by some way, his most composed innings of the series. At the end of England's first innings, Bobby Simpson made another interesting point. He compared the number of singles scored by the two sides, both of whom had batted for approximately the same length of time in their first innings. Singles are a most important component part of any big total, not only because they help the score but also because they are the means whereby the batsmen rotate the strike, with all the attendant problems that causes the bowling side. While both the Waughs have any number of big strokes in their lockers, it is always most noticeable how they play for the singles as well. With England's batsmen, one was given the impression that they regarded the single as something which just happened rather than being deliberately played for. Having played the stroke, they looked up and found the single was there, rather than playing the ball deliberately into the gap or short of the fielder so that the single could be taken. Australia scored more than eighty singles in their first innings, England only just over forty.

Much the most interesting aspect of the second day's play was the comparison between the two leg spinners, Warne and MacGill. Of course, Warne must have been nervous. This was his long awaited recall and expectations were high. No one will have known better than Warne that he was not back to his best and he hardly had the confidence now to bowl a googly, let alone a flipper. It was also the first time in his extraordinary Test career that he had to face the pressure of having another leg spinner, who had made great strides during the series, in the side with him. He will also have had to take a deep breath when, as was right and proper, MacGill was given the ball first.

Warne was thrown the ball for the twenty-second over and the entire Sydney Cricket Ground sat bolt upright. Mark Butcher was facing and he misread the length of the fourth ball, played back, was hit on the back pad and Umpire Hair's index finger was the next thing he saw. It was the perfect comeback for Warne but even after that, he never let himself go and was content to go on dropping his leg break on the spot without really ripping his fingers across the ball. On this performance, it was clearly going to be some time before he was again the bowler he had been – arguably the greatest leg spinner of all time. While Warne was deliberate and measured, taking each step with care, his rival MacGill, no doubt spurred on by the dramatic sense of challenge and showing the confidence his recent success had given him, was like a piece of quicksilver as he darted here and there, spinning the ball from hand to hand and almost running to get back to his mark.

The contrast with Warne was sharp, but the comparison between MacGill at Brisbane and MacGill at Sydney was just as acute. The country boy with a short fuse and a bit of a record now had the chance to show that he was a leg spinner who could stand comparison with the best. I wonder what his progress would have been through this Australian summer if Stewart had not swatted that innocuous full toss into deep backward square leg's hands in England's first innings at the Gabba. As it was, MacGill's confidence had grown visibly as that First Test wore on, he was not phased by his omission for Perth and then in Adelaide and Melbourne he had continued to exploit the Englishmen's endemic weakness against leg spin. Now in Sydney he scaled the heights with twelve wickets in the Fifth Test with Warne there alongside him to see for himself. Being small, like Mushtaq Ahmed and Abdul Qadir of Pakistan, and with his shirt sleeves buttoned to his wrists, MacGill gives the impression of being dartingly impish. Five wickets for 57 in England's first innings will have done him no harm; seven for 50 in the second innings will have made even Warne stop and think. MacGill was worth every single one of his wickets and watching him alone was worth the journey. He is such a splendid entertainer and there is something wonderfully infectious about a high class performer at his best when he makes it so apparent that he is hugely enjoying every moment of it.

In the first innings, all the England batsmen with the exception of Crawley, who had a beauty from MacGill, got themselves out to poor strokes having done the work of playing themselves in. If five of the first six in the Australian order had made the same solid start, almost certainly two of them would have gone on to make a significant score, as both the Waughs had in fact done. Then there is the thought that if England's batsmen had concerned themselves more with the matter of singles, Australia's lead might have been kept to 60 rather than the 102 which, with three days left and the ball turning more and more, meant that an Australian victory was the only realistic result. But far from becoming boringly inevitable, the cricket continued to provide remarkable entertainment. On the third day, Michael Slater played one of the great innings of Test cricket and if it had not been for his amazing 123 out of a total of 184, England might still just have pulled off an incredible victory.

Mark Taylor in his last Test innings, although we did not know it at the time, was caught at first slip as he pushed forward to Darren Gough. After that, Headley and Such went through the rest of the side in between Slater's strokeplay, which rivalled only the firework display on Sydney Harbour on New Year's Eve. But even so, we were all left with the slightly nasty taste that maybe Slater's was an innings that should never have been allowed to take place. When he had made 35, he appeared to have been thrown out by Headley from deep backward square leg. The television replays did not seem conclusive as Such, the bowler, was standing in front of the stumps. The third umpire gave Slater the benefit of the doubt, but having seen the replays from all the other angles, it became clear that he was out and the third umpire had given the wrong decision.

If Slater had gone then, there is little doubt that England's final target would have been very much less than 287 although it is, of course, impossible to say exactly how the Australian innings would have unwound thereafter. But now that cricket embraces modern technology, the appropriate number of cameras must be in place so that there is not the slightest chance of the game being caught with its knickers down like this again, especially at such a crucial moment. It makes the game a laughing stock if it cannot get its decisions right. The essential requirement is to have two cameras square with the wicket at each end. At least this incident, and others similar, prompted the authorities in England to arrange that these cameras were in place for the 1999 World Cup. Even then, when Pakistan played the West Indies in one of the early matches in Bristol, there was no available sideways-on replay when Moin Khan appeared to have stumped Ridley Jacobs off Saqlain Mushtaq. The ball before this incident, Saqlain had bowled Jacobs round his legs as he had swept, but Darrell Hair, the umpire at the bowler's end, was unsighted by the shot which blocked the stumps from his view. He conferred with Rudi Koertzen, the South African umpire at square leg who, in spite of an unimpeded view, for some extraordinary reason, said that he was also uncertain as to what had happened and Jacobs was allowed to stay. The laws that govern third umpires and the use of television replays state that they can still only be used in certain circumstances and this was not one of them. It is utterly absurd and infantile that although the technology is there and in this case showed quite clearly that Jacobs was bowled, those who control these things are able to restrict its use. It is yet another example of the game being made to look a laughing stock. All the world watching television can see that it is out and yet because of the mutton-headed attitude of the administrators, the batsman, Jacobs, was allowed to stay at the crease and continue his innings. Could anything be more puerile and ridiculous than that?

Slater is another impish character in appearance and style and like the other two of his ilk in the Australian side, Ian Healy and Stuart MacGill, he clearly relishes every moment out in the middle. In this series, the Australians played their cricket as if they enjoyed it, in sharp contrast to the Englishmen who seldom got beyond the hang-on-for-grim-death approach to their jobs, which I suppose is often the way with sides who are coming off second best. Slater strides out of the pavilion with an enthusiastic bounce and loves nothing more than to go for his strokes and to feel the ball racing away off the middle of the bat. He hits the ball as hard as anyone, he is twinklingly quick on his feet and a trifle impatient, which adds to his charm as does his open-faced boyish appearance. When the faster bowlers pitched short and wide or served up half volleys, they were unceremoniously cracked away to the boundary with an uncomplicated relish. Gough was driven back over his head and through mid off; he came down the pitch and drove Such over mid off for six and swept him for another; he then used his feet to make room to drive him through the covers. It was a virtuoso performance by a fine artist higher than usual on adrenaline. Slater was brilliant theatre and I can think of no contemporary batsman who communicates a greater sense of fun and personal enjoyment. I suppose it may be a fault that he only seems to makes hundreds in the second innings, which he did three times in this series, but I hope he makes no attempt to become a more scholarly performer but stays the way he is.

While Slater was batting like a windmill in a gale, wickets fell at alarmingly regular intervals at the other end, which served to highlight his brilliance. Of the others, only Mark

Waugh reached double figures before Mark Ramprakash held another extraordinary catch at square leg, right-handed high above his head with both feet far off the ground. Headley took four wickets and bowled with all the confidence he had gained from his superb effort in Melbourne, while Such made good use of a pitch now turning a long way. His final figures of 5/81 in 25.5 overs are a reflection of the damage inflicted upon him by the supercharged Slater. Slater's hundred came when he smashed Gough through mid off for four and when, finally, he cut at Headley and was caught behind, he had faced 271 balls and hit three sixes and eleven fours, figures which argue the case for an extremely well-ordered defence in amongst the pyrotechnics. He was out for 123 which represented 66.84 per cent of the total of 184. This has only ever once been exceeded, by Charles Bannerman, who made 165 out of 245 for Australia, 67.34 per cent, in the first Test Match of all, against England at the Melbourne Cricket Ground in March 1877.

England's target was now 287 which, in the conditions, was not even a remote possibility. They sensibly decided that if they were to have any chance of getting near it, they had to take the battle to the bowlers. If they went out and simply defended from the crease, they would be playing into the hands of Australia's triumvirate of spinners. The first over set the tone when Butcher cracked McGrath for three fours. McGrath, as usual, vigorously and tiresomely animated his disgust. His behaviour goes increasingly beyond the pale. Stewart drove the first ball of the next over, from Miller, to extra cover for four and all of a sudden it was looking like an exhibition match. After five overs, Miller reverted to his off breaks and after eight, he was joined by MacGill. Yet still the openers played their strokes and the fifty came up in the twelfth over. But it was surely only a matter of time. Two overs later, Warne took over from Miller at the Randwick End and Butcher came racing down the pitch to his sixth ball and was stumped by a distance. For the second time in the match Butcher was out in Warne's first over. The second wicket fell at 72 when Stewart adopted an identical approach to MacGill and also failed to make contact. In the circumstances, this stroke was batting without due care and attention at the least. In truth, it was a mindless charge. So England were 104/2 at the close and it had been stirring stuff, even if it was heavily tinged with an air of unreality.

Only six more runs had been scored on the fourth morning when Ramprakash played back to a ball from McGrath which he should have let go outside the off stump and Taylor snaffled the catch low at first slip. This was the 157th he had taken in Test cricket and, as it happened, his last. But it enabled him to beat his predecessor, Allan Border's record of 156 catches. The moon or the sun was not in the right quarter for Graeme Hick and he soon departed, bowled round his legs sweeping at MacGill. John Crawley was lbw playing no stroke at Miller who was bowling round the wicket, and the batsman walked off with the air of a man who was considering early retirement. His fellow Lancastrian, Warren Hegg, cut at MacGill and was caught behind. Nasser Hussain had watched these goings on from the non-striker's end and now reached his fifty with a delightful cover drive off Miller, but immediately afterwards chipped a ball from MacGill straight back to the bowler. England were then 162/7 and it took MacGill no time at all to dispatch the tail giving him figures of 7/50. Australia had won the match by 98 runs and the series by three matches to one. It only remained for Steve Waugh to be named as man of the series and MacGill as man of the match, before another Ashes series was wrapped up and laid to rest in the history books. The Waterford glass replica of the Ashes was entrusted to the safe hands of Mark Taylor and for England supporters the trudge up Paddington

Hill for a taxi was made to seem even steeper than usual that afternoon. The players now had to galvanise themselves for the interminable Carlton & United Series with Sri Lanka making the third side. As usual, fifteen preliminary matches were on offer before the best-of-three finals by which time surely everyone, with the possible exception of the Treasurer of the Australian Cricket Board, would be bored to tears.

The anticipated arrival of the Sri Lankans had been boiling away nicely all season in Australia. The reason for this was the continuing controversy over their off spinner, Muttiah Muralitheran's action. This had caused excitement in England when he had taken sixteen wickets in the Test Match at the Oval the previous August. David Lloyd, England's vociferous coach whose diplomatic skills are unlikely to win him a Nobel Prize, had questioned his action at a press conference in the middle of the match. This had eventually led to a verbal joust with none other than Geoffrey Boycott, but fortunately fists remained unclenched. Lloyd's outburst reeked of sour grapes. When Muralitheran had been in Australia in 1994/95, he had been called for throwing in Melbourne by Darrell Hair, their leading umpire, and in Brisbane by Ross Emerson, an umpire from Perth. Hair is a charming companion and an umpire more than prepared to take a stand, however unpopular, as he had done when England were in the West Indies early in 1998. Then, he had been prepared to give batsmen such as Jimmy Adams out lbw when they continually used their pads against the spinners pretending they were playing a stroke but with the bat tucked in behind the pad.

Hair had just written a book, perhaps emboldened by the dramatic success of Dickie Bird's autobiography, in which he had described Muralitheran's action as 'diabolical'. The Sri Lankans were most unhappy about this and were anxious that he should not stand in any of their matches in the one-day competition. Hair was censored by the Australian Board and

The groundsman at Vilamoura, Bill Sykes, tends the outfield with mower poised
and poodle to help.

Geoffrey Boycott descends on Grasse with his heavy artillery for the retrial of
1999. Max Clifford is on the left.

A picture of discontent. B[...]
Lara, left, and Ali Bacher [...]
the press in Johannesburg [...]
haven't yet seen the j[...]

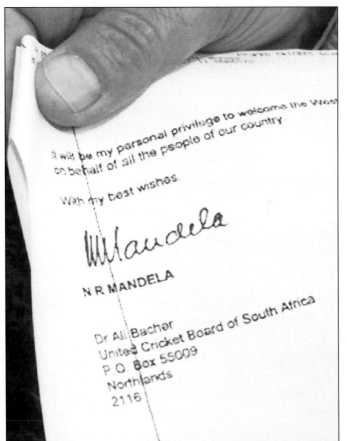

It will be my personal privilege to welcome the Wes[...]
on behalf of all the people of our country

With my best wishes.

Mandela

N R MANDELA

Dr Ali Bacher
United Cricket Board of South Africa
P.O. Box 55009
Northlands
2116

The pleading of a president.
Part of Nelson Mandela's
letter to persuade the West
Indies to honour their
commitments to South Africa

assing through a lock on the Murray River. Barry Jarman in the striped shirt, John Reid in the sun hat and HCB in a Panama. To the left, Kelly the dog enjoying a sniff.

A study in uneasiness. Shane Warne says his piece to the press at the Adelaide Oval. His grim-faced companions are Malcolm Speed, centre, and Mark Waugh.

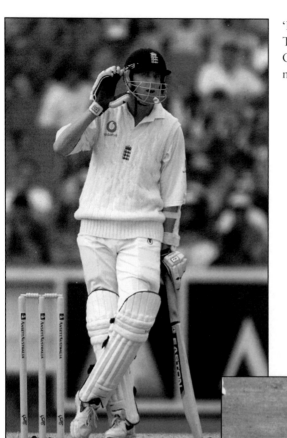

'I didn't quite get that.'
The imperturbable Alan Mullally baits
Glen McGrath at Melbourne during th
most important innings of his life.

(Righ
The Commander in MGM mode c
Bedarra Island. The look says it a
'Cut and retak

'That's no way to play
the hat-trick ball.'

Darren Gough bowls
Colin Miller in Sydney
and takes the first
hat-trick for England
against Australia for a
hundred years.

Arthur Mailey by Arthur Mailey. He surveys his stumps, the Valley of Pieces in the Valley of Peace.

No retake needed here. Bitten Blofeld in spanking form boards the boat that took us to Bedarra Island.

Laurie Bryant, aka Ben Hur, with mower cowering beneath him,
prepares even more acres for Pinot Noir.

The Valley of Peace, half an hour from the centre of Christchur
Two acres of perfection in the Cashmere Hi

'How dare you!' The Investigator, left, and the School Bully declare war.

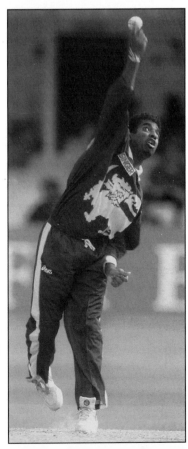

What the umpire saw. Muralitheran from fore and aft. Deformed or bent?

The condemned man.
Stewart contemplates
England's dismissal
from the World Cup.

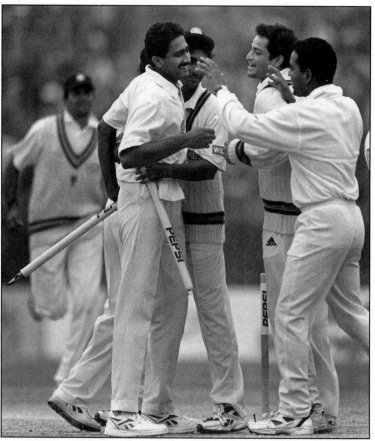

Did it really
happen? An
Kumble has
taken all ten
against Pak
and it's only
begun to sin

admitted that the timing of his book was wrong and was then told that he would not be standing in any of the Sri Lankan games. Being the man he is, it was always most unlikely that Hair would retract his opinion of Muralitheran's action. So it was not just because of his skill as a bowler that Muralitheran's arrival in Australia was being eagerly awaited. The vultures were gathering.

Although I had no more cricket to watch in Australia, there was no time for anti-climax to set in. In the latest chapter of the long-running Pakistani match-fixing circus, a Pakistani courtroom was to be set up in Melbourne two days after the end of the Fifth Test where Pakistani lawyers could cross-examine Mark Waugh and Shane Warne as a result of their recently exposed involvement with an illegal Indian bookie in Colombo. Immediately that little sideshow had finished, there was to be a full meeting of the ICC in Christchurch in the South Island of New Zealand where this same subject, and everything pertaining to it, was the principal item on the agenda. But in the meantime, Bitten and I and the Commander and his wife, Shano, had managed to find our way to Bedarra Island to explore the delights of the Great Barrier Reef.

My first visit to the Reef had been to Hamilton Island. At that time the Australian entrepreneur, Keith Williams's exciting development, aimed at turning the island into a high class resort, was in its relatively early stages. I had been so impressed that I even bought an apartment there which, in the end, went the way of all the other investments I have ever made. The development on Hamilton grew bigger and bigger, the food faster and faster and buildings higher and higher and the airport, over the hill at the back of the island, noisier and noisier. It all became too hectic and overpopulated and about as much suited for the remote desert-island holiday I was hoping for as Becher's Brook during the Grand National. The neighbouring Hayman Island was much too precious and far too expensive and when Bitten found she could come out for the New Year, I was rather scratching my head, especially as the Commander had let it be known that he wanted to explore the Reef. A friend suggested Bedarra Island of which I had never even heard. Bedarra is one of the Family Islands not far off the coast of North Queensland between Cairns and Townsville. Inevitably, it was another of those dashing discoveries made in 1770 by Captain Cook. The longer this Ashes series had gone on, the more Cook had had to answer for. By the end of the Sydney Test one felt that it would have been much better if he had managed to suppress his urge to travel altogether and got on with his garden in north Yorkshire.

We were to be on Bedarra for four days. The journey involved an early start from Sydney and after just over three hours a Qantas flight destined for Japan had decanted us at Cairns's international airport. We then had a two-hour wait before a tiny twin-engined aeroplane ferried us across to Dunk Island. We flew down near the Queensland coast and below us the country – a mixture of forest, rocky spurs and swamp, which made me think irresistibly of crocodiles – looked impenetrable. Then, we turned out to sea and in a few minutes came in to land at Dunk Island. In the tiny airport building, we were shown into a small room marked 'Bedarra Island' where the most important occupant was a fridge which dispensed all sorts of liquid goodies. We had hardly had time to swallow the first before we were ushered into a large four-wheel drive vehicle which took us the short distance to the jetty, where we found a rather superior white launch in which our bags had already been stowed, preparing to complete the last half an hour of the journey.

After we had gone through the safety drill and had set off,

the Commander's nautical tendencies came out like a rash and in no time at all he was sitting in the co-pilot's seat. For the next four days, he only spoke about port and starboard while the rest of us knew that one was left and the other right but without being absolutely sure which was which, only we didn't want to own up. We wove a determined course through the Family Islands and soon sighted our destination. Apart from a jetty, there was no other sign of human habitation visible from our boat although just before we arrived I made out one green roof in amongst the trees. Bedarra also had a Land Rover-type car which met all newcomers at the jetty and transported them back there when the time came. The distance cannot have been more than a quarter of a mile so it was a vehicle destined never to reach top gear in its entire career.

The name, Bedarra, comes almost certainly from a mispronunciation of Biagurra, its original Aborigine name, by the very first beachcomber, one E. J. Banfield, who decided he would like to live on the island. The present resort consists of only fifteen villas, set in the edge of a rain forest stretching round two lovely bays. Children and dogs are not allowed and with each villa able to house three people, only forty-five guests can be on the island at any one time. It does, unlike Hamilton Island, provide a near-perfect desert island holiday. There is a charming central dining area with a bar and a swimming pool, the kitchens, of course, are tucked away somewhere at the back, and there is accommodation for the twenty permanent staff who live on the island. The cost is paid in advance and the only slight local difficulty is getting used to the idea of helping yourself to whatever bottles of wine you want when you want. There was an extremely impressive supply but on the first few occasions I approached the fridge or wine racks to help myself, I found myself looking quickly and a trifle guiltily over my shoulder just in case anyone was watching. Aided and abetted by the Commander, we made serious inroads into their plentiful supply of Bollinger.

There were four highly qualified resident chefs and the menus for lunch and dinner were remarkable in their variety as was the choice of dishes each morning for breakfast. The 'Oeufs Benedictine Bedarra' should, by rights, have called for a new edition of the *Michelin Guide*. The shellfish was particularly delicious and one evening, by special arrangement, we all had Queensland mud crabs which are to die for, although one gets into an awful mess while eating them and the only really sensible thing is to take them into the shower with you. Our villa was extremely comfortable and the setting so idyllic I thought it would test even the Commander to shake us into anything approaching meaningful activity. How wrong I was.

After our arrival on the first day we had a very late lunch and then Bitten and I settled for glorious inactivity, extensively researching a heavenly beach all of forty yards from our villa. The water was warmer than anything I have ever swum in. Normally, I am a grade A waterfunk and the initial process of getting wet is agony but this was sheer bliss. In contrast, by the time we all met for dinner, the Commander who was now in Captain Cook mode, had walked about three times round the island and tried to hire a small boat to do the journey by sea. But as the weather was too rough he had contented himself by laying on an outing to Dunk Island the next day. It took me most of a delicious dinner to persuade him that a day lying in the sun with a book while living gently by suction, was much more my idea of fun. So, the next day he and Shano departed having given me the pitying shrug that Christopher Columbus probably gave his Number Two when he had told the boss at the last minute in Bristol that he had had second thoughts about leaving the wife and kids. A roar of engines and a gigantic plume of spray announced Arshed and Shano's departure for Dunk Island at a hideous number of knots, and left us to beachcomb and indulge ourselves in all the creature comforts Bedarra had to offer.

I knew it couldn't last and when they returned in the evening, Arshed was like a bottle of champagne which had been nicely shaken up with the cork poised to explode. With glee tinged, I fear, with a touch of sadism, he announced that the following morning we were all booked on a Big Cat that would take us from Dunk Island to the Reef and back again and spend most of the day doing it. The consolation was that Bedarra organised the most splendid picnic lunch for us with all sorts of shellfish and plenty with which to quench our not inconsiderable thirsts. We left Bedarra at some pretty ungodly hour and by now the Commander had made the co-pilot's seat his own and gave us a potted history of each small island we passed. There were many willing hands at Dunk Island to help us onto the Big Cat with our large picnic, and with forty or fifty other people on board we set off for the Barrier Reef. At the risk of being a party pooper I have to say that one ocean looks much like another to me and when it comes to looking at different coloured fish through a glass bottomed boat or whatever, my emotions are seldom stirred. As I had antici-pated, the lunch provided easily the most memorable part of the day, although I fear we were a trifle conspicuous sipping Bolly while everyone else had to make do with the fare provided by the Big Cat, which was somewhat less enticing.

We anchored at the Reef where recent rough weather had made the water rather cloudy. The fish, which we attempted to view from a sort of makeshift submarine with glass sides, were having a day off. The Commander was not in the least phased and let us know that the following day he had hired a pretty speedy cruiser, which was going to take the four of us back to another part of the Reef not normally visited by tourists. He assured us it would be just like having seats in the front row of the stalls. The Commander was becoming more theatrical by the minute. The next morning the seas were rolling along at quite a pace and, fortified by another formidable picnic, we boarded ship after breakfast and set off at a fearsome pace for the horizon. We bumped and splashed our way towards the Reef hitting some of the waves with the most tremendous bang. This drew yells of jubilation from Bitten and the Commander, while Shano and I, whose tummies were not made of such stern stuff, turned progressively greener, in my case even to the point where I actually turned down alcoholic sustenance.

On the way our delightful captain, who also owned the boat, suggested we trawled for a tuna and so two lines were baited and hooked, the boat slowed and we eagerly awaited our first bite. It took a while coming but then the rod on the left, sorry, the port side of the boat, bent like mad and the line raced out. The Commander, now in Ernest Hemingway guise with just a touch of the Izaak Walton of *Compleat Angler* fame thrown in, leapt into the chair and a mighty battle ensued. Thank goodness, the Commander was strapped in otherwise he might have been catapulted out by his intrepid prey. But inch by inch, foot by foot, he reeled in the wretched fish and eventually the Number Two lent over with a net and landed just about the smallest tuna I have ever seen. For a time it flopped fitfully around in the back of the boat and then, after the hook had been removed, it was thrown back into the Pacific Ocean with nothing much worse than a sore throat. The Commander's had been an immortal performance but some of the gloss had inevitably been taken off it by the size of the fish. We had all been waiting to take the definitive photograph of him standing proudly beside a 56-pound something or other, but this one was not even worth weighing. Alas, he was unable to put the record straight for that was the only fish he was able to attract. Almost the next time I thought of this incident, I was lying on the table in the Harley Street Clinic as John Muir, having given me an angiogram, was reeling in the tube from my heart.

We had our last splendid dinner that evening and then the next morning it was time to pack and return to civilisation. They had been four unforgettable days and a wonderful way of recharging the batteries, although I think I was probably the one who enjoyed it the most. We now had to concentrate on getting back to Sydney in time for a final farewell dinner. The next day Bitten and I were flying back to London while the Commander and Shano were setting off by car for the Snowy Mountains in New South Wales to cast their eye over some of the Australian ski resorts.

While we were being energetically uncompetitive on the Great Barrier Reef, the Hearing Rooms of the Victorian Civil and Administrative Tribunal in Melbourne had been turned into a Pakistan law court for a couple of days, complete with the country's green and white flag and the obligatory portrait of Mohammad Ali Jinnah, the founder of the nation. Within these hallowed portals, Mark Waugh and Shane Warne gave evidence to and were cross-examined by the Pakistan match-fixing and bribery Commission which had upanchored in Lahore before hoving to in Melbourne. After it had come to light that these two Australian players had accepted money from illegal Indian bookmakers in Colombo, the Pakistani authorities, quite understandably, felt that the evidence they had already given and the complaints made by Waugh, Warne and Tim May against Salim Malik, should be looked at again. However much the ACB had tried to brazen out their behaviour in keeping the Colombo incidents secret for so long, the fact that they had apparently helped with the costs of the Pakistani lawyers coming to Melbourne, seemed to indicate a willingness to cooperate at this late stage and also, perhaps, that they were not altogether sure of their own righteousness.

Mark Waugh and Shane Warne were now subjected to fierce questioning by lawyers representing the Pakistan Cricket Board and Salim Malik himself, in conditions which were altogether more formal and ordered than those which had prevailed when the Commission was sitting in Lahore and Waugh and Mark Taylor had given evidence the previous October during Australia's tour of Pakistan. There was never any accusation or even implication that Malik had been responsible in any way for the contact the Indian bookie had made with Waugh and Warne in Sri Lanka. But, as we have seen, it was Malik whom Waugh, Warne and May later accused of having offered them substantial bribes to play badly in a Test Match and a one-day international. Malik's lawyer in Melbourne, a rather dashing gentleman called Azmat Saeed, roundly and vehemently accused the three Australians of making up the story about being offered money by Malik, who had then been the Pakistan captain. It was a lively affair with Azmat scoring many points for oriental histrionics as he did his utmost to take the spotlight away from his client. The confrontations were robust and tempers became progressively more frayed.

Waugh and Warne both made statements and Waugh's, in particular, may have helped the Pakistani cause. He admitted that his involvement with the Indian bookie whom he knew as 'John' was longer lasting than he had originally admitted in that first press conference at the Adelaide Oval. 'John' had established contact with Waugh in the team's hotel in Colombo in September 1994 and his dialogue with Waugh had continued on a pretty regular basis until the following February when Ian McDonald had hauled the players in front of him during the New Zealand tour. Waugh promised that the questions he had answered had been harmless. Soon after they had met, 'John' had implored Waugh to introduce him to Warne whom he described as his favourite player. The introduction was effected the following evening in a casino close to the hotel. It was not a lucky night for Warne, and the next day in the hotel he met 'John' by arrangement and the bookie handed him an envelope saying, 'Here is a token of my appreciation. You're my favourite player.' Some appreciation, for $5,000 fell out of the envelope and according to Warne, his initial reaction was to hand it back saying that he had his own money. 'John' was then very insistent and so eventually Warne accepted the money and played with it that night at the casino. History does not relate whether or not he made good his losses of the previous evening. Warne admitted to only three subsequent telephone calls from 'John' and, like Waugh, he said the information he was asked to provide could have been picked from the radio or the newspapers and was harmless. I still find it extraordinary that it apparently did not occur to either of these two players that they were being set up for something else that was to follow. The two of them had made plenty of money out of cricket and neither will have regarded the sums on offer as especially enormous; both enjoyed a flutter themselves which suggests that they had been carefully chosen by 'John' or his bosses. Perhaps, being near the height of their powers, they rather enjoyed being singled out from the rest of the side. There was more than a touch of arrogance about their reactions to 'John' who must have been particularly pleased the way his initial contacts had gone.

Back in the makeshift courtroom there were some lively exchanges between Azmat and Warne as more details emerged about the Australians' earlier accusations against Salim Malik. Warne and May had allegedly been offered $200,000 by Malik to bowl badly in a Test Match. Waugh was then apparently also offered $200,000 by Malik at a party in

Rawalpindi if he and four or five of the others in the Australian side could be persuaded to play badly in a one-day international the next day. Azmat, whom I am sure will have been a table thumper and considerable gesticulator in the best legal tradition, asked Warne how many people had been present when Malik was supposed to have approached Waugh at that party. With that arch look of his, Warne replied that as both teams were present there must have been at least twenty-two. Warne was also asked why the Australians called Malik, 'the Rat'. The answer was disarmingly simple and something of a conversation stopper: 'Because he looks a little bit like one.' Azmat later took his life in his hands when he suggested to Tim May that the missed stumping off his bowling that resulted in the four byes that had allowed Pakistan to win the Test Match in Karachi had been deliberate. May's 'absolutely not' was mild in comparison to the answer which would have been given by Ian Healy, the wicket keeper, if the question had been put to him. Counsel for the Australian players furiously made the point that it was unforgivable to make this accusation when Healy, who is the fiercest of patriots, was not there to defend himself.

I am not certain whether anything very much was achieved in that courtroom in Melbourne during the two days it became a part of Pakistan except for a certain muddying of the waters, for which our friend Azmat may have been grateful. In the circumstances, I felt it was surprising, to say the least, that the presiding judge, Judge Qayyum, did not make the journey to Australia and it would have been fascinating to have been a fly on the wall – an Urdu speaking fly, of course – when his deputy, Judge Abdus Khawar, made his report to his boss.

While the photograph of Jinnah and the Pakistani flag were being taken down in Melbourne, the full might of the International Cricket Council had gathered in Christchurch.

The whole match-fixing and bribery business was at the top of their batting order and this time it was imperative that the august body should do something more than mouth empty words and continue on its way as a comfortable and affable travelling club. But before it could start taking brave decisions, the combined membership had to give the ICC the powers to do so. It had long been a toothless tiger because the member countries, at the last resort, refused to give the governing body control over their own affairs. The ICC was therefore in the splendid position of being able to huff and puff like mad and disapprove vehemently, wholeheartedly and unanimously about any number of issues but without any power whatever to do anything about it. We have already seen that when it did have the chance to do something constructive about Mark Waugh and Shane Warne's involvement with the Indian bookies, it had firmly resisted the temptation.

After the first day's meeting, it looked as if nothing was going to change. None of the countries wanted to surrender any of their control over their own players and what they got up to. It is interesting that the England and Australian players had already made it clear in private that they did not think the administrators had the political will to deal with match-fixing and that the issue was too hard for those in charge to cope with. They believed the Waugh/Warne affair should have been kept out of the public domain. One would like to have thought this attitude on its own would have acted as a considerable spur to the delegates as they came together in Christchurch. But after the first day it looked as if all the good intentions that had been reverberating out of Lord's and other points round the compass would come to nothing and that good old milk-and-water politics would prevail. The President of the ICC, Jagmohan Dalmiya had not been able to make the journey from Calcutta owing to a family bereavement, but he got onto the telephone to Christchurch and exhorted his troops from the nine Test playing countries to pull up their socks and do what was best for the game. But his efforts, initially, were to no avail. Then the original proposal, which had presumably been drafted by the secretariat, was redrafted overnight and there was much behind the scenes activity. This may perhaps have been inspired by the press, who will have poured considerable scorn on the events of the first day. In all probability, someone will have come forward and played the part of a powerbroker because on the second day there was a much greater unity of purpose and remarkable progress was made.

The ICC took the huge step of agreeing to appoint an independent body and to give it powers to take firm action on a worldwide basis over match-fixing, bribery, drugs and any other similar issues. In order to try to cope with all this, the member countries agreed to set up a three-man commission from high profile cricket followers not directly connected with any Board of Control. Individual countries would still have the responsibility to investigate and deal with their own affairs through their own independent processes, but if the ICC Commission was not satisfied with the way an enquiry had been held, it would have the powers either to order another or to take over itself. The punishments for those found guilty promised to be punitive in the extreme, which is right and proper, and in certain circumstances this could mean bans for life. At long last the old tiger had been dished out with some teeth but it still remained to be seen how it was going to use them, or whether a visit to the dentist was first needed.

CHAPTER NINE

Flat Kiwi Pitches and Pinot Noir

I went to New Zealand for the last three weeks of March to watch the Second and Third Test Matches against South Africa and to see a great many old friends with whom I had not caught up for far too long. For several years during the second half of the eighties and the early nineties, I had ended up in New Zealand every February to watch whatever series they were playing. I had not been back since the 1993/94 season when they had played Pakistan. In addition to writing for my newspapers in England, I also found myself being used as a commentator by TVNZ and sometimes by Radio New Zealand. I enjoyed all those visits enormously. They came to an end partly because my life took me elsewhere and partly because TVNZ, like networks the world over, had decided that commentary was best done by retired Test cricketers who were obviously the most qualified to comment on what was happening on viewers' screens. I also think that by then, the long-suffering New Zealand audience had had more than enough of all my silly comments.

I had greatly enjoyed commentating with two of New Zealand's former opening batsmen, John Morrison and Glenn Turner. Morrison, whose nickname 'Mystery' fitted him well because of his unfathomable inscrutability, was, in his quiet way, always ready for a laugh. But he appears to have subsequently packed it in and has become a city councillor in Wellington. I am sure the city will benefit from his wisdom and the council meetings will be much more entertaining for his contribution. Glenn Turner was the most prolific batsman New Zealand has produced. What's more, had he ever opened the innings with Geoffrey Boycott and they had both been out for nought, the atmosphere in the dressing room would have made that of a sepulchre seem exhilarating. They both took their batting seriously. Also working for TVNZ was Richard Hadlee, who still tended to guard jealously the secrets of being a great seam bowler. Ian Smith, the former wicket keeper-batsman was just making an impressive start and then there was one of my favourite New Zealanders, Bob Cunis. He had bowled for the Kiwis at an energetic, bustling fast medium. He always spoke the truth as he saw it, was a bit of a maverick and a delight with it. His job up in the north of the country was to look after young offenders at a rehabilitation school which I am sure he does brilliantly and with a happy touch. Although tough, he is a kind man with a great sense of humour.

I also had a great time on radio with Jeremy Coney, who in the first half of the eighties had captained that wonderfully successful New Zealand side that never lost a home series in the decade. This included an extraordinary victory against Clive Lloyd's formidable West Indian side in an immensely unpleasant and controversial series in 1980. The West Indies had felt that the world and, crucially, the New Zealand umpiring, was against them. In the latter they may possibly have been right but even so it did not justify barging over an umpire at the point of delivery, kicking the stumps down and threatening to pull out of the tour and go home. In the radio box, Coney is extremely funny and his no less admirable sparring partner was John Parker, another Test opener. Parker has now moved on but Coney continues and his humour is as wonderfully refreshing as his comments are always lucid and to the point. Their main commentator, Brian Waddle, does a fine job interacting with him, too.

Having not been to New Zealand for six years, it was gratifying to be recognised at some unearthly hour in the morning at the enquiries counter at Auckland airport. New Zealand is the friendliest and most delightful of countries. The realisation of this starts the moment you step outside the aeroplane, for me now close to twenty-four hours after leaving London. In Auckland the people working at the airport seemed pleased to see you even at just before five o'clock in the morning. Immigration officers smiled, customs officials said 'please' and 'thank you' as if they meant it. I pushed my trolley for ten minutes along the outdoor walkway from the International to the Domestic terminal. I was booked on the first flight that morning to Christchurch where the Second Test began the following day at a cricket ground which I had presumed was Lancaster Park, although it now masqueraded under the strange name of 'Jade Stadium'. It was a pleasant walk at the start of a lovely day and when my trolley and I arrived at the domestic terminal the lady who checked me in on the Christchurch flight could not have been more helpful. As a general rule, airports are hell but I had been at Auckland for about an hour and a half and I had never for a single second had to fight my own corner, which was a relief and most unusual. It was only just over an hour to Christchurch and then a moderately talkative taxi driver delivered me to the ParkRoyal Hotel in the city centre. There, thanks to the efficiency of Andy Haden, the former All Black who looks after my life in New Zealand, they were expecting me.

Christchurch is the most relaxed of cities, especially for someone who is used to the bustle of London and Europe. It is almost a garden city and in much of it bricks and mortar are comfortably outnumbered by flowers, trees and greenery. The drive in from the airport sets the tone. The road is wide and the houses on either side are well set back with big gardens, all of which are beautifully looked after. Unless it is the rush hour there never seem to be that number of cars on the road and boy racers who pass you on two wheels at hundreds of miles an hour are few and far between. As you approach the city, you drive into Hagley Park, a huge green oasis which seems to go on for ever and dominates Christchurch rather as Hyde Park envelops West London. It has some most handsome trees, any number of cricket clubs, the joyous clash of hockey sticks and the thumping noise of rugger balls being kicked into the next parish. Whenever I have driven past or through Hagley Park, there always appears to be something going on. A small, busy river runs along one side and in the city centre itself you are for ever walking over little bridges with tumbling water underneath. The centre is also dotted with squares and tree-lined pedestrian precincts. There is a strong Indian influence in the street names and the bright spark who thought he would give the West Indies a mention as well made the same mistake that I had made at school. In Christchurch, they have spelt it 'Barbadoes' Street. If there is a better reason than poor spelling, I have never heard it.

Christchurch possesses two excellent second-hand bookshops, which act like a magnet on me wherever I find myself there. Before lunch on my first day, I had already found a good copy of J. D. Salinger's *The Catcher in the Rye,* a

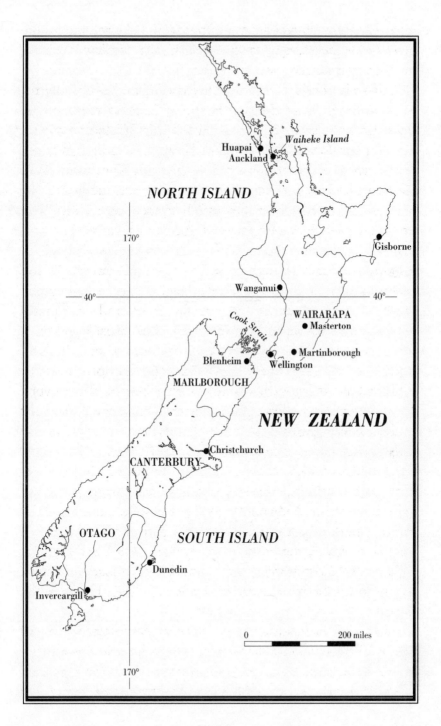

reasonable one of Noël Coward's *Middle East Diaries* published on poor paper in 1944 and an excellent *A Pelican at Blandings* by P. G. Wodehouse with the incomparable dust-jacket by Osbert Lancaster depicting that arch bounder Alaric, Duke of Dunstable, wearing bright yellow pyjamas with a coronet and the letter 'D' on the chest. He has a bottle of Vichy water in his right hand. Although he normally preferred stronger stuff, he was about to use this as a blunt instrument to bean Lord Emsworth, who had strayed into the Duke's room during the night wearing an elderly, hirsute dressing gown and, tripped up by a cat, had knocked over a table. All scintillating stuff and one of the great Wodehouse scenes. I thought this was a pretty good haul for my first morning in the country. After the walk back along the river and through the gardens to the hotel, I was able to gloat over my catch.

Lancaster Park was built for rugger, which has always taken pride of place in New Zealand, but cricket is played there as well. The ground is in a semi-industrial area but it has the most lovely backdrop of the Cashmere Hills. Nevertheless, I have never thought that cricket lies easily in rugby stadia. It makes cricket seem a poor relation and the game a trespasser on another's territory. Now, lo and behold, with a wave of a bank manager's wand, Lancaster Park had been transformed into 'Jade Stadium', a name which was being thrust most aggressively down all our throats. It was being used twice a minute, it seemed, on all broadcasts and in alternate paragraphs when it came to the papers.

Sadly whoever ran Lancaster Park (as I have every intention of continuing to call it) became aware of the possible benefits of attaching a sponsor's name to the ground. Test Matches and Rugger Internationals are played there almost every year, as is a good deal of extremely important domestic sport. Enough to have a potential sponsor licking his lips. After all, it was not that long ago that the committee at the

Oval in London felt compelled, by financial necessity no doubt, to stoop and rename their famous ground as 'The Fosters Oval'. But at least that's not as bad as 'Jade Stadium'. When Lancaster Park was put up for grabs the first commercial organisation to rise to the bait was The Auckland Savings Bank with, from what I heard, quite a princely sum. Then, at the last moment, those who ran the ground realised that it might not be to everyone in Christchurch's liking that the famous Lancaster Park should now carry the name of a major North Island city. The ASB appear to have been given the heave-ho at the last moment as a result. But the idea of a named sponsor taking over the ground did not go away. The money had made itself heard. A replacement had to be found and a local Canterbury computer-software billionaire saw his chance. His company is called Jade and he unbuttoned around NZ$400,000 (£130,000) a year, which was actually cheap at the price. For the exposure that so much top-level sport would bring to the name, a realistic fee must be somewhere in the neighbourhood of a million and a half dollars.

It was all put into the right perspective by one of Canterbury's oldest and most famous sportsmen, a man who played rugger for his country at Lancaster Park and captained New Zealand at cricket. Walter Hadlee is also famous for being the father of Richard, Dayle and Barry, all of whom played cricket for New Zealand, although Barry only managed to make the one-day international side. He told me during this Second Test Match that he had first played rugger at Lancaster Park in 1927 as a schoolboy in a warm-up game before either an international or a domestic final. He was not happy about the new name of 'Jade Stadium' and also reckoned that it had been significantly undersold. He had managed to reconcile it to himself by regarding the stands and the amenities they contained as 'Jade Stadium', while the playing area remained unyieldingly 'Lancaster Park'.

It would be hard to imagine a much more tedious Test Match than this Second of the series. The weather played a big part but so too did the strange attitude of Hansie Cronje, the South African captain, who might still have made a worthwhile attempt to win the match, even allowing for the rain. New Zealand were not to be blamed because injury had robbed them of three of their best players, Stephen Fleming, their captain, Craig McMillan, a dashing middle order batsman, and Chris Cairns, a formidable allrounder. They were most unlikely to win and a draw was always going to be a good result. New Zealand cricket does not have great depth and they were never going to be able to make up for the loss of three such important players. New Zealand in this form were never a match for the super-efficient, methodical South Africans who leave nothing to chance but, Jonty Rhodes and Allan Donald apart, play the game without much flair.

Pitches in New Zealand are a problem for they tend to produce extremely dull cricket. In the First Test in Auckland, the groundsman had used glue on his pitch to make sure the cracks did not open and it did not break up as the game went on. By all accounts, the game had been about as interesting as watching the glue dry. Eden Park is not the most satisfactory of Test venues with its very short square boundaries and, like Lancaster Park, it gives the strong impression that cricket is intruding. The South Africans had been put into bat by Dion Nash and had managed to amass 621/5 and so one can say, without fear of contradiction, that it had not been one of the game's more successful gambles. Daryll Cullinan compiled South Africa's highest ever individual Test score of 275. South Africa's score was the highest ever made in a Test Match at Eden Park and, rather curiously, Cronje declared their innings when they were one run short of the highest total ever made by South Africa. New Zealand replied with 352 on a pitch which was becoming more lifeless by the minute and although they had to follow on, they were more than comfortably placed at 244/3 when the whole business was mercifully laid to rest.

At Lancaster Park, New Zealand again won the toss but this time Nash decided to bat. Donald and Shaun Pollock did not waste much time in showing that this, too, was not necessarily the best of decisions and they were bowled out on the first day for 168. After that, South Africa, who were not helped by the rain, laboured on for three and a half days over 442/1. For a time, their principal objective seemed to be to make sure that their opener, Herschelle Gibbs, reached his first Test hundred. This he achieved in 383 minutes having spent an unconscionable time over the last twenty runs. The principal objective now became to make sure that Gibbs scored his first Test double century, or so it seemed, and when at last he had done so we had all grown noticeably older. Cronje had declared by the time the weather allowed a belated start on the last day and New Zealand were able to make sure of another draw. How much better it would have been if Cronje had declared when South Africa were 120 or so ahead and then unleashed Donald and Pollock on the fourth day. If they had taken four wickets then, they would have had an excellent chance of winning on the last day in spite of the rain. But they were obsessed with the need to make a huge amount of runs in the first innings to avoid any chance of batting in the second. I am not sure why.

Much the best part of the five days for me at Lancaster Park was the chance to catch up with Dick Brittenden, who is the patron saint of New Zealand cricket writers and was for many years the cricket correspondent of the *Christchurch Star*. He has long since retired but he joined us in the press box on four of the days and was at his most irrepressible. His wife Joy, who is a considerable golfer, was away playing in a competition and so Dick was off the leash. He was an exact contemporary of Walter Hadlee. Dick has written many books about New Zealand cricket and is as near as possible their official historian. He told me that sadly he had been forced to sell his big collection of cricket books because he and Joy were moving into a smaller house and space was at a premium. I made a return visit to Smith's Bookshop and bought a copy of *The Book of the Two Maurices*, which is an account of the MCC side in Australia and New Zealand in 1929/30 by two of the participants, Maurice Turnbull and Maurice Allom. They played four Test Matches in New Zealand after taking on only the state sides in Australia. The book had come from Dick's collection.

Much my most enjoyable cricketing experience while I was in Christchurch came on the Sunday morning at that unique ground, the Valley of Peace, tucked away in the Cashmere Hills. David Elder, who managed the successful New Zealand side in Australia in 1985/86 when Richard Hadlee and Martin Crowe were at their best, drove me out on a damp morning for my third visit to the Valley. It is less than half an hour from the city centre and yet the setting suggests that it is far deeper into the country. It is almost certainly the smallest serious cricket ground in the world although this statement will probably have Bill Sykes reaching for his measuring tape in the Algarve. Before the recent small addition on one side of the ground, it had covered less then two acres. Even so, boundaries still count for two and four rather than four and six. It all began in the 1920s when the Christchurch Cinematograph Company, run by Harry Waters (whose son runs the Valley of Peace today), needed a ground where the staff could play cricket on Sundays. This was quite a problem because almost all sports grounds were closed on Sundays. It was solved for them by a Miss White who farmed at the Huon Hay Valley in the Cashmere Hills and agreed to lend them a paddock provided they cleared it, at a rate of one shilling a week from every player.

Intriguingly, the ground is found at the end of a narrow winding lane and is surrounded by trees. When Harry Waters' employees first played there, Miss White, a considerable benefactress of the Roman Catholic Church, lived in the house just above the ground. One day, she looked out at the cricket and was horrified to see lots of women watching. She described them as 'painted hussies' and made it abundantly clear that if the Cinematographers wanted to continue to play there, 'painted hussies' would not be allowed. The ground has been forbidden to the fairer sex ever since and this is, I believe, why it is called the Valley of Peace. When I was last there a few years ago, Jeremy Coney turned up with a lady and there was much muttering behind the backs of hands before she beat a hasty retreat. An exception to the rule had been made in 1978 when a party was held to celebrate the fiftieth anniversary of the ground. A much more unhappy exception was made on the Sunday morning of my visit this time. The previous Sunday, a stalwart of the club, the seventy-four-year-old Eric Jackson, was batting and was four not out when, standing at the bowler's end, he collapsed and died. A week later when I was there, his son and American daughter-in-law and their daughter were invited to the ground to take part in a touching little ceremony on the spot where he had died. For all the constant forecasts of the imminent demise of cricket, I have no doubt that while the game still prospers as it does in the Valley of Peace, there is not too much to worry about.

I left Lancaster Park just before the end of the Test Match on the fifth day, the Monday, at the start of what proved to be an extraordinarily hectic week. I flew that evening on a small, bullet-like aircraft to Blenheim at the top of South Island where I was to transfer my allegiance from cricket to wine. As I mentioned at the start of the book, Richard and Johnny Wheeler had bought half of Clayvin, a 35-acre vineyard near

Blenheim. I had asked myself to stay at the charming vineyard house; as it happened I was to be their first guest. John Thorogood, their deputy managing director, and his wife Juliet had just come out to Blenheim, much more in the capacity of interior decorators than wine merchants, and I had two splendid days with them. Pinot Noir is one of the up-and-coming grape varieties in some parts of New Zealand. As far as Pinot is concerned, Marlborough, where we were, is probably second in the batting order to the Wairarapa in the south of North Island where I was aiming for the following weekend. Central Otago may feel slightly miffed not to have had a mention so far. The Pinot I drank from there certainly entitles them to be buckling on their pads to come in at the fall of the first wicket.

Of course, in both places, in Blenheim and Martinborough, which is the centre of the wine industry in the Wairarapa, I was lucky enough to find myself among some pretty discerning winemakers and I tasted some quite delicious wines. Blenheim is the most lovely part of the world. It is a charming country town where nothing seems to move at breakneck speed. The surrounding countryside is a mass of vines except in those areas where for climatic reasons they will not flourish. Land on south-facing slopes will not get enough sun and the microclimate is tremendously important. It may be significantly different for two neighbouring pieces of land with only a road between them. Lack of sun or cold currents of wind can mean that soil that should be ideal for grape production simply will not work. Generally in Blenheim the climate is as blissful as the scenery with the mountains in the background. These mountains are splendidly shown on the labels of Cloudy Bay wine. This image comes from a photograph of the mountains taken by Kevin Judd, the Cloudy Bay winemaker who is also a highly competent photographer. Judd came to Cloudy Bay in 1985 and it was his original Sauvignon

Blanc which not only put Cloudy Bay on the map but probably did more for the worldwide impact of the New Zealand wine industry than any other individual wine.

At Clayvin the southernmost part of the vineyard is perfectly placed, rising gently on a north-facing slope, which is why it is such a sun trap. There the majority of the grapes are Pinot Noir and Chardonnay. The 1999 harvest was just beginning. The Wheelers' partners, George and Ruth Fromm, who are Swiss, also own the Fromm Winery which makes the wine a mile or two down the road from Clayvin. That winery is presided over by a tall German, Hatsch Kalberer, who is bearded and intense and makes the most delicious wines. They began to produce there in 1992 and the wine was mostly a blend sold under the name La Strada. I was there for two days, and on the first night we dined at a splendid bistro in Blenheim called Bellaficos which would have stood comparison anywhere, and there we drank some delicious Chardonnay made by Hatsch. Later we drank some of his excellent 1996 Pinot Noir.

Both mornings at Clayvin were relatively gentle as John and Juliet went about their business as interior decorators. Juliet showed great talent but John started these two days by having to take back and change most of the things he had bought the day before which, I suppose, was progress of a sort. While they kept the upholsterers in Blenheim on their toes, I wrestled unconvincingly with my computer and it was not until lunch time approached that we joined forces. One amusing diversion was the appearance on the evening that I arrived of a black cat, which was friendly and obviously wanted to muck in. By the time we had gone out to dinner it had been irrevocably christened 'Blowers', recognition of a sort, I suppose.

By the time we left for lunch the following day, Blowers seemed sad to see us go. With John's steady hands on the wheel we set off for Jackson's Road, which is to winemaking in Blenheim rather as Hatton Gardens is to the diamond industry in London. Allan Scott's winery was our first objective because it incorporates a delicious winery restaurant. Sitting in the sun or the shade, as it suited, we had a lunch that could not be faulted and my green mussels in a white wine sauce were the best I have ever eaten. I was in mid-mussel when we were joined by an old friend of mine, Graham Thorne, who had only recently left Auckland to come and live in Blenheim. His arrival is always heralded by a certain amount of noise and there is now rather more of him than when he played for the All Blacks. He and his wife Briony had come to Blenheim after his short but meaningful political career had foundered at the whim of the voters of Onehunga, near Auckland. They had bought a sizeable house in Blenheim and thirty acres attached where he was planning to produce his own wine. The vines he had planted were now in their second year. They also had a vineyard restaurant which opened the day I left Blenheim. When I was in Auckland ten days later, Graham asked me to do a commercial for the restaurant over the telephone with the local radio station in Blenheim. I dread to think what it sounded like but he rang me just before I left for London and told me that The Gumdigger's Dog, as he had most intriguingly called it, was doing great business.

Graham joined us for lunch and afterwards, when John and Juliet found the call of the interior decorating business too shrill to ignore, they left me in his hands. By then we had met Kevin Judd himself who had also been lunching there and he suggested we should go with him to Cloudy Bay, further along Jackson's Road, and tackle his tasting room. He gave us his 1997 Pinot which he said was the best he had ever made. It had a delicious nose and a taste to match and we never moved away from it. Then we went on to Graham's new house, called appropriately enough, Thornedael, where everything was

218

being made ready for the grand opening of The Gumdigger's Dog the next day. Of course, we had to celebrate that.

After an early lunch at another winery restaurant, not a patch on Allan Scott's or, I am sure, the *haute cuisine* of The Gumdigger's Dog, the Thorogoods drove me to the airport. It was a twenty-minute flight across the Cook Strait to Wellington. Soon I was comfortably accommodated in the ParkRoyal Hotel where I got ready for what I knew would be a splendid evening with one of New Zealand's great characters, Laurie Bryant. With his wife Sally, he was giving me dinner at a 'splendid bistro'. Laurie always has restaurants and shops and even barbers tucked away just off the main road, as it were, all of which are 'rather special'.

Laurie began life in Dunedin and having festooned himself with all sorts of degrees at the University, he set off for London. He became a journalist and soon found himself working for the BBC. Laurie has nothing if not an old-fashioned BBC voice of which Lord Reith would have thoroughly approved. While at the BBC, he was spotted and for three years he became a courtier at Buckingham Palace. A visit to the downstairs loo at his country house just outside Masterton always goes on for longer than you anticipate as the walls are plastered with photographs of a young, slim and fit Bryant going about his royal duties. So sylph-like was his figure in those days that it was a moment or two before I spotted him. In the intervening years, far from running to seed, he has become a considerable panjandrum in the business world. If his girth has increased with his status, it is no more than one would expect. He founded and ran his own public relations business in Wellington. He has now sold out to an international conglomerate although he still fits into the chairman's seat – just. He is, too, a lobbyist of great repute and knows the tributaries and back alleys of politics and parliament as well as anyone.

There are many adjectives which would suit Laurie, but the one built especially for him has to be 'stately'. There is something of the galleon in full sail when he approaches. P. G. Wodehouse wrote of Beach, Lord Emsworth's butler, that when he walked across the lawns at Blandings, he made his entrance 'as a procession of one'. Beach would have picked up some tips from Laurie. He has become a tremendous friend, as has Sally. For years I stayed with them in their house in Thorndon, on the edge of the parliamentary quarter in Wellington. This time, I spent three nights with them at Masterton, which developed into a wine rather than a cricketing adventure. We surveyed the three acres of Pinot Noir he has planted next to the house and we did rather more than just sample his cellar. Laurie has a thing about Australian wines and Penfold's, of Grange Hermitage fame, is represented in just about every year of its considerable existence. He also has a great liking for the Shiraz or Syrah grape variety. Laurie had moved their splendid house to its present position by trailer in two halves which, for people living in houses made of bricks and mortar, sounds highly improbable. With houses largely made from wood, this seems to be accepted practice, in New Zealand, at any rate. He has a big garden and one of my favourite memories this time was of him sitting resolutely on his tractor mower as they scooted round the lawns with Laurie reminding me more than mildly of Ben Hur. Even the mower seemed apprehensive.

I had first met Laurie ten or twelve years before when I was in Wellington covering a Test Match. He had known Mark Turner, my uncle, and he rang me out of the blue to ask me if I would be prepared to go up one evening to Wanganui and talk to the boys at the Collegiate where his son, Nicholas, was at school. I agreed and that was where it all began. Now Laurie's splendid walk, with Sally in close attendance, brought him into the ParkRoyal and after tasting a bottle of Kevin

Judd's Pinot Noir in my room, we set off to a packed but excellent bistro where Laurie received the equivalent of royal treatment. He had brought with him ample liquid refreshment which predominantly bore an Australian birthmark. After a lengthy catching-up process, Laurie and I had plans to make. The next day, after the close of play in the Second Test, I was catching the eight o'clock flight to Auckland where, the next day, I was to talk to the Luncheon Club at the Sheraton Hotel. My plan then was to take a taxi back to the airport and catch the four o'clock aeroplane to Wellington where Laurie was going to meet me and propel me in his car to Martinborough, a difficult seventy miles along a tricky, winding mountain road. After dinner at The Martinborough Hotel, I was to talk to about a hundred and twenty people. Timing would be of the essence. I am ashamed to say I watched only the first day of the Test Match at the Basin Reserve, purpose-built for cricket and the best of the major grounds in New Zealand and also probably the largest roundabout in the world. The home side's inadequate batting was again exposed and this time South Africa's batsmen left their bowlers time to win the match and the series with it.

The audience at the Sheraton laughed in all the right places and it was about a quarter past three when I leapt aboard a taxi and headed for the airport. For the first ten minutes everything went according to plan. Then, just as we joined the dual carriageway, there was a horrendous accident about a third of a mile in front of us. An aged banger, full to the brim with Pacific Islanders, lost control on a downhill bend at more than a hundred miles an hour. It ended up as not much more than a piece of scrap metal after bouncing, repeatedly it seemed, off both crash barriers. It was amazing that anyone was left alive. We did not move for well over an hour as police cars, ambulances and even helicopters arrived. I missed two aeroplanes but after much frantic mobile telephoning, I just made the 5.30 and Laurie was waiting for me at Wellington airport an hour later. His Mercedes was all set to go as if we were competing in the Le Mans 24-hour race. This illusion continued as Laurie, with masterful control, did his best to beat the lap record between Wellington airport and The Martinborough Hotel. There can't have been more than a second or two in it and I felt as queasy as Shano and I had done careering across the Pacific Ocean to the Great Barrier Reef with the Commander just over two months earlier. I was soon back on course, though, and we had a delightful evening with Mike Laven, a charming Englishman who owns the hotel, together with his friends and neighbours. To make sure it was even more convivial, Pallisers, a Wairarapa winemaker, contributed substantially to our well-being. Mike's sister, Kate, helps run the Lord's cricketing website and is a press box colleague and so it was something of an in-house evening for me.

I slept well that night. The next day, Laurie had all sorts of plans for deep research into the vineyards of Martinborough. There were also one or two invitations to follow up from the night before. The day was given impetus by an article in the Wellington morning paper, *The Dominion*, about the Martinborough Vineyard, one of the four original wineries set up in the Wairarapa in 1980, which gives you an idea of how young it all is. In the course of this article, their 1996 Pinot Noir was described as being arguably the best red wine ever to have come out of New Zealand. Of course, it was our first port of call and after tasting some Sauvignon Blanc, which was almost luminously fruity, and some passable Chardonnay, Laurie and I both bought a bottle of the aforementioned Pinot for NZ$60, not far short of £20. I am happy to say that mine survived the journey home and still awaits a corkscrew.

The night before, the dinner had also been attended by Clive Paton, the owner of and winemaker at Ata Rangi Vineyard, another of the original four. He had promised Laurie and me a bottle of his 1996 Pinot Noir and we took him at his word. That, too, awaits consumption. He showed us round the winery and told us that one of his four huge steel wine tanks was yet to be named and he had decided upon 'Blowers'. I was suitably pleased and thought that a black cat in Blenheim and a wine vat in Martinborough wasn't bad going in the space of four days. We then had lunch with the former head of the New Zealand Navy, Vice-Admiral Sir Somerford Teagle and his wife while surrounded by four or five acres of vines he was growing himself on either side of the house. Wine was not just all-embracing in the Wairarapa, it was obsessional. Yet it was only in the late seventies that a soil scientist had discovered the close parallels between the climate at Martinborough and that in some important wine-growing areas in France, especially Burgundy. He did not want for converts.

I left Masterton a couple of days later by a train which took me back to Wellington. It was not a particularly memorable journey except for two curious things. I was first surprised to discover that the railway line belonged to a company in Wisconsin. Then, as we approached Wellington with a large bay on the lefthand side of the train, this American theme was taken further. My attention was attracted by a talkative small boy who was sitting with his father across the gangway. After closely studying the bay for a while, he asked his father, 'Is that where the Titanic sank?' Fair enough, at his age. Then it was the father's turn. 'No,' he began, 'that was in America, in Alaska.' And we pottered on into Wellington station.

Before my return to London, I had a few days in Auckland. Apart from a day's visit to Invercargill at the bottom of the South Island I did not have much planned. In spite of that though, it was a week which seemed to acquire a momentum of its own as it went along. The week before at the Sheraton lunch I had met Steve Nobilo whose huge family business supplies the wines at such occasions. Steve had promised to take me round their vast commercial operation on my return to Auckland. They produce the equivalent of 325,000 cases a year including bulk sales. Steve's father, Nikita, who is still alive, emigrated from a Croatian island in the Adriatic at the start of the forties and at once began to plant vines in Huapai, about twenty miles northwest of Auckland, where the business has remained.

In addition to the eight-hectare vineyard in Huapai, Nobilo's have large vineyards in joint-venture ownership with Maori Trusts in the east of North Island and more joint-venture vines in Marlborough. They also buy in grape juice from other parts of the country and acquire some from as far afield as Argentina. Over the years they have sold vast amounts of White Cloud, a sweetish white wine which they ship across in bulk to northern Europe and particularly Scandinavia. Something like seventy per cent of their mass-produced wine is sold outside of New Zealand and it is Nobilo's who make the Poverty Bay Chardonnay which is served on British Airways. They also make small quantities of extremely drinkable top-of-the-range Chardonnay. The difference could hardly have been more dramatic between the almost non-stop operation I saw at their winery in Huapai and the small, more intimate, carefully crafted production I had seen taking place in Martinborough and Blenheim. Before we left, Steve introduced me to his father and mother who are well into their eighties and extremely distinguished. They live in a modern house by the side of the winery of which he is naturally immensely proud.

My next wine adventure was entirely different and under-lined the comparison I have just made. I took a taxi one morning to the ferry terminal about ten minutes from my hotel and bought a return ticket for the journey to Waiheke Island, which takes barely an hour. Several years earlier, I had been to the island to stay with a friend, Stephen Lunn, and he had introduced me to Stonyridge, a vineyard owned by Stephen White, who made the most exceptional Cabernet Sauvignon-based wine, Stonyridge Larose. When I had returned to London then, I was lucky enough to have been able to buy a couple of cases of the 1993, which awaits the Millennium at least. This superb wine is sold at London's Premier Cru night club, Annabel's, which says much for the palate of whoever buys their wines.

It was a sunny day and a most pleasant hour on the ferry. Auckland Harbour may not be as spectacular as Sydney's. Of course, it has neither the Opera House nor a bridge of quite the same curvaceous authority, but nor is it overlooked by thickly populated suburbs in the same way. We backed in most skilfully to the jetty at Waiheke and I soon found a friendly mini-bus driver who, for four dollars, was prepared to drive me the few miles to Stonyridge, dropping one or two others off along the way. It is the most beautiful island and if you work in Auckland there must be a great deal to be said for living on Waiheke and commuting daily by ferry.

When I descended from my mini-bus, lunch was in mid-course, as it were, and packed out. I was glad I had let Stephen know I was coming over as he had kept a table for me. I began with two sensational glasses of Chardonnay which came from Gisborne and ended up with two glasses of the 1997 Stonyridge Larose which still had enough tannin for me to have an enjoyable and lengthy chew at each mouthful. It was full of heavenly flavours and we will be well into the third millennium before it will be near its best. The lunch, fish followed by tarragon chicken, was also word perfect. Stephen himself was eating with a most amusing American from California who had, about twenty years ago, given him his first job in a vineyard. Stephen had also worked for a time with Aimé and Véronique Gibert in Montpellier in the south of

France where they produce the remarkable Mas de Daumas Gassac, also made predominantly from Cabernet Sauvignon. It seemed strange to find a number of their wines on Stephen's list in faraway Waiheke Island. I moved over to their table when they had finished lunch and then those of us going back to Auckland, which included the American contingent, caught another mini-bus back to the four o'clock ferry. On the return journey the television was showing pictures of the one-day international at Eden Park between New Zealand and South Africa. Hotly, unrewardingly and indecisively, we debated the respective merits of cricket and baseball for the rest of the journey. The Americans were mystified by what they saw on the screen but they enjoyed a vigorous display of six-hitting by Daryll Cullinan.

After a quick change at my hotel, I caught a taxi to Eden Park where I was looked after most hospitably in two boxes. One of the assistant managers of the hotel had asked me to join him in the first, from where I watched New Zealand straining to come to terms with a big South African total. Inevitably, without Fleming, McMillan and Cairns who were still unfit, they crumbled. I watched their final disintegration high up at deep third man. I had been invited to this second box by that ubiquitous Moorfields-trained eye surgeon, Hylton Legrice, one of my oldest friends in New Zealand. Even allowing for the desultory state of the cricket, it was a jolly evening. This was the first cricket match under flood-lights at Eden Park; they helped enormously in terms of the atmosphere and also managed to give the impression that the ground had not been designed exclusively for the use of rugby footballers. The lights seemed to soften it no end. I would love to watch a rugger international there because then I am sure that I would then see Eden Park in an entirely different light.

It was on my first visit in 1974/75, when I had joined the Radio New Zealand commentary team for the series against

England, that New Zealand's last man, Euen Chatfield, was almost killed when he was hit on the head by a bouncer from Peter Lever. Helmets were not worn in those days. Chatfield collapsed at the wicket and swallowed his tongue. It was only the quick thinking of Bernard Thomas, England's longstanding physiotherapist who had raced out onto the ground, that saved him. Thomas realised at once what had happened and with his finger managed to hoick Chatfield's tongue out again. It was not until Kerry Packer's cricketing revolution two years later that helmets began to become standard equipment.

In Auckland I was asked by the general manager of the Sheraton to a wine dinner one evening in the hotel. The dinner was being held in order to taste and celebrate the wines from the same Martinborough Vineyard that Laurie Bryant and I had visited the week before. Their winemaker and part owner, Larry McKenna, was going to talk about his wines and one of those which was to be poured was the 1996 Pinot Noir Reserve of which Laurie and I were the proud possessors of one bottle each. It was the most relaxed evening and, to show what a small world it is, the couple I sat across the table from were the mother and father of Anna, the lovely girl who is the assistant manager of the Chelsea Ram, that celebrated pub which, wonderful to relate, is situated not much more than a minute and half from my front doorstep in London. The proceedings that night at the Sheraton were presided over by a local master of wine, Bob Campbell. He spoke fulsomely of Larry McKenna and his wine, both of which he clearly knew extremely well. He began by telling the story of how, when a party of winemakers from Europe had met McKenna, one of them, Robin Don, who makes wine at Elmham in West Norfolk, had described McKenna (who is more than a touch pugilistic in appearance) as looking more like a night club bouncer than a winemaker. A bouncer with an unusual touch, he might have added. The 1996 Pinot was the hero of the evening and I only wish I knew enough about wine to be able to do it justice. I also enjoyed the Pinot Gris with which we had kicked off before dinner.

The next morning I had to make a hideously early start to catch an aeroplane for Christchurch which left Auckland just before six o'clock. It was only by doing this that I was going to be able to make the connection which would decant me before lunch in Invercargill. With the taste of that Pinot still in my mouth – a wine has to be of an exceptional quality to defeat my toothpaste – I remember little of the journey or the changeover in Christchurch where I was definitely on automatic pilot. But I must have got it right because we landed in Invercargill at almost eleven o'clock.

It may sound paradoxical but there is a rather warm feeling of isolation about Invercargill. It is only just over an hour in the air from Christchurch and it must be less than that from Dunedin. We flew over a rugged, rocky, mountainous terrain for much of the way before hitting the fertile southern coastal strip, but in terms of actual distance, Invercargill is not that far removed from the rest of civilisation. For all that, it is almost falling off the bottom of New Zealand, it is the southernmost city in the world and the nearest civilised spot to the South Pole. All these factors take their toll and if you live there it is not surprising that, psychologically at any rate, it seems a hell of a long way from anywhere. I have written earlier in the book that there used to be something of the same feeling in Perth. There is a strong spirit of self-dependence and self-reliance in Invercargill. There are, too, any number of rich characters almost all of whom seemed to turn up at the Invercargill Licensing Trust Luncheon Club to whom I was speaking.

It was getting on for ten years ago that the Luncheon Club was set up and it happened that I was their first speaker, so it was a most happy reunion. I was met at the airport, just as I had been all those years ago, by Gary Muir who is part of the Licensing Trust and who organises the Luncheon Club. He is a great extrovert with a tremendous sense of humour and a great companion. He drove me first to the local television station where I was closely interrogated about cricket in all parts of the world. We went from there to the sprawling hotel where the lunch is always held and after another interview and some photographs, there was time for a glass of wine while the 400 guests threaded their way into the huge dining room.

As you will have gathered by now, I am a great supporter of Invercargill. While Gary Muir was driving me about, I felt there was something slightly strange which I couldn't put my finger on and then suddenly it came to me. There is hardly a building in the entire city which is more than two storeys high. This gives it all a mildly flat feeling. I am glad to be able to say that Invercargill is never far from my mind because when I first went there to speak, I was given an amazing blown-up photograph which had been taken by Owen Jones of the *Southland Times*, the local newspaper. It was taken during the extremely bad-tempered Test Match against the West Indies in Dunedin early in 1980. Michael Holding, who had opened the bowling for the West Indies, had had an overwhelmingly confident appeal for a catch behind against the New Zealand opener, John Parker, turned down. The ball had appeared to have hit him on the glove. With Parker standing in his crease looking decidedly sheepish, Holding had followed through to the batsman's end and, with a stylish kick that any footballer would have envied, uprooted two of the stumps. The photograph catches the moment when the stumps are airborne but upside down. This picture hangs prominently in Norfolk and whenever I look at it, I am reminded of Invercargill.

They were an excellent audience and my only problem after that was to get a seat on the four o'clock aeroplane back to

Christchurch. If I failed, I would not get back to Auckland until eleven o'clock which would have made it a long day. The four o'clock out of Invercargill was full but the Licensing Trust's powers of persuasion are legendary and the two charming pilots agreed to let me sit with them on the flight deck in the jump-seat. This is always a great experience and after they had radioed on to Christchurch to get me onto the connecting flight to Auckland, I was back in my hotel in good time for dinner.

The few holes I had left in this hectic week were filled with lots of lovely extras. Dinner at Antoine's in Parnell owned and run by the uncle of Nathan Astle, New Zealand's opening batsman, was as rewarding as ever. I had a lovely dinner with the Legrices and Hylton showed off his considerable knowledge of wine to excellent effect. I had the great luck one afternoon leaving the Sky Television studios to run into Martin Donnelly who had scored a double century for New Zealand in the Lord's Test Match in 1949. He had made his life across the Tasman in Sydney and was visiting New Zealand now because the nine surviving members of that 1949 side, which drew all four three-day Test Matches, had been having a reunion during the Wellington Test Match. Donnelly was one of the great left-handed batsmen, although because of the war and his business career he played all too little cricket. I also had a long Sunday lunch with my old broadcasting friend Tim Bickerstaff at his house out by the Bombay Hills where I caught up with much of the latest gossip. Tim also told me that surfing through the internet, he had become the first man in New Zealand to get hold of some Viagra. He refused to lend me some. Then, in no time at all, it was the final journey to the airport and the long flight to Heathrow.

Alas, within two weeks I was at the Harley Street Clinic, but that was no fault of New Zealand's.

CHAPTER TEN

Lara's Genius in the Nick of Time

When we left them, the West Indies players had effectively held their Board to ransom while holed up in a hotel at Heathrow airport. Having successfully twisted the relevant arms, they left for Johannesburg, but too late to play in the opening one-day game of the tour, not that that would have greatly concerned them. But having won all their battles with the Board, aided and abetted by Nelson Mandela's missive, one would have liked to think that at least they would have piled into their aeroplane one happy family, united behind Brian Lara. Incredible as it may seem, one or two of the players missed this rather important aeroplane, surely not by mistake.

Yet, no sooner had the bulk of the party arrived in the first aeroplane at the Jan Smuts airport than the news broke that one of the more dependable of their number, Jimmy Adams, had cut his hand so badly trying to dissect a bread roll on the flight that he was at once ruled out of the tour. It was not long before he was on his way back to Jamaica. Modern bread rolls have clearly attained new levels of militancy and bullet-proof gloves, helmet and visor would seem to be the minimum requirements when a waiter approaches with the bread basket. There were other stories that filtered through about how the captain and one of his fast bowlers had become embroiled in a bout and a half of fisticuffs. Adams had tried to separate them, the story goes on, and had picked up this nasty knife injury for his pains. But maybe the bread basket was just putting this about in a belated attempt to salvage a shred or two of honour.

If, after their Heathrow triumph, the West Indies were a happy and united side in South Africa, determined to give of their best, their cricket did little to reflect it. Inevitably, the story centred on Lara. By now he had become such an enigmatic figure: defying his Board at every turn, not living up to his ability with the bat in his hand, with a punctuality problem which suggested he wore a watch purely as an ornament and with man management abilities that would qualify him for a leading role in Fawlty Towers. Neither was he a bundle of fun, seeming to see the dark side of life round every corner and to be riddled with the insecurities which so curiously seem to bedevil some people born with exceptional talents.

The West Indies Cricket Board had, with good reason, refused to accept him when he was chosen as captain by the Test selectors in 1997. He had kicked over the traces too often and their message was: the job won't be yours until you get yourself more together. Of course, there was an outcry in different parts of the Caribbean, especially in his own Trinidad. The Board showed its weakness by giving in to public opinion a year later when the selectors again came up with Lara's name, this time to succeed Courtney Walsh. Although the circumstances of their first objection had not changed, they now bowed to public pressure and appointed Lara, who will, by then, have been convinced that the Board was public enemy number one. While Lara was too big for his own boots, the Board had vacillated to an absurd extent. The battle-ground of the Excelsior Hotel in Heathrow was already being prepared.

It was especially surprising that the President, Pat Rousseau, had accepted Lara. Rousseau can be a persuasive and a dominant character and Board decisions are probably more a reflection of his views than anyone else's. Rousseau likes to surround himself with Jamaicans and he cannot have been happy to see one of them, Walsh, now make way for Lara. Lara's side now beat a thoroughly inept England, 3–1, although the captain's tactical acumen did not play an enormous part in this West Indian triumph and nor did his batting. In the field, he appeared to speak only to carefully selected colleagues and not with any great frequency. You did not have to watch the West Indies in the field for long to gain the impression that they were not the most united of sides. Captain Walsh had created a greater sense of cohesion than his successor. Lara obviously enjoyed the trimmings that came with the job: the popularity, the attention of the media and the general adulation. He was lucky that his first two Test Matches as the official West Indies captain were played in Trinidad where he was further insulated against criticism by the applause of his fellow countrymen.

Many people close to West Indies cricket will have been distinctly apprehensive about the style he was likely to bring to the job. If theirs was the common-sense, practical point of view, it was in direct opposition to the public perception of Lara. The mass supporters of West Indies cricket badly needed another super-hero, another Viv Richards figure. They had watched spellbound as Lara had made 375 against England in 1994 and then gone on to make 501 for

Warwickshire against Durham. He was their man and they didn't want anyone to try and take him away from them. But Lara's genius began to founder on the shaky character of the man himself who was getting his priorities into a frightful muddle and was relishing fame and fortune without any longer being concerned about scoring runs and winning matches.

He had undoubtedly changed as success had come to him. I remember interviewing him in the West Indies not long after he began his career and he was as charmingly helpful as he could be. For the last year or two if we happened to pass in the hotel or on the ground, I have been lucky to receive an acknowledgement at all. Now that he had at last achieved the position he had craved for so long, it seemed reasonable to suppose that he would start to behave himself in a manner which was in keeping with the job and that he would not go out of his way to antagonise his employees. But it was clear that he and his vice-captain, Carl Hooper, still bore massive grudges against the Board.

Lara was inevitably appointed to captain the side in the one-day tournament for Test-playing countries in Bangladesh in October 1998 and for the West Indies first official tour to South Africa which followed. We all know what happened between the end of Bangladesh and the start of the South African tour. The captain and his deputy had made up their minds to take on Rousseau and his Board and they will have had the support of the West Indies Players Association headed by Walsh. They won the day as they knew they were bound to, after shutting themselves up in a great display of team unity in that Heathrow hotel while the waiting world, with all its vested interests, visited and pleaded on bended knee. One would have thought the whole saga would have bonded the side together in a major display of unity as they rushed to catch the aeroplane to Johannesburg. But apparently discontent still bubbled and personal animosities within the side continued unabated with the odd bread roll now thrown in.

It was only a year earlier that the Australian Players Association had threatened strike action for better terms and conditions from their own Board. Although this was put into cold storage so that the South African tour of Australia could proceed, matters were eventually settled to the satisfaction of almost everyone. One has heard that Mark Waugh was still not that happy, but now that the revelation that he took money from Indian bookmakers has emerged, he may feel it is wiser to continue to sit on his hands. These twelve months of the 1998/99 season have been electrified, if not illuminated, by the bribery and match-fixing hearings running in the law courts of Lahore for about the same length of time as *The Mousetrap* in London's theatreland. Now that the West Indies have screwed their Board into the ground, players everywhere are growing increasingly restless about what they consider to be the small percentage of the total amount of money coming into the game that finds its way into their pockets.

This was, of course, the reason that Kerry Packer in 1977 had found the leading players of the world so receptive to his plans to form World Series Cricket in opposition to the establishment game. Thanks to him, the pay for the best players, at any rate, went up sharply, but in the intervening years the authorities have again been guilty of taking their eye off that particular ball. There is an enormous amount more money in the game these days because of sponsorship and television rights and yet all too little has been getting through to the pit face. The prize money for the players at the 1995/96 World Cup on the Subcontinent was derisory when seen as a percentage of the money grossed from all sources. As we have seen, players round the world are once again beginning to flex their muscles as they go in search of a better deal for themselves. Perhaps as a result, the authorities were much more generous over prize money in the 1999 World Cup in England.

I have not the slightest doubt that all the Boards of Control will feel that right is on their side and to some extent one can understand their thinking. The game has for ever been short of money and now that there is rather more, they feel they are right to take a parsimonious approach to guard against poverty in the future. In one sense, few people would argue that the Board in Pakistan does not have right on its side in the face of all the accusations of skullduggery by which, if true, some leading players have lined their pockets to a considerable depth. One has then to reconcile this with the fact that a Pakistani Test player receives the equivalent of £200 a match. If he lived his entire life in Pakistan, he might not feel he was too badly done by, but Pakistani Test players spend much of their lives in the Western world where incomes, like prices, are very much larger. Naturally, they want to compete and need more money in order to be able to do so. With their Board always pleading poverty and also adopting a strong feudal attitude to their relationship with the players, small wonder if the players themselves do not then look to bend the rules so that they can hold their own in London and other Western cities. It is easier to do so if you live in a part of the world where bending the rules is just about a full-time occupation.

The English authorities even began to feel the crunch in the build up to the World Cup over the matter of the contracts for the England players. The number of employees at the English Cricket Board at Lord's rises at an alarming rate and we are always told how much more professional, up-to-date and user friendly they have become. It seems that almost their sole occupation is to make sure that the England players are looked after properly and that their needs are met. It was in the first half of November that, entirely by chance, I ran into the ECB's Director of Operations, Major-General Simon Pack of the Royal Marines. I was travelling from London to Brisbane and, knowing that that famous obituary writer, Johnny Woodcock was sitting upstairs in the bubble on this jumbo, I asked one of air hostesses if she would take him up some claret. We had been drinking Château Beychevelle 1990 which I knew he would enjoy. I told her that he was grey haired and distinguished with a charming smile. A few minutes later she told me the deed had been done. It was some time later, when we were about to arrive in Singapore that she came back to me with a long face and told me that she had given the wine to another grey-haired gentleman upstairs who had turned out not to be Mr Woodcock at all. I said I hoped he had a charming smile.

Anyway, I didn't get off at Singapore and those of us on board were milling around towards the front of the aeroplane when the grey-haired gentleman who had received the Château Beychevelle introduced himself as Simon Pack. Although I had never met him, I knew who he was and I am relieved to be able to tell you that he did have a charming smile. He was going to Brisbane where the First Test was about to begin and in his bag was a draft copy of the contract for England's World Cup squad. This draft did not suit the players and the issue went backwards and forwards between them and the ECB like a yo-yo and was only settled just before the competition began. The players, led by the captain Alec Stewart, who is nothing if not money conscious, were demanding and probably unreasonably greedy. It all made for a most unedifying spectacle, which reflected the new approach by the players around the world to the financial side of things. It also more than hinted at the feudal manner in which these matters had been handled for much too long by the various boards of control.

So what happened to Lara's West Indians in South Africa? Naturally, no one had worked harder to make sure the tour took place than Ali Bacher, the Managing Director of the United Cricket Board. No one understood better than he, how important this tour was for the coloured communities in South Africa. We have seen that immediately the crisis broke out he was on an aeroplane to Heathrow where he will have found himself involved in tricky negotiations. He helped solve it in the end but left the airport saying that it would be easy to envisage it all breaking out again. It is not known whether that was a vote of no-confidence in the West Indies players or their in Board. Or both. By that stage one would have hoped that the West Indies players would have fully realised the significance of their first official tour to the multi-racial South Africa. It would have been nice to think that having already caused their hosts considerable last-minute embarrassment, that now they had their way, they would have taken the joint decision to put their best feet forward. Not a bit of it, though.

There is one potentially formidable but slightly hazy figure in all of this. Clive Lloyd, who had captained the West Indies through much of their success in the late seventies and eighties, may be a man of firm views but it is his way to speak them quietly. Throughout the present period, he was employed by the West Indies Board as the team manager. I would be surprised if he did not have an inkling of the troubles that were brewing while the team was in Bangladesh. If he did, he was unable to stop Lara and Hooper from jumping on an aeroplane to London when they should have been taking the side to Johannesburg. If he did know what was going on, did he, as their employee, alert the West Indies Board that there was trouble ahead? When the action began, there was something delightfully Grand Old Duke of

York-ish about Lloyd's progress. Looking as lugubrious as ever, he collected the remnants of his troops after captain and vice-captain had scarpered, and took them to Johannesburg where they apparently awaited events, not to say instructions, in their hotel.

The Lara-Hooper-Walsh axis in London then demanded that Lloyd bring his players back to Heathrow, which is what he did. They came on more than one aeroplane and Lloyd was, by all accounts, on the same flight as Ali Bacher who was bearing the all-important missive from Nelson Mandela. Their conversation would have been excellent value. Back in London, Lloyd was in the uncomfortable position of having a foot in both camps but if you are as tall as he is, maybe you can keep them far enough apart to ease the burden. As soon as the negotiations were complete and the issues resolved, Lloyd led his troops back again to Johannesburg although, with one or two missing the plane, even then he did not have a full contingent. It is a moot point as to whether from then on he was able to exercise the control he will have wanted.

But when the West Indies eventually returned home after the South African tour and Australia were upon them, Lloyd came out of his corner. 'We've lost the cricket ethic,' he said. 'There's a lack of professionalism, of passion, of pride. We worked very hard for our success when I was captain but you don't see that sort of discipline now. We've got very complacent and unfortunately there are too many people involved in the management of the game who don't have any knowledge of cricket.' Although he kicked hard with both feet, it was impossible not to feel that he was making an each-way bet.

To be fair, the West Indies were bedevilled by injuries in South Africa. The first replacement, precipitated by that recalcitrant bread roll, was on his way to replace Adams before a ball had been bowled. Floyd Reifer, a left-hand batsman from Barbados, was quickly plucked out of the 'A' tour of

India and Bangladesh. The two veteran fast bowlers, Walsh
and Ambrose, had managed to miss the original flight from
London – it is hard to know what to make of that – and
immediately he arrived, Ambrose had to have a toe-nail
removed. I hope that the steward had not dropped the bread
basket on his foot. Ambrose's preparation for the First Test
consisted of a back-breaking twenty-five overs. Worse
followed when Walsh twisted his ankle on the first day of the
opening first-class match and two days later was found to be
suffering from tendonitis of the left knee. But no one in the
side will have given more than these two on the field and they
took thirty-five wickets between them although they only
played in four Test Matches each. Being the trooper he
is, Walsh recovered from all his leg problems and took
seven wickets in the First Test going past Malcolm Marshall,
the coach, as the highest West Indian wicket taker with a
haul of 377.

And on it went. A shoulder injury badly affected Dinanath
Ramnarine's leg breaks and googlies and after being given a
long bowl in the second match of the tour, against Free State,
his tour was finished. Rawl Lewis was summoned across the
Indian Ocean as his replacement and found himself getting
ready for a Test Match two hours after he had flown in from
Bombay. In the first innings of the First Test, Carl Hooper
pulled a groin muscle and had to have a runner in both
innings. He was forced to bat at number seven in the second
and only managed to bowl four overs in the match. During
this Test Match, two of the non-combatants, Merv Dillon and
Junior Murray, had to go to hospital with food poisoning.
Never a dull moment.

It was something of a surprise they only lost the First Test
by four wickets, but things did not improve. It was Shaun
Pollock who had done the principal damage in Johannesburg
with nine wickets; Pollock and Allan Donald did it together

in Port Elizabeth; it was Pollock again, in Durban; Jacques Kallis led the way in Cape Town and Donald was the main executioner at Pretoria's Centurion Park. The West Indies had shown fight in Johannesburg but after that it was a procession. South Africa won by 178 runs in less than three days at Port Elizabeth, by nine wickets on the fourth day in Durban, by 149 runs in Cape Town (although that match at least went into the second session on the last day), and by a massive 351 runs in four days at Centurion Park.

Not that one would have guessed it, but the United Cricket Board in South Africa were also having their own problems, albeit of a very different nature, when the West Indies players condescended to put in an appearance. In March 1998, in order to frustrate a demonstration during the Test against Pakistan at Port Elizabeth, Ali Bacher, the UCB's Managing Director, had made a statement that South Africa should no longer have an all-white national team. The issue became less urgent when Makhaya Ntini, Paul Adams and Roger Telemachus won places in the side. But by the time the West Indies tour began, these three had fallen by the wayside, victims of loss of form and injury, while the form of Herschelle Gibbs was not yet good enough to get him in.

So an all-white side was chosen for the First Test Match. This prompted Sports Minister, Steve Tshwete to say to his parliamentary constituents in the Cape that the days of 'Lily-white' teams at international level in rugby and cricket were numbered. The problem was tackled at once by the UCB and they made it clear to their constituent members that coloured players must be included in all national teams. A special committee with considerable powers was set up to see that this was carried out. As far as racial integration is concerned, the government is treating sport in the same way as business or any other aspect of life. The committee has the duty to make sure that the provincial sides select more coloured players so that there is a bigger pool from which the Test selectors can choose.

While all right-thinking people would agree wholeheartedly with this, there is always the danger that political correctness can cause problems where none should exist. It was in Washington at around this time that a bureaucrat found himself summarily dismissed from his job for showing marked racist tendencies, when he said that a colleague a little higher up the ladder was 'niggardly' in his distribution of money. When a perfectly good word is used in its correct sense and this interpretation is put upon it, it makes you wonder where we are going. The issue of political correctness arose in South Africa when the former Test allrounder, Brian McMillan, was roundly ticked off for using the apparently accepted term of 'coolie creeper' to describe a ball which barely left the ground when it was bowled. Although this particular phrase has obvious dangers and is probably best avoided, a gentleman called Mr Brian Basson, who is the Director of Umpiring and Playing Affairs for the UCB, apparently went on to say that he thought 'chinaman', 'chinese cut' and 'whitewash' – all age-old cricketing terms – were in danger of inviting a racist interpretation and should be avoided. After this extraordinary addition to the debate, McMillan found plenty of support when he described Mr Basson's comments as a 'load of crap'. I can't wait to meet Mr Basson, for half of me feels sure that he doesn't exist and that I missed him in the pages of *Alice in Wonderland*.

The West Indies plight in South Africa made one wonder what further indignities may befall them when their two old warhorses, Courtney Walsh and Curtly Ambrose, have taken their creaking limbs into retirement. After losing the Test series 5–0, they then lost the one-day series 6–1. Their main problem in South Africa was their inability to make anything like enough runs. Lara passed fifty three times and

Chanderpaul and Jacobs both had their moments with the bat, but there was not a single West Indian century in the Test series. It was here that Lara's lack of leadership and example was most felt. As a batsman at his best, Lara combines supreme skill with genius and it can be the most explosive mixture. The West Indies are no longer the side they were, which means it is imperative that their one batsman of true class should score runs with much greater consistency than Lara had managed for the thirteen Test Matches since he had scored his last hundred.

Having put it across his main enemy, the West Indies Board, Lara had now become a self-confident gambler and probably felt that nothing could touch him. In South Africa, with Lara very much to the fore, the West Indians threw their weight around everywhere except on the field against South Africa. They were at all times anxious to demonstrate that it was they themselves who ran the show and how dare anyone get in their way. They set about trying to curtail the responsibilities of their coach, Malcolm Marshall, who had forgotten more about the game than any of them knew. He had also played first-class cricket in South Africa and his knowledge of the disciplines required to make a success of your game in that country should have been of crucial importance to his side. As it was, the players tried to marginalise him. They then turned their attention to Dennis Waight, the Australian from Sydney who has been their physiotherapist since the Packer revolution in 1977. The players demanded fewer and shorter physical training sessions as they felt that his routines were too demanding. I wonder if, looking back on it even now, the players have any idea of how badly they let down themselves, their countries, West Indies cricket and the millions of coloured South Africans who had so eagerly awaited their first official tour, some of whom might have been inspired to take up the game.

The signs of approaching disaster had been growing within West Indies cricket for a number of years. In 1992 when they were still on top of the pile, it was Malcolm Marshall who had said in an interview, 'Everything seems to be going down the drain. There is no respect, no manners.' When former captain Rohan Kanhai, who was the team coach at the time, let his Board know that he had been sworn at in public by some of the players, their immediate reaction was to sack Kanhai and not the players concerned. It was then the turn of former fast bowler Andy Roberts to take on what was fast becoming a poisoned chalice. He also was none too impressed by the 'attitude problems' he found in the side. It was just about the oldest recipe of all for disaster. Ill-discipline off the field leads in no time at all to ill-discipline on it and once the Test team had been affected, the whole of West Indies cricket would not be long in following.

In 1995 and 1996 Lara had led revolts against his captain, Richie Richardson, and when the first one, in England, did not succeed, he left the team in a huff. Richardson, a good man, was treated intolerably and it was greatly to his credit that he stuck it out as long as he did. When he threw in his hand, the incredibly perceptive Board promptly sacked Roberts. So, victory again for the rebels. Desmond Haynes, their former opening batsman, was ignored when he said, 'I warned them [the Board] that others would start to catch us but they didn't listen.' He also said, 'How come the best team in the world have the worst Board?' When senior players like Lara, Hooper and Ambrose were reported for serious disciplinary infringements, the Board would issue weighty cautions and it was business as before. The players knew they could go on suiting themselves as they would get away with it. In the end, and entirely predictably, the Board bowed to the increasing pressure of public opinion and not only made Lara captain but also gave Hooper the vice-captain's job, as if unaware of the disciplinary record of either.

It almost seemed that the West Indies Board had prepared the ground for their own ultimate humiliation with immaculate thoroughness. This moment arrived when Rousseau and Dehring fastened their seat-belts in the aeroplane in Antigua, which was to take them scurrying across the Atlantic to that hotel at Heathrow in answer to the summons they had received from the players they had first sacked as captain and vice-captain and then called back to Antigua – an order that had been ignored. The journey to London was on its own an admission of defeat. The Board had finally burned its own clothes.

For many years West Indies cricket had been extremely lucky to find former players of the calibre of Jeff Stollmeyer, Gerry Gomez, Allan Rae and John Dare to run the game in the Caribbean. Of course, the job became more difficult as the islands and territories acquired their independence and the Board became more insular in approach. The representatives from the various countries came to the meetings determined that the most important part of their job was to further the interests and the representation of their own people rather than the best interests of West Indies cricket, which was just about the only unifying force within the region. It was now more important than ever that the Board should be in strong hands which, preferably, came from an established cricketing background. Unfortunately for West Indies cricket, the supply of old players of the calibre as administrators of those I have mentioned above ran out.

It can be seen from this that the Board has to take a heavy share of the responsibility for what went on in South Africa and at Heathrow just before. The players themselves will have been greeted by the West Indian equivalent of a deafening silence when they returned home to prepare for the Australians. The Caribbean was deeply upset and disillusioned by what had gone on in South Africa, not least as a late reminder of their abhorrence of South Africa's former racial politics. The West Indies public at last seemed to be prepared to face the truth. The irresponsible behaviour of Lara was roundly condemned and he had to take the blame for the lack of team spirit and discipline.

I believe it may have been the realisation that he was fast losing his power base with the people of the West Indies that accounted for the astonishing change Lara was now to show, both as batsman and captain in the series against the Australians. Lara had felt for some time that he could do no wrong and suddenly he found that this vanity had blown up in his face and that he had been rumbled. The Emperor didn't have any clothes now.

The improvement did not happen at once. The selectors stayed with Lara and the pusillanimous Board reappointed him as captain for the first two Tests of the four-match series and issued him with a string of instructions he had to obey if he wished to be considered after that. Along with Lloyd and Marshall, Lara was blamed by the Board for the South African humiliation. The captain was now given what Rousseau chose to describe as 'specific performance targets' by Mike Findlay, a former West Indies wicket keeper who was chairman of the selectors. After a Board meeting in late February, which cannot have been the jolliest of gatherings, Rousseau had said that weak leadership was responsible for the performances in South Africa and that Lara had been told the facts of life. There was no mention that the vacillation by the Board over which Rousseau presided had contributed handsomely to what had happened.

Almost the last time these two had met had been in that Heathrow hotel in October when Lara had been the one to call the shots. It was a bit like Cain and Abel at the beginning of time when brotherly love got badly left at the start.

Speaking on radio and television, Rousseau went on to say, 'We have told Mr Lara that he needs to make significant improvements in his leadership skills. We believe he has it in him to fulfil his potential but we are not prepared to wait indefinitely for these qualities to emerge.' Lara now had to convince the selectors that he was able to improve his relationship with the other members of the side, that he would make sure that his own discipline was up to scratch and that he would make a conscious effort to get on with the coach and manager.

The Board still got it in the neck. Andy Roberts, normally a man of few words, was soon onto the attack. 'The West Indies Cricket Board played true to form by demonstrating a lack of guts in reappointing Brian Lara as captain. We have to get rid of them. They are only concerned with personal ambitions.' Strong stuff. Roberts was not the only former player to join in the criticism of the Board and even the Prime Minister of Barbados, Owen Arthur, felt compelled to add his little bit: 'The Board has not been as decisive as the situation warrants.'

I happen to believe the selectors were right to offer Lara one last chance on these terms. If Lara had lost the captaincy, the authorities would maybe have had to settle for a prolonged period of mediocrity as far as the international game was concerned. Being the man he is, Lara, without the captaincy, might easily have become a disruptive influence within the dressing room and he would also have been unlikely to have been productive with the bat. One only has to look at his record before he eventually succeeded Courtney Walsh to know that this was almost bound to have been true. He could not have helped himself. Golf had become his passion and would increasingly have been the reason for his lack of punctuality on the cricketing front. He would rather have played another couple of holes than have turned up at the nets on time.

There is no doubt about Lara's genius as a batsman even if it has constantly been distracted and sat upon by a flawed character. If West Indies cricket was once again going to hold its head high in international competition, it could not do so without Lara. He was the only player they had capable of reaching the heights whereby one man can win a cricket match at this level. As we were soon to see against Australia, he was, therefore, the one man able to pull a fickle part of the world away from the lure of American sport, which had been proving so strong, and back to cricket. To dispense with Lara and not give him a clearly stated last chance would have been to condemn West Indies cricket to mediocrity, which might ultimately have led to terminal uncompetitiveness. This would have been folly of an impressive nature, rather like asking Sherlock Holmes to come along without the pipe which so helped his deductive agility. I think Findlay and his fellow selectors need congratulating for holding their nerve and making one last effort to bend Lara to their will before getting rid of him altogether.

It was just as well they did not appoint him for one Test Match at a time either, although amid the ruins of the First Test in Port of Spain it was possible to see that Lara had been pulled up short by all the criticism thrown at him. It was apparent that the need to reform had hit home and the indignity of being treated as something less than a god on his own doorstep in Trinidad had got through to him. He now knew that he had to show them. It was the biggest test of character he had ever faced, especially as he had already alienated just about everyone in his own dressing room. It was probably the first time in his life he had been forced to stop and think and conduct a thorough self-examination. He had sought help, too. He had shrewdly asked the advice of Rudi Webster, a well-known sporting psychologist who once bowled at fast medium for Warwickshire. Webster is a remarkable man and he undoubtedly played a considerable part in the transformation of Lara and his side. He managed to reinvigorate them both. His cheerful approach to the job, as a friend who wants to help rather than a schoolmaster who wants to instruct, had much to do with it. In a surprisingly short time he had players who had reached just about rock bottom beginning to believe in themselves again. But Webster's success with the team hinged on Lara's rejuvenation. Without that, none of it would have been possible. Lara had also looked for help from a religious figure in Trinidad, which may have been a new departure.

After Australia had won the toss in the First Test, Lara had soon shown that he was a more involved captain than before and at last he began to communicate with his players. He was now bothering with the minute-to-minute mechanics of captaincy in an innings in which Walsh took the three wickets he needed to take his tally to 400. When the West Indies came to bat, Lara made 62 and was back to near his best when he was run out by a brisk flick at the stumps from short leg. The West Indies then collapsed and Australia led by 102. After that, a typical second innings hundred by Michael Slater, full of exciting strokes, put the match beyond the West Indies' reach on a pitch which had never been that easy for batting. Even so, all the good that had come out of it was effectively undone when in 19.1 overs the West Indies were bowled out for just 51, their lowest score in 71 years of Test cricket. Glenn McGrath and Jason Gillespie bowled unchanged and left West Indies cricket in an apparently even greater sense of disarray than when they had returned from South Africa only days before.

What now happened reads like pure fiction. Yet it was a story born out of hard, rocky and horribly uncomfortable fact. The First Test, although ultimately horrendous for the

West Indies, had shown that Lara had been giving thought to turning a sharp mental corner and had taken the first steps, even though the eventual result will have done much to hide the fact. The unpalatable truth had hit him. He was on his own and he knew it and no amount of bullshit, bravado or swagger was going to save him now. He had to produce or else. For the first time in his cricketing life he had been asked to show what he was made of. Not everyone thought he was capable of providing an adequate answer.

For all the discernible signs of change at Port of Spain, that earth-shattering collapse had reverberated round the Caribbean. The public rounded on the players and their anger must have been a trifle disconcerting, to say the least. The caravan now moved on to Jamaica and after the first day at Sabina Park, Lara must have felt that the gods were against him. After bowling out Australia for 256 with Steve Waugh making exactly a hundred, the West Indies had collapsed to 39/4 by the end of the first day. It was happening all over again. But the one glimmer of hope for Lara and the West Indies was that he himself had not been dismissed. The thoughts that must have gone through his mind that evening could form the ultimate definition of confusion. He would have been forgiven for thinking that his reign as captain of the West Indies had just four more days to run and Rudi Webster will have felt that he was going to have his work cut out to settle him down that evening. Yet, in view of what happened the next day, maybe Lara was cool and composed and knew exactly what to do.

He could not have wished for a better partner than Jimmy Adams. They batted throughout the second day with Lara's flair for extravagant, breathtaking strokeplay combining perfectly with Adams's dogged defence and his ability to put away the bad ball. It has to be said that with the Australians expecting the collapse of the previous evening to continue, they bowled as if they felt the job was done and without quite their usual consistency. It was an easy pitch to bat on, too. That said, the Australians are surely the hardest side in the world to deny victory when they scent it as strongly as they will have done now. It was on this day that Lara raised himself back onto the plinth he should never have left. His determination was magnificent, his strokeplay both glorious and emphatic and he was always in command in the way that only a batsman of his talents can be.

Disbelievingly at first and then with growing exuberance, the West Indian public welcomed him back into their hearts. Their hero had shed his feet of clay at the very last moment and was dancing once more to a tune they were able to recognise and rejoice in. At breakfast that morning in the Caribbean, few people will have wanted to talk about cricket if they could possibly avoid it. By the time it had grown dark that evening, no one was talking about anything else. Lara had not only saved himself, he had given back a sense of pride and self-respect to the many nations of the cricketing West Indies. He had fulfilled their slender hopes. It was a wonderful innings from a man who had managed to summon up the strength of character to defeat all his personal gremlins and to provide the perfect answer to his multitude of critics. It was not the innings of genius he was to play in Barbados in a few days' time but it was something extremely nice to be going on with. Lara was the main architect of this extraordinary West Indian recovery but he could not have done it without the sterling support of the self-effacing, always understated Jimmy Adams, who kept him company while they added 344 runs in this all left-handed partnership. They had dismayed the Australians and visibly strengthened the backbone of the West Indies. Lara was eventually caught behind by Ian Healy off Glen McGrath for 213. The Australians were bowled out for 177 in their second innings, leaving the West Indies to score three for victory in their second innings and they won the match on the fourth day.

Lara won't now have been sitting nervously by the telephone keeping his fingers crossed that Mike Findlay would call him and ask him to captain the side in the last two Tests but, even so, he had not yet fully settled his account. It was his first hundred in fifteen Test Matches and in South Africa he had presided over the most humiliating performance ever put up by a West Indies side when at times they had probably rightly been accused of not trying. Now he had made an excellent start to his rehabilitation, but it amounted to a stay of execution rather than a final departure from the condemned cell. Ten days of frenetic reflection and anticipation followed the Kingston Test Match. No one in the world relishes their triumphs and the success of their heroes more joyfully and all-consumingly than the West Indians. Then the two sides gathered at the Kensington Oval, Barbados. An Australian side which has cornered its prey and then watched horrorstruck as it has leaped over the fence and run off just as they were closing in for the kill, is always likely to be even more dangerous next time. There is, too, no more determined cricketer than Steve Waugh and it was not part of his plans to come to the West Indies and lose his first Test series as his country's captain.

The truth of this was soon shown when, after Australia had won the toss on an excellent pitch in Barbados, Steve Waugh made a small matter of 199. With help from Ricky Ponting, who also made a classy hundred, Australia amassed 490. Then, in double-quick time, the West Indies found themselves reeling at 98/6. Worse still, Lara when on eight had edged Jason Gillespie to Ian Healy and had walked back to the pavilion enveloped by a stunned West Indian silence. But then Sherwin Campbell and Ridley Jacobs put on 153 and with the tail-enders doing their stuff, the West Indies clawed their way to

329, although they were still 161 behind. Courtney Walsh now dug deep and took 5/39 and Australia were dismissed for 146 in their second innings leaving Lara's team to score an improbable 308 to win. They were given a solid start but the middle order still did not know what to make of it and when Adams again found himself coming out to join his captain the score was 105/5. The Australians were steamed up, sniffing a victory which was surely not going to jump the fence and get away this time. Lara and Adams were under even fiercer pressure now than they had been at Sabina Park.

But from his very first ball Lara took control like a consummate ringmaster. While he was always composed in defence, his selection of strokes was brilliant and his obvious belief in his ability to do the job never faltered for an instant. Through a long, hot day his concentration never wavered until right at the end, and even then he got away with it. When he played the pull to anything at all short, it was as if no mortal had ever hit a cricket ball harder; when he late cut it was with charm and delicacy and perfect timing and when he launched himself into one of those all-consuming drives through the offside, it suggested he had taken the art of batting onto a new level. Each one was as bewildering in its power and certainty as it was in its placing. The statistics of the innings are as irrelevant as the number of notes in Beethoven's Ninth. The one was a work of genius as much as the other and there was no need for the statisticians. The Australians wore the blank astonishment of soldiers who have raised their rifles, pulled the trigger, and had the nasty shock to find that nothing happened. They were powerless in the face of this onslaught.

He and Adams put on 133 and when Adams departed, 70 were still needed. Ridley Jacobs and Nehemiah Perry – they do some funny things at the font in the Caribbean – departed ten runs later which left only Ambrose and Walsh. But what wonderful support they now gave their captain. Ambrose, with a bat in his hand that reminded one more of a toothpick than a weapon of war, not only made twelve invaluable runs but he stayed with Lara while 54 were added. When Gillespie disposed of him, only six more were needed. Courtney Walsh, whose batting has become an amusing party trick at the end of the West Indies innings, strode out all arms and legs and tried to make sure that no one thought this was a laughing matter. By now Lara had begun to falter. When he had made 145, he was dropped behind and, almost overtaken by exhaustion, he began to flash and fiddle outside off stump. Walsh brought an air of mildly curious solemnity to the other end rather like a venerable archdeacon preparing to have words with a member of the congregation who has kept his hand in his pocket when the collection bag passed by.

Walsh dug out a yorker with a scholarly precision not many people knew that he possessed. Eventually a no-ball and a wide brought the scores level and Gillespie came bounding in to bowl to Lara. The ball was up to the bat and instinct took Lara into another scorching cover drive which sped away through the field to the boundary. Bedlam followed. This was, beyond a doubt, Lara's greatest innings and so remarkable was it that some old hands even found themselves wondering if it was not perhaps the best ever played by any batsman at any time. Lara had made 153 not out and by the time he had staggered back to the pavilion the slate had surely been wiped clean. Every now and then, genius will stand a game of cricket on its head. Lara had done it now at Kensington just as Ian Botham had done it at Headingley in 1981 when he made 149 not out and after following on, England had beaten Australia by nineteen runs.

Just for good measure Lara now struck a hundred in 84 balls in the Fourth and final Test in Antigua, which was nothing more than a joyful and extraordinary demonstration of superiority. It was as if he was merely playing with the Australians but this time their nerve held and they won the match by 176 runs and the series was drawn at 2–2. But it is Lara's performances that will be remembered long after the result of the series has been forgotten.

Lara had redeemed himself in a manner which had called for remarkable character. His game was in ruins when he returned from South Africa, his captaincy was on the line and his life must have been in turmoil. He left it late but in the end the pressure, the ignominy and the realisation he had let a proud people down, had enabled him to find the right path. He has, of course, set himself a benchmark for the future. It goes without saying that he will not always play innings like those three hundreds against Australia and, like everyone else, he will make his share of low scores. What he cannot do is go back to his old attitude. He has now shown that he under-stands the responsibilities he has to show as captain of the West Indies. He cannot again ignore them. The old days of ill-discipline and lateness are no longer on the agenda and he must be more rational and diplomatic in his dealings with his Board, too. It may very well be that he is now in a position to orchestrate change here and that West Indies cricket will soon be run by people who understand the game better. That seems a prime requirement which at the moment is fulfilled only by their admirable chief executive, Steve Camacho, a former Test opening batsman.

It is thanks to Brian Lara that children in the Caribbean are once again rushing out onto the beach or any piece of open land with a makeshift bat in their hand shouting to their chums, 'I am Lara.' Cricket is alive again in the West Indies. But it will always need nurturing and, with the close competition from American sport, more so now than ever. Having become the hero of these youngsters, Lara must not now let them down. That is the biggest of his new-found responsibilities. The biggest irony of all is that Lara's deeds against Australia have almost certainly saved and maybe even extended Rousseau's tenure of office as President of the West Indies Board.

My only complaint about his performances is that I had chosen to go to New Zealand and not the West Indies, but then they make very much better wine in New Zealand.

CHAPTER ELEVEN

The School Bully Strikes in Adelaide

While all this had been unfolding, there had been a fair amount of skulduggery going on in other parts of the world. From the depths of my sybaritic rain forest on Bedarra Island I watched on television England's impressive victories over Australia and Sri Lanka in Brisbane at the start of the World Series Cup. By the time I had returned to England about a week later, normal service had been resumed in all ways but one. Defeat was again back on the agenda, but Graeme Hick had started to make hundreds. I wonder if there has ever been a more irritating player than Hick in the entire history of cricket. It is as though he is a genius with dirt on his hands. How could such a talented batsman be so alarmingly inconsistent at the top level? What goes through his mind? The answer to that would probably produce a considerable medical treatise.

Those initial results in Brisbane had made it look as if England would walk their way into the best-of-three finals against Australia, but by the time the three sides had reached Adelaide for the Australia Day weekend, England were slipping and Sri Lanka were not yet out of it. The first of the three games, between England and Sri Lanka, besides being a remarkable game of cricket, produced one of the most appalling scenes ever to have been enacted on a cricket ground. Arjuna Ranatunga, behaving exactly like the School Bully, elected to treat one of the umpires, Ross Emerson (a regrettable choice, as we shall see), rather as Mike Gatting had Shakoor Rana in Pakistan in 1987. The School Bully, unlike Gatting, got away with it on the field of play at the time and afterwards, too, when confronted by the ICC's terrifying Code of Conduct. England had made 302/3 after being put in and Hick's 126 not out was his second hundred of the competition. This surely was an invincible total. Yet Mahela Jayawardene outdid Hick with an even more brilliant century and when Muttiah Muralitheran hit the winning run, two balls remained.

Emerson is a former police officer from Perth who now likes to describe himself as an 'investigator'. This makes him a member of the same illustrious profession engagingly and courteously graced by such as Sherlock Holmes, Hercule Poirot, Miss Marples and Lord Peter Wimsey. Emerson, the Investigator, would probably argue that his single greatest piece of sleuthing consisted of the deductive processes he brought to bear on the case of the recalcitrant off spinner, Muralitheran's action. But I doubt it put him in line for his deerstalker hat. In all honesty, I saw it as nothing more than major interference in headlong pursuit of self-importance. As well as trying to make a name for himself, the Investigator was attempting to justify the stance he had taken up in Brisbane four years earlier and also to back up Hair for publicly labelling Muralitheran a chucker in his autobiography. It is impossible to believe that he did not make the journey from

Perth to Adelaide with his mind made up that he was going to call Muralitheran for throwing, come what may. There is no doubt that the Investigator was the catalyst for all that followed, not that this takes any of the blame away from the School Bully.

It was not, alas, a match which will be remembered longest for its result. The problems had begun when the Australian Cricket Board had picked the Investigator to stand in this match with Tony McQuillan. In January 1996, in a one-day international in Brisbane, these two umpires had no-balled Muralitheran for throwing seven times between them. By all accounts, the Investigator had got it wrong then, for he continued to call him when he had reverted to bowling orthodox leg breaks. He called him when standing at the bowler's end, too, which made it look like a preplanned exercise, for he is a short man without an obviously treble-jointed neck. Before Sri Lanka came to Australia this time, their Board had shown considerable concern about the appointment of Darrell Hair for any of their matches. He had called Muralitheran for throwing in the Boxing Day Test at Melbourne in 1995. Hair had not won a medal for tact when he 'called' Muralitheran in his recent autobiography, describing his action as 'diabolical'. The ACB had not been pleased. Yet it is difficult to believe they were unaware of the likely consequences of appointing the Investigator and McQuillan for this match in Adelaide and, who knows, maybe they did it in order to get one back at the Sri Lankan Board for complaining about Hair. What a glorious muddle it was.

I have mentioned the controversy over Muralitheran's action in Chapter Eight. His action may look strange, but I do not believe he throws. Most significantly, Ian Chappell wrote, while it was all going on in Adelaide, that he did not consider that Muralitheran's action gave him an unfair advantage. It is important not to forget about his deformed arm and the

259

double-jointed wrist which effectively turns him into the only wrist-spinning off spinner the game has ever known.

In Adelaide Muralitheran was brought on to bowl the sixteenth over of the match. The Investigator was standing at square leg and one can picture the great sleuth biding his time before he made his burst for freedom. Or perhaps I over-estimate him and he was merely trying to pluck up courage to fulfil what he may have seen as his destiny. In that first over he held his breath and kept his mouth shut and his magnify-ing glass in his pocket. Muralitheran came back to bowl his second over and for the first three balls the Investigator was apparently entirely satisfied with his rectitude since, as far as one could gather, he did not even clear his throat. But as Muralitheran bowled the fourth ball, he leapt into action. The cry of 'No-ball!' rang across the Adelaide Oval and his right arm shot out sideways to signal the same to the scorers. With a brilliance bordering on genius, he had detected something that no one else on the ground or indeed in the television audience had been able to see. His relentless search for clues had brought home the bacon. Soon after he had done the deed, he may have begun to feel that even a former police-man's lot is not a particularly happy one because he was to become an object of ridicule, not to say contempt. But first he had to suffer the School Bully.

After making the call, the Investigator signalled to the Sri Lankan captain that this had been the first ball of Muralitheran's with which he had been unhappy. To make sure everyone understood, he pointed to his own elbow. It was extremely unfortunate that a bowler who had taken more than two hundred Test wickets should have been made a fool of in this way. The accepted procedure for an umpire who is unhappy with a bowler's action is for him to have a word with the match referee who will report the matter to the ICC and the bowler in question will be put under photographic scrutiny. The reason for this procedure is to prevent exactly what happened now when the intrepid Investigator, for reasons of his own, decided to ignore the accepted procedure and highlight Muralitheran in the most embarrassing manner. Of course, it is possible to understand the anger of the Sri Lankans. But the behaviour of their captain, the School Bully, was intolerable. For his pains he should have been banned from international cricket for a long time.

The School Bully advanced upon the Investigator and did a bit of finger wagging before leading his troops to the boundary's edge in front of the main stand. There the players were met by the Sri Lankan officials and the match referee, the former South African captain, Peter van der Merwe. For a few minutes the future of the competition was in doubt. The School Bully and the team's manager, Ranjit Fernando, who is the most reasonable and charming of men, telephoned the chairman of their Board of Control, Thilanga Sumathipala in Colombo to seek instructions. Fernando later said there was not the slightest chance of the Sri Lankans packing it in, but in all probability that was belated diplomacy.

Eventually the players went back to the middle and now the School Bully moved into overdrive. Muralitheran finished his over but the confrontation continued. Muralitheran immediately changed ends and bowled round the wicket. He asked the Investigator to stand up to the stumps – a bowler is allowed to ask the umpire to stand where he wants – but Emerson was unwilling to do so and this brought the School Bully strutting in. He insisted that the Investigator, who now seemed to be becoming less sure of his ground, stood right up to the stumps. He was mindful, no doubt, that the Investigator had found his clues three years before when standing at the bowler's end which, far from being easy, underlined his genius. When the Investigator showed a certain initial reluctance to comply, the School Bully showed his true colours and apparently said, 'I'm in charge of this game. You'll stand where I want you to. If you don't stand there, there won't be a game.' At a blow, he had swept his way clean through the ICC's celebrated Code of Conduct.

All eyes were now on McQuillan at square leg. He had also called Muralitheran in Brisbane three years before but now he either thought that Muralitheran had reformed his action or simply didn't want to know. Attention then switched back to the School Bully who was strutting about the place as if he was Napoleon at half-time at the battle of Waterloo with a touch of Attila the Hun thrown in. He revealed himself as one of the great finger waggers and obviously he had picked up a number of tips from Mike Gatting.

The School Bully's behaviour was indefensible but the Investigator would have brought a saint out in a cold sweat. In this game he showed that he was a poor umpire as well. In Sri Lanka's innings he failed to refer a run out against Jayawardene to the third umpire. He gave the benefit of the doubt to the batsman and the replay showed that he was out. He turned down Darren Gough's more than reasonable appeal for obstruction against Mahanama and he presided over a seven-ball over from Gough. They all added up. Then there were the other incidents. When play restarted, Mahanama seemed to knock deliberately into Gough in mid pitch and at the end of the same over, Alec Stewart appeared to walk deliberately into Mahanama which, if he did, was conduct unbecoming from an England captain. The game became increasingly unpleasant and yet the umpires never tried to exert their authority.

If that famous Code of Conduct had meant anything, the School Bully would have considered himself extremely lucky if he had got away with only a six-match suspension. Although the Sri Lankans may have felt that they were the victims of an Australian plot, this is not entirely borne out by the fact that their Board had taken the precaution of retaining the services of an Australian lawyer before arriving in the country. When their aeroplane landed, one Brendan Schwab, a senior associate in a posh firm of Melbourne solicitors, was already buckling on his pads on their behalf. Schwab himself said that his brief was broad although confidentiality forbade him to enlarge upon that. When they had been in Australia three years before, the Sri Lankans had been accused of ball-tampering, gamesmanship and throwing. The players were also said to have been unduly petulant and had refused to shake hands with the Australians at the end of a disagreeable one-day series – kids' stuff in all honesty.

Sri Lanka seemed, therefore, to be covering their backs before the start. I could not avoid the impression that after the great Investigator had called Muralitheran, the School Bully then worked to a preconceived and well-rehearsed plan of campaign. It wouldn't surprise me in the least if, possibly with Mr Schwab's help, they had come to the conclusion that the much vaunted Code of Conduct was most unlikely to stand up in a court of law. The School Bully was able to besport himself as he did, having a pretty good idea that the ICC could not touch him. It says a fair bit about the ICC that even if this scenario had occurred to them, they had not apparently done anything about it. Or maybe it was simply that they felt that the ICC was a gentlemen's club and that its members would not work against the governing body from within. I suppose there must have been an attempt to persuade all the member countries to accept the Code of Conduct. The fact of the matter was that a set of rules or Code of Conduct was in place for all international cricket which did not apparently stand a chance in a court of law. I only wish that Gilbert and Sullivan had still been around to set to words and music the incredible situation which unwound in Adelaide.

Peter van der Merwe, the match referee, was soon made aware of the legal possibilities. His own intuition may have had something to do with it but you may be sure that the Sri Lankans will not have been slow to raise every possible legal obstacle. What is all too clear is that van der Merwe himself was hopping mad at the School Bully's disgraceful behaviour, but sensed that his hands were tied. At the end of a two-hour meeting in Adelaide, van der Merwe made the decision that the disciplinary hearing into the School Bully's conduct would be adjourned until a later date. The wires between Adelaide and London will have burned red hot, with impotence as well as impatience. Van der Merwe felt unable to detail the specific charges to be brought against the Sri Lankan captain. He said warily, 'Certain points have been raised by Ranatunga's legal representatives which I have referred back to London for advice. We have to get the right answer even if it takes time.'

One does not have to be related, even distantly, to Einstein to be able to interpret this. On the day the School Bully did his bit, van der Merwe will have rung the ICC in London and will have said that he wanted to throw the book at him. He will also have mentioned the legal noises which were coming from the Sri Lankan dressing room and their likely intention to contest any arbitrary sentence in the law courts. Van der Merwe was frustrated because this was surely an open and shut case if the dear old Code of Conduct meant anything. Right was indisputably on his side and yet he was as powerless as he might have been if Delilah had got to work on him with the scissors. Mention of the law courts will have set all the bells ringing in London and van der Merwe will have been told to do nothing until further notice. Hence the outcome of that first meeting in Adelaide.

The School Bully, meantime, was engaged in outrageous delaying tactics. He launched a noisy and robust defence and made much of the rule which states that umpires are obliged to submit their match reports within one hour of the game ending. The Investigator had been late with his but it is hard to blame him. He will have had much to put down and after all the kerfuffle that will have gone on when he left the pitch, he will have been extremely pushed to file his report in time and should have been allowed an extension. But the awful majesty of the law was now firing on all twelve cylinders. The next hearing was scheduled for Perth later in the week where, as luck would have it, England were playing Sri Lanka the following weekend once more under the vigilant eye of the dreaded Investigator. Neither did the ACB cover themselves with glory in this entire episode because they set up a situation which had the predictable consequences we have seen. Don't tell me they could not have foreseen exactly what was likely to happen. But now, with lightning footwork, they acted and, in a slightly portentous statement, said that the Investigator had been 'stood down' from the match in Perth, not because of what had happened in Adelaide – of course not – but because of his medical condition.

Van der Merwe presided over the second meeting in Perth. He will have been told that the likelihood was that if he suspended or banned the School Bully with immediate effect, the decision would be hit for six in the courts. It was a farce. The meeting lasted for five hours and there were two lawyers present representing the ICC and two more looking after Sri Lankan interests. The net result was that the School Bully received a six-match suspension which was suspended and he was fined a whacking seventy-five per cent of his match fee. The Sri Lankans are paid the equivalent of about £80 a match and so the School Bully had narrowly escaped bankruptcy by having to fork out all of sixty quid. He had got away with it, as I suspect he always knew he would, and his insufferably arrogant behaviour had cocked a snoop at the ICC, their beguiling Code of Conduct and anyone else

265

who cares about the sport of cricket.

Van der Merwe did his best when he said afterwards, 'The unfortunate happening has cost Ranatunga,' – a moderate dinner for two with plonk – 'and I told him this, a great deal in the popularity stakes. And respect is something he and I will both lose by this decision.' The School Bully will have taken just about as much notice of these words of warning as the oceans did when King Canute sat on the sand and exhorted the tide not to come in. Van der Merwe also said, 'I am very disappointed that the disciplinary panel were compromised by a number of legal representatives. In future, the ICC will take the lead to ensure that lawyers will not be present at hearings. I warned Ranatunga that his every action in the next twelve months will be closely monitored and scrutinised.' There are a number of people who come out badly from this whole charade and the Sri Lankan Board of Control's performance was as bad as any in the way they did handstands to defend the indefensible.

I still wonder what would have happened if, that first evening at the Adelaide Oval, van der Merwe had handed out an immediate six-match suspension to Ranatunga. Would the Sri Lankans have broken their agreement with the ACB and gone straight home? Would they have attacked the ICC in the law courts for upholding their Code of Conduct? I'm sure they would have made a lot of noise but I wonder if the Sri Lankan Board might not have backed down when the full picture of their captain's behaviour had been understood. No doubt they would have been made to realise the consequences for their future in world competition. I believe it would have been a risk worth taking.

The goings on in Adelaide had rather submerged a sad story to come out of South Africa earlier in the new year. Makhaya Ntini, their young, coloured fast bowler, who had toured

England in 1998, had been accused of raping a girl in the pavilion of his home ground in East London. Ali Bacher had spoken strongly in his support saying that he had every reason to believe that Ntini had been set up. In the meantime, the selectors had left him out of the side to tour New Zealand. It was at about the time of the goings-on in Adelaide that he was found guilty. One can only imagine that his future in South African cricket is in some doubt, although Bacher is a good chap to have on your side.

The School Bully's behaviour was still the topic of conversation in Australia when, the day after the cricketers had left Adelaide for Perth, Mark Taylor announced that he had decided to pack it in. He had said after the last Test against England that he was going to consider his future. He now said that after winning the Adelaide Test and making sure of keeping the Ashes, his enthusiasm had not been quite so sharp and he had decided the time had come. When the current one-day series was over, the Australians were going to the West Indies. Taylor had to let the selectors know his decision before they chose the side. Shortly beforehand Taylor had been voted the Australian of the Year and he had acquired a remarkable celebrity status at the end of his career, much of it originating from that noble declaration in Lahore the previous October that had left him not out on 334, thus equalling rather than surpassing Don Bradman's record.

It is almost impossible to fault Taylor as a captain, a batsman, a catcher or a human being. He had taken over a strong Australian side from Allan Border in 1994 and moved it on to new levels in that he maintained the record and yet turned it into a more entertaining, more watchable side. The beauty of Taylor was that, unlike so many contemporary cricketers, he never demeaned the game, never thought for a moment that he was bigger than the game, never did anything but respect it. He was not interested in headlines and, in an age when money apparently rules everything, he never lost sight of the fact that cricket was a game and that the essential reason for playing it was for the enjoyment that was to be got out of it. He was not a glamorous cricketer. He worked hard for all that he achieved but then those achievements were considerable. There was a small matter of 7,525 Test runs, more than any other Australian except his predecessor, Allan Border. He made nineteen Test hundreds and, in 104 Test Matches, hung onto 157 catches, mostly at first slip, which happens to be one more than anyone else.

Although his record was remarkable, it was his character which will cause him to be remembered and cherished the longest. He was blessed with a sense of humour and, just as important, a sense of proportion. In the tightest of finishes when the pressure was extreme, or in moments of despair, Taylor never lost sight of where he was and what he was trying to do. He was a natural communicator who handled the authority that went with his job firmly but always gently. When he was under attack, both from the fast bowlers and the critics, he never flinched. He looked them unrelentingly in the eye and told them the truth. He never tried to deceive anyone. Eminently reasonable, he was always prepared to listen to another point of view. Those who were there will never forget the exceptional way in which he carried himself on his last tour to England in 1997. When the tour began, he could not find a run nor locate the middle of his bat to save his life. For all his record, the critics were on his back at once and even Ian Chappell and Dennis Lillee were saying that he should go.

The First Test was in Birmingham and in the first innings Taylor failed again and when he walked off the ground he was desperately close to resigning his commission. But his nerve held and in the second innings he made a sterling hundred. Although Australia lost the match, Taylor had answered his critics in the only way possible and his position was never queried again on that tour. At press conferences during that match he was exemplary. He never looked for excuses and handled the media with such courtesy that they were the ones to feel embarrassed and not Taylor. For all his shuffling walk and baggy-trousered appearance, Taylor had a quiet but indomitable confidence in all that he did. The game without Taylor and his example will be the poorer wherever it is played.

While the Sri Lankans and Mark Taylor kept everyone busy in Australia, great deeds were being enacted on the western side of the Bay of Bengal. For the first time since 1987 the politicians had allowed India and Pakistan to do battle in the Test arena. Pakistan went to India for two Test matches, in Chennai (Madras) and Delhi. The tour was surrounded by interminable political problems from which the cricketers happily remained immune. It is worth remembering that the cricketers of India and Pakistan are all the best of friends. The animosity only appears from beyond the boundary, but it is usually of such an intensity that it cannot be ignored. The immediate danger came from the extreme Hindu parties in India. The right wing Shiv Sena had, through its leader, Bal Thackeray, promised mayhem on a grand scale if the tour took place. By way of flexing their muscles, they had ransacked the Indian Board of Control's offices in Mumbai (Bombay) and then dug up the Test pitch in Delhi causing the two Tests to be swapped round. But by the time Wasim Akram and his team arrived in Chennai, these Hindu militants had bowed to pressure and publicly suspended their plans to disrupt the tour. Nonetheless, security was maintained at an extraordinary level.

The two matches were an unqualified success. It was a fairy story blessed by the gods of both sides. The Indians were generous to their opponents and the Pakistani players, especially Wasim Akram, entered fully into the spirit of it. At the First Test in Chennai, the spectators showed immense patience and control as each one of them was searched on entering the ground. They were rewarded with some breathtaking cricket and a thrilling finish.

Pakistan won the toss and batted carelessly especially against Kumble who took 6/70. Yousuf Youhana and Moin Khan enabled them to get as far as a disappointing 238. India's reply was unconvincing, especially against the off spin of Saqlain Mushtaq, who picked up 5/94 including Tendulkar for nought. For no good reason, he came charging down the pitch to his third ball and skied it to point, which only goes to show how pressure can get to even the coolest of thinkers. Only Rahul Dravid and Saurav Ganguly passed fifty and so at the halfway stage the game could hardly have been more delicately poised with India gaining a lead of 16.

In Pakistan's second innings, Shahid Afridi, who had achieved a great reputation as a one-day player but was taking part in only his second Test Match, put Pakistan in the driving seat. His glorious strokeplay was disciplined by a sound defence and good judgement. Javed Miandad, the coach, had made it his job to try and teach Afridi about Test cricket and on this evidence had made an outstanding start to the job. Afridi's 141 took him 191 balls and included 24 boundaries. His best support came from Inzamam-ul-Haq, who reached fifty and ran no one out. Pakistan were all out for 286 after Venkatesh Prasad, in a fearsome spell, took the last five Pakistan wickets for no runs in eighteen balls.

India were left to score 271 to win and on the fourth morning they collapsed against pace and spin to 82/5. At this point Tendulkar was joined by Nayan Mongia. Tendulkar was magnificent and if ever an innings was needed to show that he is the best of all contemporary batsmen, this was it. But if

Tendulkar was the one player who could win the match for India, Pakistan had their own match winner in off spinner Saqlain Mushtaq. The battle between the two of them was cricket at its very best. The ball was turning and lifting but Tendulkar played Mushtaq always with respect, sometimes with suspicion and usually with authority. Once Tendulkar might have been stumped by Moin Khan when he used his feet to try to drive. Moin was unable to take the ball cleanly and Saqlain banged his head on the ground in frustration while Mongia came down the pitch and did his best to calm Tendulkar. Mongia himself played a fine innings, reaching his fifty sweeping Saqlain for six. But then he tried to hit Wasim Akram back over his head and was caught at mid on. Maybe, after that six, Tendulkar should have returned the compliment and tried to quieten Mongia.

The drama intensified when it became clear that Tendulkar was suffering from painful back spasms. It hurt every time he hit the ball, but he knew that if he was out, India had had it. He played two slightly frantic straight drives for four off Wasim which spoke of his agitated frame of mind. He then had a last desperate heave at Saqlain and skied the ball to mid off. Saqlain and Wasim now closed in for the kill taking the last three wickets without conceding a single run and Pakistan were home by twelve runs. Saqlain's 5/122 gave him match figures of 10/187. Wasim said later, 'I have long said that Tendulkar was the best batsman in the world and today we saw one of the best innings.' It had been a remarkable game of cricket in the skill, the excitement and the closeness of the result, but also in that it was played without incident and when Pakistan won deep in India, they were cheered as they ran a lap of honour around the ground afterwards.

Four days after this dramatic First Test Match, which served to underline the futility of the eternal conflict which puts relationships between the two countries on a more or less permanent war-footing, the sides met again in Delhi where the pitch had been successfully repaired. This turned out to be another remarkable contest, not for its closeness, but because Anil Kumble, the Indian leg spinner, took all ten wickets in the second innings, only the second bowler in history after England's Jim Laker to perform this feat in a Test innings.

India won the toss and thanks to the extravagant strokeplay of their new opener, Sadagopan Ramesh, supported by sixty from Azharuddin, they made 252. Saqlain took his regulation five wickets, again for 94 as he had in the first innings in Chennai, figures which show that the Indian batsmen were eager to attack him. When Pakistan batted, Shahid Afridi's 32 was their highest score and they were bowled out for 172. Kumble, perhaps testing the water, took 4/75. Another fine innings by Ramesh who was out for 96, and useful runs from Ganguly and Srinath took India to 339 in their second innings and the scene was set.

But first of all, Saeed Anwar and Shahid Afridi put on 101 for the first wicket with little apparent difficulty. Srinath was expensive and so, too, was Kumble in his first spell before lunch, his first five overs costing 25 runs. Immediately after the interval, he changed ends and gave his sweater and cap to Tendulkar to give to the umpire. In that over, Afridi felt for one wide of the off stump and was caught behind. 'I think a little superstition helped,' Kumble said later, 'because whenever we felt we really needed a wicket afterwards, I would let Sachin take my sweater and cap again. It always worked.' Ijaz Ahmed was hit on the toe as he pushed forward to the very next ball and was lbw. Four overs later, Inzamam-ul-Haq was bowled by Kumble off the inside edge playing from the crease and two balls after that, Yousuf Youhana was leg before shuffling defensively across his stumps. Pakistan had slumped from 101/0 to 115/4. Twelve more runs had been added when Kumble had Moin Khan caught low down at slip by Ganguly and only another single had come after that when Saeed Anwar thrust forward and was caught off bat and pad at forward short leg. In the afternoon, Kumble had taken 6/33 in 16 overs. It took him 33 balls to pick up the last four amid scenes of frenzied excitement. Salim Malik swung across a top spinner and was bowled, Mushtaq Ahmed played forward to one which turned and lifted and was caught at silly point and, next ball, Saqlain, moving forward, was lbw.

With the eighth and ninth wickets going down to the final two balls of Kumble's twenty-sixth over, he had to sweat it out at third man while Srinath bowled an over in which he could so easily have taken the last wicket. What Kumble did not know was that Azharuddin had had a word with Srinath and told him to bowl wide of the stumps to give the leg spinner the chance to take all ten. 'By that stage,' Azharuddin said afterwards, 'they were so far behind that we were going to win and there are not many situations where a bowler has the chance to take all ten.' Srinath even bowled two wides in his effort to comply. Wasim survived the hat-trick ball from Kumble but two balls later got an edge onto his pad and it flew to short leg. The deed was done and the leg spinner finished with 10/74. Kumble is modest, unassuming and shy, which made it even more delightful that he should have achieved such a remarkable feat.

'After I had taken the sixth wicket, I thought I might have a chance of all ten. I was not particularly nervous because I knew it was a matter of destiny. If I was destined to get ten wickets, then that is what would happen. My first reaction was how good to beat Pakistan. In that moment I had forgotten it was my tenth wicket.' He dedicated his achievement to God, his family and his team mates in that order. He even said that he thought the match award should have gone to the Indian opening batsman, Ramesh, who had made 60 and 96. He added that every time he left home his mother told him to take a hat-trick and he was frightened that she would now instruct him to take all ten.

Appropriately, the series had ended level at one match each and it was a triumph for the two captains, Wasim Akram and Mohammad Azharuddin, who had both made it clear before the start that they were only interested in playing attacking cricket.

In this short period, Test cricket had been done a power of good all round the world, from Melbourne to Delhi and Chennai to Barbados. One of the main reasons for this had been the brilliant efforts of the spin bowlers – MacGill and, to some extent, Warne and then Saqlain and Kumble while Mushtaq Ahmed had had his moments as well. Kumble is perhaps the most unlikely of these. One is more likely to find him coming out of the assistant manager's office behind a hotel reception desk than walking off a Test ground with ten wickets in one innings under his belt. He is a diffident hero and so different from most wrist spinners who tend to be buoyant extroverts, which probably helps them cope with the moments of disaster which are so often their companions. Kumble is not a big turning leg spinner either, although he now tweaks his leg break more than he did. He uses his height well to make his top spinner and his googly bounce and this has brought him many of his wickets, as has the extra pace of the top spinner, which has undone many a batsman who has prepared to play it off the back foot and has found himself plumb lbw as the ball hurries on.

These two splendid Test Matches in India had brought to an end the pattern of interminable draws which has disfigured so many of the Test Matches the politicians have allowed these two countries to play in recent history. It was a delightful coincidence that the first ever Asian Test

Championship, held immediately after these two matches, should have brought them together again in the preliminary round. They now played in Calcutta and it was another cracking game of cricket. India had reduced Pakistan to 26/6 on the first morning, helped by some superb fast bowling by Javagal Srinath, who finished the match with 13/114, before Moin Khan, determined as ever, took them to 185. India replied with 223 before Saeed, dropped in the slips when two, made a magnificent 188 to help Pakistan to 316 in their second innings. India now needed 279 to win, but their second innings was marred by the appalling behaviour of the big crowd when Sachin Tendulkar was run out for nine in a most bizarre incident. He was going for an easy enough third run. He ran while looking at the fielder and did not see that Shoaib Akhtar was backing away from the stumps as the throw came in and effectively blocked his path. Tendulkar tried to complete the run by unwittingly pushing his bat right through Shoaib, who in an instinctive reaction to the collision lifted the bat in the air and away from safety. The third umpire had no alternative but to give Tendulkar out angering the crowd who proceeded to hold up play and continued to do so on the last day as Pakistan moved towards victory. In the end, the security forces removed all the spectators from the ground and the final wickets fell in front of an empty stadium. It was said that the security forces were none too gentle, either, in the methods they used to clear the ground. It is a part of the world where emotions are often uncontrollable whether you are breaking the law or enforcing it.

A great many runs were amassed in the competition with ten centuries being scored in the remaining three matches, including doubles by Ijaz Ahmed and Inzamam-ul-Haq in the final when Pakistan beat Sri Lanka by an innings and 175 runs. In Pakistan's qualifying match against Sri Lanka, Wasim Akram had taken a hat-trick and he did so again in the final when he struck in Sri Lanka's second innings with the fifth and sixth balls of his first over and the first of his second. It was the first time a bowler has taken hat-tricks in successive Test Matches. Jimmy Matthews, the Australian, took two hat-tricks in the same match against South Africa at Old Trafford in the 1912 Triangular Tournament in England, amazingly the last time before this that a Test Match had been played on neutral soil.

The resumption of Test cricket between India and Pakistan was a triumph for the game. But after the Calcutta crowd's behaviour and even before bringing Kashmir into the equation, no one would be sanguine enough to suggest that the politicians will agree to this happening again on a regular basis. As we have seen, Australia's visit to the West Indies was also a glorious victory for Test cricket, but no sooner were our backs turned than the West Indian crowds got up to all sorts of tricks in the one-day series, which left a most unpleasant taste in the mouth.

In both Georgetown and Bridgetown, crowd invasions and bottle throwing put players at grave risk and it makes one wonder when administrators will come to their senses over the issue of crowd control. It is something worse than madness to allow highly emotional people to bring large bottles made of glass and full of alcohol into the grounds on these occasions. Drunkenness on its own causes bad enough problems; empty bottles as missiles quite another. This was illustrated all too starkly when one, at Kensington Oval, Barbados, thrown at great velocity, missed the Australian captain Steve Waugh's head by no more than a foot. This incident was seen on television and this particular bottle was apparently propelled by someone sitting in the most expensive seats in the house, in the Sir Garfield Sobers pavilion.

The first incident occurred at Bourda in Georgetown where they had not made sure the gates were properly manned. The crowd considerably exceeded the small capacity of the ground and twice towards the end of the fifth one-day international, hundreds of spectators invaded the playing area. Rain had reduced the match to thirty overs a side and the first invasion took place when the West Indies had bowled twenty-nine of their thirty overs. The crowd seemed to think the match had finished although there was still one over to be bowled with Australia needing four more to win. It took ten minutes to clear the ground and even then the huge number of security police made no attempt to make sure it did not happen a second time.

When the last over was bowled by Keith Arthurton, Steve Waugh was unable to score off the first five balls. Four were therefore needed from the last if Australia were to win and three if they were to tie. Waugh drove towards long on and while he and Shane Warne set off on their run chase, another major invasion was already in progress. They had run two when Stuart Williams's throw reached Arthurton who took off the bails. At the other end, Waugh had turned for an improbable third run but by then the pitch was thick with spectators, the stumps had been pulled up and one chap even tried to pinch Waugh's bat. Fortunately, the match referee, Raman Subba Row, a former England batsman, was no stranger to this sort of thing at Bourda. Six years before, he had been presiding there when Ian Bishop needed two from the last ball for the West Indies to beat Pakistan. As Bishop sprinted through for the second run, Wasim Akram, who was standing by the stumps with the crowd descending on him, dropped the throw-in from the fielder. Subba Row had declared that match to be a tie and he will not have required outside assistance to make the same decision now.

The last two games of the seven-match series were being played in Bridgetown and Australia won the first, giving them a 3-2 lead in the series. The second game was watched by at least 14,000, which almost certainly exceeded the official capacity of the ground and, to the spectators' immense delight, the West Indies looked like winning with ease. Australia had made 252/9 and the West Indies were cruising along at 138/1 from 28.5 overs. Shivnarine Chanderpaul now pushed Brendon Julian towards mid on and he and Sherwin Campbell set off for a quick run. In the general confusion between batsmen, bowler and fielders, Campbell was rammed amidships by Julian, who is about three times as big, and sent sprawling. Michael Bevan fielded the ball, took off the bails at the wicket-keeper's end and Campbell was given out.

In moments, the ground was covered with bottles, which came from all directions. When it became clear that cricket could not continue for quite a while, the Australians followed Campbell. It was as he neared the pavilion that Steve Waugh almost had his head knocked off by that bottle. It took three quarters of an hour to clear the ground and then Gary Sobers himself announced that the Australians and the match referee had agreed that Campbell would be allowed to continue his innings. Steve Waugh said the decision had been taken in the interests of cricket but the fact that the police had told the Australians they could not guarantee their safety if play did not continue will also have been taken into account. The West Indies went on to win and Campbell, who was out for 62, was made Man of the Match and Man of the Series. So, all in all, it had been a pretty good day for mob rule.

When it was all over, the most telling comments came from Steve Waugh. 'We were risking our lives again for a game of one-day cricket. If it keeps on like that, there's no point in us playing.' It is impossible not to agree with every syllable. Events like these have happened too often in the West Indies, and indeed on the Subcontinent, although alcohol is obviously no problem there. The safety of the players is of paramount importance and if the relevant Boards do not take action now to prevent this sort of thing continuing, they should forfeit the right to hold international matches on the grounds concerned. It is as elementary to stop spectators bringing bottles of booze into the grounds as it is to make sure that the ground is not filled beyond its capacity and that there is a big enough police presence to cope with any likely trouble. Nor is it beyond the capability of man to arrange for more effective safety fences to be built.

It is extraordinary that the game should have a governing body and yet no semblance of cohesion in the methods used to prevent these incidents arising. Are we going to have to wait until someone is killed before the responsibility for the players is accepted by the home Boards, all represented on the ICC? The present situation is an utter disgrace and reflects appallingly on all those concerned. I will be amazed if a similar scene to the ones above is not enacted somewhere in the cricketing world at a one-day international or Test Match in the not too distant future. And we will all be deafened by the distant clicking of tongues and the pious voices saying how dreadful it is and that something must be done. Please, someone, prove me wrong.

CHAPTER TWELVE

Australia's Seven in a Row

I must own up. During the 1999 World Cup in England I was unable to watch a single ball bowled live. Doctor's orders decreed that I should spend much of May and all of June in the depths of Norfolk as my bypasses and I tried to learn to live together. The World Cup consisted of twiddling the knobs on my television set in a fevered and sometimes unsuccessful attempt to locate the right channel. It was so much easier to keep the radio tuned to 198 metres longwave and simply switch it on and off. I found it much more enjoyable, too, but then I suppose I would say that. Aggers and CMJ and co. did a masterful job, telling me all that I wanted to know and leaving the imagination free to wander and paint its own pictures. The visiting commentators were splendid also and none more so than that lively and attractive lawyer from Barbados, Donna Symonds who, I am sure, will have been enjoyed for good solid cricketing reasons and not just because she belongs to the distaff side of things. In fact, as I listened to *Test Match Special* (which, in the circumstances, should probably have been renamed *One-day Special* or *World Cup Special*) I kept feeling, Talk Radio take that.

It would not be the truth to say that the World Cup was on everyone's lips in North Norfolk from 14 May to 20 June, but there was a ripple of interest. It is a part of the world which gives itself over, body and soul, to looking after the interests of those who spend their holidays and their loot on the Broads, but Ralph and Georgina, in their village store in Horning, were still always up to date with the latest news. It wasn't really cricket weather in Hoveton and Wroxham or Horning, either. For all that, England's victory over Sri Lanka in the opening match made a few people sit up and no doubt a few mainbraces were spliced in exultation. 'Ranatunga, go and eat cake,' just about summed up the local consensus of opinion. There was a shrug of the shoulders when England went down to India and out of the competition, a mild ripple when Australia and South Africa locked horns in the two best matches and, after the apology for a Final, a slight feeling that Pakistan might have been up to their old tricks again. Lance Klusener would have been given the freedom of the parish and so too, rather grudgingly, would Steve Waugh and Shane Warne. As a rule, we in Norfolk don't mind who wins as long as it isn't Australia.

It was a competition in two parts for me. I had the time to read every word that was written in the papers. The match reports were one part of the competition while the tittle-tattle, the filler paragraphs at the bottom of the page and the diary items were the other, a part I would probably have missed through lack of time if I had been actively involved. I remember reading on the 14 May, which was the day after I had returned to Norfolk, that David Lloyd, the ever garrulous England coach, had been prepared to go on record saying that the England players were excited at the prospect of the battles ahead. That made me feel much better.

But in spite of this revolutionary new attitude, the England World Cup squad did not get off to the most gracious of starts in the warm-up games against the counties. They were based in Canterbury and one evening, when Manchester United were playing the European Cup Final, Graham Thorpe elected to watch television rather than go with the rest of the side to an official function. He claimed tiredness and was rightly fined a thousand pounds by the management, which should have taught him a lesson about teamwork. If this is an indication that the England players are now going to be made to be more aware of their responsibilities, which they so often seem to have forgotten of late, it can only be for the good. 'I'm alright, Jack' attitudes have been too prevalent for too long. The England party had only travelled as far as Chelmsford when, in their game with Essex, Adam Hollioake was spotted making a rude sign to one section of the crowd. He was presumably ticked off but the management were reluctant to comment, which I hope does not mean that double standards were being applied. One of the stranger aspects of this year's cricket has been the way in which the Hollioake brothers have both disappeared as serious contenders for places in the England Test and one-day sides. We have already seen how the younger, Ben, wasted his chance to make an impact in Australia through lack of effort, while Adam is now at best a fringe player in one-day cricket at international level. Fringe players should be careful what they do with their fingers.

Even before the tournament started, Pakistan's inestimable captain, Wasim Akram, was on the war-path. He was most upset by the shortness of the beds provided for his players in a hotel in the West Country, where they were playing a practice match. There's nothing worse than having your toes sticking out of the end of the bed, especially if you've forgotten to bring your bedsocks with you. Wasim was seldom happy with the practice facilities at the smaller grounds and a couple of times when it rained the day before a match, his players were unable to use indoor nets because they had already been given over to corporate hospitality and the tables were laid. Wasim never missed the opportunity to make his feelings known. He clearly believed that attack was the best form of defence.

I didn't think that the genius who dreamed up the opening ceremony would be awarded the Nobel Prize for anything very much. Fireworks, at ten o'clock in the morning, have to be something pretty special to make an impression. The few bangs and flashes we had now would have had poor old Guy Fawkes turning in his grave in despair. But maybe they whetted the appetite for what was to follow. The intrepid Tony Blair, who has been uncharacteristically guarded about his love for cricket, stepped forward to address the multitude. But his early gems fell on deaf ears because the Lord's electrician had forgotten to turn on the supply of electricity to the PM's microphone. It might, I suppose, have been a political statement; it might also have been a brave attempt to save money. But it was much more likely to have been caused by early morning incompetence. It is fair to say that the World Cup was given a muted start.

Tony Blair was to get his own back later when his government announced (in the middle of a competition where the emphasis is on teamwork) that it was opposed to team sports in schools. Presumably some clever clogs had persuaded them that competition is bad for children. But it is human nature to compete, and surely it is the competitive edge which brings the best out in children. Those that succeed at school are probably better suited for the struggles of later life. Did not Mr Blair compete with Mr Brown for the leadership of the

Labour Party and with someone or other at every other stage during his rise to the top in politics? Was he not helped by the know-how he picked up at school at Fettes and later in the cut and thrust of life at Oxford University? He is the leading protagonist in the most vibrant competition in the country as he strives to beat the Conservative Party and to push them into a permanent backwater. Do Mr Blair and his ministers and spin doctors not wish to prepare the next generation to continue this battle? The back pages of all our newspapers would be given over to articles on sunbathing and picnicking if man and woman were not eternally and gloriously competing on the sports fields of the world. In another section of the same papers the world's businessmen can be seen at one another's throats and on it goes. These are battles that have to be won and the best possible preparation is needed, not only to beat the opposition but also to learn how to get the best out of your own team. What is school for if this is not part of what it teaches?

Mr Blair's old enemy John Major, who has always loved cricket, was to feature in the competition as the subject of one of Sporting Index's more unusual bets, calling on punters to estimate the number of times that the ex-PM would be spotted at World Cup matches. The first spread was 9 to 10. It was a seller's market for he made only two visible appearances and was apparently lecturing for much of the time in the United States. The World Cup was, of course, a potential field day for my friends at Sporting Index. Compton Hellyer and Lindsay McNeile had been refusing lunch for weeks to prepare themselves, with the odd session at the gym thrown in. The public were given all manner of betting possibilities to consider. But what Sporting Index had not anticipated was the expensive joust they were to have with the white Duke ball used for the competition. This ball swung uncontrollably from the first delivery to the last. Ever since white balls were first introduced by Kerry Packer's World Series Cricket in 1977, they have swung more than their red counterparts. Before the start, Sporting Index's spread for the number of wides bowled during the forty-two matches was 260–280. The umpires, to a man, must have bought at 280, since during the competition they combined to signal a total of 979 wides. 'Ouch' cried the collective voice of Sporting Index. By the end, each wide was costing them £700. But even if this kept them on their toes I daresay the dear old Index were coining it in from all sorts of other directions.

Shane Warne may by now have been treating bookies with some degree of caution, but he soon ran into trouble in his new role as a journalist. Like several of the best players, he had been employed to write a newspaper column throughout the World Cup. There must always be an inherent danger in this and Warne stepped over the mark in one of his first offerings for *The Times*. He wrote an extremely critical piece about the behaviour and the attitude of the Sri Lankan captain, our old friend the School Bully which, while more than justified, is against the rules. Players are not allowed to criticise one another publicly in this manner. Warne wrote, 'Yes, there is plenty of animosity between Arjuna and myself. I don't like him.' He went on to explain how this had come about and it was no surprise that it earned him a two-match suspension, which was itself suspended. I wonder when anyone will actually be punished there and then for doing something wrong.

So Warne may well have been cheering as England put it across the School Bully and his cohorts in such convincing manner in that first grudge match at Lord's. But, horror of horrors, the seats in the front of the pavilion were all but empty and gleamed with a mocking whiteness at the rest of a full-house crowd. As we have seen, a lively and vociferous section of the membership of the Marylebone Cricket Club had been up in arms because they had had to pay to sit in their own pavilion and watch the World Cup. Was this, then, a boycott? Apparently not, for what had happened was that many of the members who had bought tickets for the pavilion had decided to go and sit with their families, in the stands such as the Warner and the Allen, which are specifically reserved for members, their families and friends. These stands were packed to overflowing and inside the pavilion the Long Room was chock-a-block. There were no signs that the empty seats in the front of the pavilion were part of a protest by members who had thrown tantrums because they had been made to pay for their tickets. It is worth pointing out that MCC had negotiated for 8000 tickets to be available for members of the club for all three World Cup matches at Lord's at a discount of twenty-five per cent. The reaction of the protesters could only make one wonder if they were fit to be members of the club in the first place. For £182 a year it much surely be the best value for money in England.

There was an intriguing moment in that first match at Lord's. One of the few MCC members who braved the seats in front of the pavilion (and had probably been written off as a blackleg by his fellow members as a result) had brought a bottle of champagne with him. When the time came to open it, he got to work on the cork a trifle carelessly and it exploded over the rails and onto the outfield in front of the pavilion. Those who heard the pop probably thought that it was one of the fireworks which had forgotten to go off earlier. It was not long before this celebrated cork put itself in line for the Man of the Match award when it stopped a Sri Lankan stroke from reaching the boundary. And this at Lord's.

Away from London, Pakistan were beating the West Indies in Bristol in front of a full-house crowd of 8,000. This was an occasion which brought the West Country ticket touts out of honourable retirement for just about the first time since

W. G. Grace and Gilbert Jessop used to pack them in (although I suppose Walter Hammond had his moments as well). But not content with the victory, and missing the point by several thousand miles, the Pakistan manager, Zafar Altaf complained afterwards that if this match had been played on the Subcontinent, it would have been in front of a crowd of at least 100,000. He didn't say how many of the 100,000 would have outwitted the gatekeepers.

The point is that the World Cup is a vehicle to be spread evenly around the cricket-playing world. That day at Bristol may only have been able to produce a crowd of 8000 because of the smallness of a county ground laid out more than a hundred years ago. Nonetheless, the day will have done wonders for the game in that part of England. People will have come along who never normally get the chance to watch international cricket. It will have been the talking point for a long time before and for some time afterwards and it will have helped regenerate local interest in the game. The fact that the ground could have been sold out more than once illustrates the interest and enthusiasm this match raised. The World Cup is not only about money, something Mr Altaf seemed to have forgotten. Of course the ECB could have increased the takings by scheduling matches like this on the Test grounds. South Africa played India in front of 5000 at Hove where the touts also had the day of their lives and the ground could have been sold out many times over. But the success of this or any World Cup should not only be measured in terms of its financial outcome. Spreading the gospel is just as important. I think it is right and proper that the World Cup should come every twenty-five years or so to Hove, Taunton, Northampton, Chelmsford and eight other county grounds. When the competition is next held in the Subcontinent, Mr Altaf can lick his fingers, rub his hands together and count his rupees. I am sure they will come to a huge amount more money, but so what?

It's Just Not Cricket!

It was at the small ground at Hove in the match between South Africa and India where an observant match referee, Talat Ali from Pakistan, noticed that two of the South African fielders, Hansie Cronje and Allan Donald, were wearing ear pieces and it transpired that they were connected by radio to Bob Woolmer, their coach, in the dressing room. It was not a two-way system and the plan was that if either Cronje or Donald needed to hear Woolmer's views, they made a prearranged hand signal and the coach came on the air. The South Africans had checked that there was nothing in the laws specifically to prevent this, but as it was done surreptitiously without asking anyone if it was in order, it gave the impression of being a little too close to sharp practice for comfort. The use of radios in this way was then banned. But it would not surprise me if they became a regrettable new part of cricket before too long. Football and tennis forbid coaching during a match, golfers don't go into endless huddles with their coaches during a round and cricket should take the same view of on-field coaching.

Umpires intervened again when, in the first throwing accusation of the competition, Kenya's twenty-year-old medium-pace bowler, Jimmy Kamande, was reported for chucking in their match against Zimbabwe at Taunton. The umpires, Doug Cowie of New Zealand and Javed Akhtar of Pakistan had reported him. It was a bit of luck for the organisers that it was a minor bowler from a country which stood no chance of qualifying for the later stages. They will have been happy that the Investigator, Ross Emerson, was still recuperating in Perth and they had made sure that Darrell Hair did not get another look at Muttiah Muralitheran.

Sometimes, though, the players were able to put one over the umpires. Shane Warne, who has the shortest of fuses when things are not going his way, did a Hollioake finger-wagging routine to a section of the crowd who were getting at him in Australia's match with Scotland at Worcester. He had a great piece of luck not to be spotted by the match referee, Ranjan Madugalle from Sri Lanka, who is in every sense the best of eggs and would undoubtedly have come down hard on Warne. Maybe the two-match suspension he had been given earlier would have been brought into play. Surprisingly, Australia made rather a meal of beating Scotland. Warne can be something of a fair weather friend, for if everything is going well he is the cheerfullest of chaps, but if life and luck is against him, he finds it impossible to suppress the dark side of his character and he becomes only a fairly nice chap.

Together with Mark Waugh, Shane Warne may have been interested in the news that now came hot foot from Ahmedabad in central India that no less than ninety people had been arrested for illegal bookmaking. The two Australians will have shared a knowing look and wondered if 'John' was one of those involved. Other, sadder news came from India during their side's visit to Grace Road, Leicester. Sachin Tendulkar's father had died so Tendulkar immediately flew back to Bombay for the funeral and missed India's game with Zimbabwe when, in an extraordinary last over, Henry Olonga, one of their fast bowlers, took the last three Indian wickets of Robin Singh, Javagal Srinath, and Venkatesh Prasad, and Zimbabwe won by three runs.

Then, in another upset, the very next day at Cardiff, New Zealand put it across the Australians by five wickets after Geoff Allott had taken four wickets and Roger Twose had finished things off with a robust 80 not out. It later emerged that Twose, a former Warwickshire batsman who had discovered Test cricket in New Zealand, found a curious way to pass the time before their crucial Super Six match against India. He was busy the day before taking a business management exam as part of a degree course at Massey University in New Zealand. John Graham, the New Zealand manager and a former headmaster, was the invigilator for the three-hour exam.

Tit-bits such as these were often much more interesting than most of the thirty qualifying matches. The competition had begun on 14 May and mercifully the rain held off enough to prevent it being hijacked by Duckworth and Lewis and their incomprehensible method for working out revised targets in rain-affected matches. Nonetheless, the pitches favoured the seam bowlers in the early matches. Scores of not much more than 200 were enough for the side batting first and although the crowds were excellent, the entertainment value suffered. By the time we had got to the Super Six stage, the weather had improved, more strokes were being played and more runs scored and bigger totals were the order of the day. Spinners came into their own, too, which greatly helped the entertainment. How much better it would have been if the World Cup had begun, rather than ended, on 20 June. That would have meant that the tournament would have been in direct competition with Wimbledon and the Open Championship and other major sporting events. It would also have meant it would have been almost impossible to have fitted in the four-match Test series against New Zealand which followed the World Cup. Nevertheless, the English authorities should have made a bold and confident statement about cricket and staged it later, instead of apologetically tucking it away in a rather damp and murky corner when the weather cannot make up its mind whether it is summer or not. Anyway, there still would have been time for at least a couple of Test Matches afterwards. Perhaps television schedules were the stumbling block and money always seems to have the last word.

The opening game in which England dismembered Sri Lanka should have done wonders for the hosts' confidence but sadly it was a result which only flattered to deceive, as did

Alec Stewart's innings of 87 not out. The fateful weekend for England was 29/30 May when Zimbabwe astonishingly outplayed South Africa and won by 48 runs. It was an unthinkable result and when, the following day, India beat England by 63 runs, England had failed to qualify and Stewart had been in charge for the last time.

Then came the biggest laugh of all: namely the fiasco of the much vaunted World Cup song, 'All Over the World'. With a stroke of pure genius it was released now, after England had suffered the ultimate humiliation of dismissal at the qualifying stage. I wonder what would have happened if 'Good King Wenceslaus' had been released for the first time on Boxing Day. A London radio station offered a holiday abroad to the first person who rang in and sang a few bars of 'All Over the World'. The offer remained open for two hours without a single call. The song burst into the charts in the 184th position before disappearing without trace. It was reckoned to have sold about three thousand copies and in time may, I suppose, become a collectors' piece. The ECB was, of course, quick to blame the marketing policy of the record company, BMG, who are part of the Sony Group.

The World Cup finances were constantly under review. This aspect of it got off to a rather unseemly and, one felt, unnecessary start with a semi-public argument between the ECB and Alec Stewart and presumably the other leading England players, about the World Cup contracts for the England squad. Simon Pack of the ECB and Château Beychevelle 1990 fame, had flown to Brisbane the previous December with a draft copy of the contract which the players obviously didn't care for. Like so many others around the world, as we have seen, the England players were putting their feet down for more money and better terms. It is easy on these occasions to regard the players as serf-like employees downtrodden by feudal overlords and to take their side. When I heard strong rumours that the England captain had recently told a newcomer to the Test side that in his first Test he could play for himself and his country and that after that he was only playing for the money, I was not nearly so sure.

The World Cup became strapped for money when the marketing boys (who we had been led to believe had got the best deal for everything over the years), could only run to ground four main sponsors out of the eight originally planned for. There was probably a combination of reasons for this. The marketeers will almost certainly have been guilty of an arrogance stemming from a belief in their own publicity handouts that cricket in England was as resoundingly popular as ever, if not more so. More than a decade of constantly coming second had taken its toll, however, and those with big enough budgets were looking for something with higher impact and profile. It seems clear that those concerned did not get on with the job of selling the competition early enough. This was part of the arrogance. They must have felt that they had a sure-fire winner on their hands. Another reason, which sadly could not have been helped, was the serious illness which knocked Terry Blake, the head of marketing for the ECB, out of the firing line at a particularly crucial stage.

Profits were not going to be as high as had been originally hoped but this still cannot excuse the single most shoddy act of the World Cup. The ECB refused to pay the county scorers who performed during the competition saying, as far as one could gather, that the honour which went with the job was recompense enough and they would have to be satisfied with their expenses. In relation to the entire budget of the World Cup this was peanuts indeed and a contemptibly petty act. It is extraordinary what apparently sane men can occasionally get up to. I am sure that any day I will be given another, more rational explanation. Whether I shall believe it is another matter. The powers-that-be were busy claiming that this would be the most profitable World Cup ever. This was a spurious claim simply because the World Cups in India and Pakistan in 1987 and 1996 had both produced colossal profits which, because of obscure Subcontinental bookkeeping methods, were not officially recorded. It is impossible to escape the impression that the finances of the 1999 World Cup were comprehensively cocked up.

More financial acumen was shown by those who betted on Bangladesh to beat Pakistan in the last qualifying match of all. Pakistan had just got the better of Australia by ten runs – it was after this match that Steve Waugh said that all Australia now had to do was to win their next seven matches. But somehow Bangladesh now managed to beat Pakistan by 62 runs and although this remarkable result may have had no bearing on the competition, it appeared to have made a few people much the richer on the Subcontinent. It was said that bets were taken at 33/1 and then at 16/1 against Bangladesh and there were many people who felt that such an extraordinary upset could only have been contrived. In other words, this was a match where the result must surely have been fixed. We may never know. Pakistan have always been an unpredictable side but for some it stretched the imagination to believe that having conquered the West Indies, Scotland, Australia and New Zealand, they should now be outplayed by Bangladesh. I can understand why this result left a great many people scratching their heads. But then didn't Zimbabwe beat South Africa and isn't this the essence of one-day cricket? You pays your money and takes your choice.

When the smoke had cleared from the qualifying round, South Africa, India and Zimbabwe had joined Australia, Pakistan and New Zealand from the other group, in the Super Sixes. As well as England, Sri Lanka, the holders, were out and heading home. We soon heard that the School Bully had finally been sacked as captain. His brother, Dammike, the Chief Executive of the Board, had presumably kept him in position until now but the World Cup exit, after all those shenanigans in Adelaide, meant that the time had come for the School Bully. Another side making an early return home were the West Indies. It was a thunderous surprise to learn that having got home Shivnarine Chanderpaul was arrested in Guyana for shooting a policeman. It transpired that this was not the result of high dudgeon over the West Indies' early dismissal. Chanderpaul was reported to have been with his girlfriend in Georgetown, the capital, when he was surprised by a light being shone at him. He is a licensed gunholder and, thinking they were being attacked, he drew a pistol and let fly. The policeman sustained minor injuries to the wrist and Chanderpaul was arrested. The moral is obvious: leave your pistol behind when you take your girlfriend out.

At the risk of sounding idiotically unpatriotic, it was in many ways a relief that England were no longer involved for it meant that I would not have to sit through the endless agony of at least three more lengthy engagements. I was able to save my nerves for the almost daily and interminable contests involving Tim Henman on Wimbledon's Centre Court, which were no less taxing to the system. But at least I could now sit back and enjoy the cricket.

England themselves could now concentrate on the approaching appointment of David Lloyd's successor as the England coach. The ECB had been lukewarm when Lloyd had asked them about an extension to his present contract. He had been offered alternative employment by Sky Television and he must have known that the chances were that he would be sacked by the Board. As it happened, with England failing to make the Super Sixes, he wouldn't have had a chance of being offered another contract. His successor was likely to come from four names. The ECB and Lord

MacLaurin, the chairman, were known to favour Bob Woolmer, whose present contract with South Africa ended after the World Cup. Woolmer had been visited by that celebrated imbiber of Beychevelle 1990, Simon Pack, the Director of Operations at the ECB, who had flown to South Africa to discuss it all with Woolmer. Initially, Woolmer appeared to have shown enthusiasm but refused to consider doing the job until after England had toured South Africa in 1999/2000. He wanted a lay-off from the game and rumour had it that he was likely to be offered a sizeable contract by Talk Radio, who were involved in a relentless search to find the ideal radio commentary team. In the end, he pulled out just before the end of the World Cup and I think it was clear enough that his soul as well as his body was now firmly entrenched in South Africa. In the end, though, he decided to go back and look after Warwickshire, whom he had coached with outstanding success in the early nineties.

Jackie Birkenshaw, who had just steered Leicestershire to their second County Championship title in three years, was also in the frame. The Zimbabwean, Duncan Fletcher, was the third. He had captained Zimbabwe and then coached Western Province in South Africa and was in charge of Glamorgan when they won the Championship in 1997. Fletcher had an impressive reputation and it was felt by all those who played under him that he had the great ability to make players raise their game. The fourth contender was Davenal Whatmore, the former Australian Test player who was born in Sri Lanka and who had masterminded their World Cup victory in India and Pakistan in 1996. In the end, after Woolmer's withdrawal, the choice was made from Birkenshaw, Fletcher and Whatmore, all of whom were interviewed by the England management committee. It was after the World Cup had finished and just before the start of the series against New Zealand that Fletcher, whom the papers had already made the hot favourite, was appointed, by which time Hussain had taken over the captaincy. David Lloyd had announced that he would have had Birkenshaw as his successor, but when he didn't get the job, Lloyd said, rather surprisingly, that being English had counted against Birkenshaw. That sounded a bit double-Dutch to me.

By the time the qualifying round had come to an end, South Africa's Lance Klusener, the farmer from Zululand, was already well on the way to becoming the player of the competition. He is an admirable cricketer, not least in the whole-hearted and uncomplicated way in which he plays the game. He wields a bat weighing an ounce or two over three pounds as if he were using a pitchfork in a hayfield. He runs into bowl with bouncing enthusiasm and an honest intent to make the batsman pay for it. He is no slouch in the field, either. It was a dreadful irony that somehow seemed to encapsulate the greatness of cricket that after all his fearless feats of hitting it was his extraordinary misjudgement which was to cost South Africa a place in the Final. He began his heroics in South Africa's first match, against India, when he contented himself with making twelve not out in four balls to take them to victory by four wickets. He had earlier claimed three wickets. He showed he had really got the taste for it against Sri Lanka when he smashed 52 not out in 45 balls, taking his team to 199 for 9. He then picked up three more wickets. He smote 48 not out in a mere 40 balls against England although he then had to be content with only one wicket as England's batting was blown to pieces by the others. A small matter of 5/25 followed against Kenya and, although South Africa then lost to Zimbabwe, Klusener contributed 52 from 58 balls. This little lot had won him three Man of the Match awards.

Another major contributor in the early matches had been Neil Johnson, who had gone to Zimbabwe after being passed by in South Africa. Roger Twose did well for New Zealand and Jacques Kallis, surely the best allrounder in the world, never wasted an opportunity for South Africa. Shoiab Akhtar was soon showing Pakistan's opponents that he is the fastest bowler in the world, even if he might be a trifle too petulant for everyone's taste. Sachin Tendulkar and Rahul Dravid made memorable runs for India. Inzamam-ul-Haq's running between the wicket's put the fear of Allah or, in the case of Yousuf Youhana, a Christian, the fear of God, into all his partners. Two old stagers, Courtney Walsh and Wasim Akram played important roles and by the end the Australians were beginning to hit their target and the Waughs and Glenn McGrath were in the headlines. And so it came to the Super Sixes.

In the first match at the Oval, after Australia had made nearly 300, McGrath, in the best opening spell of the tournament, removed three Indian batsmen including, as his first victim, Tendulkar, caught behind off the perfect outswinger. Then it was Klusener again when South Africa beat Pakistan by three wickets at Trent Bridge. The insatiable Zulu hit 46 not out from 41 balls to take his side to victory and collect a fourth Man of the Match gong. After rain had given Zimbabwe the one point against New Zealand which seemed likely to see them through to the semi-finals, India played Pakistan at Old Trafford. With fighting going on in Kashmir, this was considerably more than just a cricket match but, mercifully, the spectators on both sides behaved themselves pretty well in the circumstances. Apart from the usual Subcontinental enthusiasm, which included the odd fire cracker and a pitch invasion or two, it was commendably calm. The Pakistani supporters must have been sorely tempted to misbehave for their side was outplayed by India, who won by 47 runs. There were, of course, match-fixing rumblings after this result, too.

Johnson's 132 for Zimbabwe at Lord's may have been in a

lost cause after Australia had reached almost 300, but it was heroic stuff and enabled Zimbabwe to leave the ground with their heads held high. It was Kallis, with both bat and ball, who for once shaded Klusener and enabled South Africa to beat New Zealand while Saeed Anwar's century at the Oval saw Pakistan dispatch Zimbabwe. After keeping India to 251/6 at Trent Bridge, Roger Twose steered New Zealand home by five wickets and India back home by the next flight. Twose's strokeplay also meant that Zimbabwe would be scurrying back to Heathrow if Australia put it across South Africa in the final game of the Super Sixes.

And what a game this turned out to be. South Africa ran up a score of 271/7 and the main contributor was Herschelle Gibbs with an outstanding 101. But this was the moment when Shane Warne decided to take a hand and show the world that he was anything but a spent force. His ten overs cost only 33 and he took the important wickets of Daryll Cullinan (who has often found Warne hard going) and Hansie Cronje, who was lbw for nought. But then Australia lost their first three wickets for 48, and it looked as if they would also contribute to the traffic jams on the road to Heathrow. They had to beat South Africa to stay in the competition and this was the fifth of those seven matches Steve Waugh had said they had to win. But the one man this synopsis of events did not allow for was Steve Waugh himself. As ever, he came to the crease with his chin sticking out, full of bloody-minded intent and proceeded to play one of the great one-day innings. The pressure was enormous. With three wickets having already fallen, whatever else he did, he had to avoid getting out. At the same time, the required run rate had to be kept to a manageable figure and all this against a truly formidable bowling side even without Kallis, who had been unfit to take his place because of a pulled stomach muscle.

Waugh's method is irresistibly effective rather than

sublimely glamorous. In spite of his consistent success over the years, the lack of aesthetic beauty in his game has not brought the word genius readily to mind. But if this innings was not heavily tinged with genius I don't understand the meaning of the word. Under dramatic pressure, which always seems to bring the best out of this remarkable cricketer, he played almost the perfect innings. His judgement was supreme. Singles and twos were pushed and scampered; bad balls were dismissed to the boundary; occasional calculated risks were taken. He found an invaluable partner in Ricky Ponting with whom he added 126 for the fourth wicket. It all hinged, though, on one dreadful moment of South African expectation and exhilaration which turned into frozen disbelief and tortured despair, all in a split second. Waugh had made 56 when he played Klusener off his pads to midwicket where Gibbs, the hero of the day to that moment, appeared to swallow an easy catch. One can only guess at what went through Gibbs's mind when he felt the ball against his fingers. He will have known this was the moment Australia were beaten.

Uncontrollable joy must have overtaken him like a surge of electricity and barely had the ball touched his hands when he began to throw it aloft in modern macho style. Alas for him and South Africa, the ball had other ideas and while his hands were lifting towards the heavens, the ball trickled ignominiously out of his fingers like that last piece of recalcitrant coal off the end of the shovel, and went to ground. Rightly, the umpires ruled he did not have control of the ball and Waugh's innings continued. The South Africans, and Gibbs in particular, must have had a dreadful foreboding that that was the last chance they were going to get from him. Ponting was then out but Michael Bevan, who bats like a left-handed greyhound, and Tom Moody, tall and apparently unconcerned, played important supporting innings while Waugh went on batting like a colossus with just the touch of a solid and trustworthy pyramid thrown in. I shall never forget one shot: he suddenly unwound a contemptuously dismissive slog at Steve Elworthy for no better reason than he felt like it – for the ball was no different to many others – and dispatched it far into the crowd at straight midwicket. A gigantic risk at such a moment – for anyone except Steve Waugh. From his bat, it looked a racing certainty. He hit the winning run with two balls to spare having made 120 not out from 110 balls: incredible statistics in such a match. With an enormous wink, Fate now decreed that these two sides would meet again in their next match, the second semi-final, at Edgbaston.

The first semi-final, at Old Trafford, was almost an anticlimax as another hundred by Saeed Anwar took Pakistan to a nine-wicket victory over New Zealand, who had got through at the expense of Zimbabwe thanks to Australia's victory over South Africa. Edgbaston on 17 June was not going to be a place for those of us who were nursing recently completed heart bypasses. It was bad enough on television. The South Africans had talked themselves into a state of optimism which they had based on the return of an almost fit Jacques Kallis to their side. His absence, they persuaded themselves, had made the difference at Headingley. At the same time, that first victory had given Australia the confidence they needed and Steve Waugh wasn't saying much. He would make a wonderful poker player.

It was impossible not to make comparisons between the characters involved in these two matches between Australia and South Africa, both collectively and individually. No side has been more unrelenting in its approach to cricket over the years than South Africa. When they walk out onto a cricket ground, it is as if they are taking their own and their country's very reason for existence onto the field with them. It is as though there are involved in a permanent process of self-justification in all that they do. They are the personification of 'All for one and one for all'. As cricketers, their aim is combined efficiency rather than giving a free rein to skill and flair. It is no laughing matter. That much is seen from a look and a listen to Ali Bacher, who runs South African cricket almost single-handedly. He captained a great South African side when they beat Australia in South Africa in 1969/70, although as a cricketer he was not one of the strongest links in the side. He had qualified as a doctor but when South African sport was overtaken by the world's hostility to apartheid, Bacher, himself a radical opponent of apartheid, took on the job of trying to keep South African cricket together during those years of isolation, and wonderfully well he did it, too. No single sporting body did more to break down the barriers of apartheid within the confines of their own sport than the cricket administrators and Bacher must take the credit for that. What's more, since the abolition of apartheid he has led the United Cricket Board of South Africa firmly in the right direction. Whether he would have found it any easier with more of a sense of humour we shall never know, but it may be that obsessive and intensive characters do not find things to laugh about as often as others. If South Africa's cricketers were better able to laugh and happier for individual players to break the mould, maybe they would win rather more matches.

There is no harder side than the Australians and no side that is more dedicated to winning but hard though they are, they have a sense of humour and on a particularly good day even Steve Waugh has been known to have a chuckle. Their approach is more flexible than South Africa's. They accept and allow and indeed expect individuality to flourish. It is this which, in my belief, enables them to rise to greater heights in times of crisis. I shall never forget the faces of the two captains during these matches. I never felt that Steve Waugh was in uncharted territory. He has seen enough of the rough side of things in his cricketing life not to be phased when they go wrong. He was not a man on a mission, he was just a man who was bloody determined to win, shit or bust. If he lost, he would have had a good swear, a drink and would harbour no grievances at the same time as being extra determined not to let it happen again. He is harder than granite. He stands in the gully totally involved in the present doing everything he knows to make it work. Like Cronje, there is not a flicker of emotion, but there is no dark sense of foreboding either. He will not have felt the Fates were against him. I doubt he has too much time for the Fates.

Hansie Cronje, as picked up by my television set, was dark and brooding at mid off as he watched a messianic dream disappear. South Africa had been the favourites and most especially so in their own eyes. For them, it was almost as if victory was preordained. But then it began to go wrong. Disbelief was written all over Cronje's face in the field at the very end at Headingley. At Edgbaston, it was almost impossible to see his face in the closing overs apart from the odd fleeting glimpse the cameras allowed us. I should be surprised if disbelief was not also then written large. He had done all that could have been expected of him and at the last, when the tap had been turned on, horror of horrors, nothing came out. I felt that he was almost mesmerised by what was happening at Headingley and was only able to follow the preordained course. If the roles of the two captains had been reversed, my gut feeling is that Steve Waugh, while no Mark Taylor, would, together with his players, have been marginally more likely to have come up with something to change the outcome of the match.

Cronje put Australia into bat in the semi-final and only Steve Waugh and Bevan, who both fought their way past fifty, withstood some wonderful fast bowling from Donald and Pollock. They shared nine wickets between them, which seemed appropriate as they had both played on that ground for Warwickshire. They were backed up by the usual superb South African fielding inspired as always by Jonty Rhodes, who was one of the joys of the competition, and a total of only 213 meant that Australia had the dickens of a fight on their hands. South Africa were given just the start they wanted when Kirsten and Gibbs put on 48 in twelve overs for the first wicket. Early wickets eluded McGrath, Fleming and Reiffel. It developed into a situation where a combination of desperation, class, and a mental attitude tinged with bloody-mindedness can suddenly combine to produce a match winner. Steve Waugh's great chum is Shane Warne, who had flexed his fingers in the match at Headingley in a manner ominous for South Africa. There is no cricketer who is more aware of and responds better to the big occasion than Warne. He is a natural show-off and what better place than centre stage before a full house in a World Cup semi-final? (The Final, of course, and we will come to that in just a moment).

Warne now came on to bowl the eleventh over. The man, it had been said, who had lost the googly and the flipper, now smiled as he spun the ball from hand to hand as if he was King Herod who had just stumbled across a nursery school. It was less than two months since he had been dropped by the selectors for the final Test against the West Indies in Antigua. In his newspaper column he had been plaintiffly describing himself as a one-day bowler. But the batsmen will have now felt more nervous than Warne, who had issued a reminder to his opponents up at Headingley. In his second over here he produced a real fizzer which pitched outside Gibbs's leg stump and must have hummed as it spun across him before hitting the off. It was not quite the freak ball with which Warne had bowled Mike Gatting at Old Trafford – that astonishing first ball in Test cricket in England, which must have turned a yard and a half – but it was a blood relation alright. In Warne's next over, Kirsten swept as countless others before him have done without taking the precaution of moving some part of his body behind the ball, and was bowled. Two balls later, Cronje, coming forward, was hit on the boot and given out caught at slip for his second nought in two matches against Australia. His walk back was not a joyful affair. Warne walked off later with the superb figures of 4/29 in his ten overs and the Man of the Match award as well.

Warne's bowling was irresistible, his body language irrepressible. The bounce, in his feet and of the ball off the pitch, the spin, the variety and the sheer joy of it all, revealed that the greatest leg spinner ever to have spun a cricket ball was back in business. When Cullinan was thrown out by Bevan, South Africa were 61/4 in the twenty-second over. Kallis was now joined by Rhodes and just for a while Steve Waugh seemed to take his eye off the ball. Australia's two lesser bowlers, Moody and Mark Waugh, from whom he had to collect ten overs, came on in partnership. Kallis and Rhodes pricked up their ears and suddenly began to find the boundary again after a barren spell of sixteen overs. The asking rate was still seven an over, however, when Rhodes, for no apparent reason, pulled Reiffel to deep square leg and departed, head down, like a man doubting the meaning of life. The Australians perked up no end. Warne now came back to bowl his last two overs and off the fifth ball of his second, a rather indeterminate stroke by Kallis gave Steve Waugh a simple catch at extra cover and he clasped the ball as if with eight hands rather than two. That was one which was not going to get away. We were in the forty-fifth over and 39 more were needed with four wickets to fall.

In the next over Fleming bowled Pollock off the edge and three overs after that, with Klusener trying to find his bearings, Boucher swung at McGrath and was bowled all over the place. Two runs later, Elworthy was eventually given out after the third umpire, Steve Bucknor, had looked at every possible replay about three times each. South Africa were 198/9 needing sixteen from eight balls. Difficult but anything is possible when Klusener is alive and kicking. Somehow, he now managed to drive a full toss from McGrath to long on where it flew through Reiffel's outstretched hands and over the boundary for six. A single from the last ball of the over meant that nine were needed by South Africa from the last over and Klusener was on strike. Fleming ran in and bowled and Klusener picked up his bat as if he had taken it to Pamplona for the bull run as a defensive weapon and the bull was upon him. The ball soared away to the straight extra cover boundary and the Australians watched dumbfounded. Fleming tried again and this time the bat seemed even lighter in Klusener's hands and the ball went away a fraction straighter for four more. The Australians now looked like a side that had taken two in the solar plexus. At the start of the over they must have felt they were going to win. After two balls they were certain losers.

One run was now needed from the last four balls of the match. It seemed rather an anti-climax as the Australians all came in to save the single. Fleming bowled again and Klusener drove to mid on where Lehmann picked up quickly and, with a sprightly Donald out of his crease backing up, narrowly missed with his flick at the stumps at the bowler's end. Three balls to go, one run to win. Fleming again. Klusener drove this time just past the stumps on the offside. Donald has been roundly condemned for not running instantly Klusener started, but when the ball is driven back so close to the stumps the non-striker can't move until he is sure the bowler cannot field the ball. Of course, these were exceptional circumstances but at times like these old habits die hard and Donald waited and watched. He knew there were two balls left but to his amazement a noise like a puffing grampus announced the imminent arrival of Klusener in the crease beside him. He was so shocked that he dropped his bat before setting off on the loneliest trek ever undertaken by an Afrikaner. The ball had been picked up, meanwhile, by Mark Waugh running behind the bowler from mid off and, seeing what was going on, he threw to Fleming who was well down the pitch. He relayed it on to Gilchrist who caught it as if it was the Cullinan diamond and stumps flew in all directions with poor old Donald still well short of the halfway mark. The scores were tied at 213 but by dint of having beating South Africa in that Super Six game at Headingley, Australia won on a superior run rate by the frighteningly small margin of 0.19, scarcely the blink of an eye. Has there ever been a better game of one-day cricket? Almost certainly not and there may never be another to equal it. What a pity it had to be the semi-final and not the Final. It seemed so dreadfully cruel on South Africa and it was an awfully hard result for them to take. But Australia's nerve had held in the tightest of situations twice in the same week and no one could say they didn't deserve their success. Alas, that final ball will have left Lance Klusener with a nightmare which could only be rivalled by that of Jean Van de Velde when he so spectacularly failed to win the Open at Carnoustie later that summer.

The final was almost bound to be an anti-climax but was it a farce as well? It was certainly all strung about with hideous possibilities. Wasim Akram won the toss for Pakistan and batted first on a bowling morning. There was moisture in the pitch and the air, and the ball moved around extravagantly. Even so, Pakistan collapsed so ignominiously it was truly impossible to believe. They were bowled out for 132 and lost by eight wickets with 29.5 overs to spare. Again Shane Warne did not waste the moment. He tortured some disorientated middle order batting and finished with 4/33 from nine overs. He may not have bowled as well as he had done at Headingley but it was well enough for him to pick up another Man of the Match award. In Australia's last three games in the competition he had taken a small matter of ten wickets for 95 runs in 29 overs. Not bad for a chap who had apparently lost it.

Questions were being asked even before the prize giving had begun. Had the match been fixed? Of course not, the honourable Pakistanis replied, but maybe without total conviction. It was absurd even to speculate that something as prestigious as the World Cup could possibly have been thrown. But was it? A great many accusations were being thrown around and the match-fixing enquiry in Lahore was still running. We have already seen that some key players left Pakistan for England and the World Cup the day they had been summoned to answer questions before the Commission. Was the last laugh theirs? One cannot avoid that question. Had the unscrupulous had a big chortle and decided to watch 30,000 at Lord's pay a hundred pounds a ticket to come and see a final which had already been decided? The Prime Minister of Pakistan, Nawaz Sharif, was exceptionally quick to ask the Commission in Lahore to run their eyes over this one too, and I daresay his hasty reaction will have made a great many people believe that it was indeed fixed. Match-fixing or not, it was a sad end to a competition which had been made by those two matches between Australia and South Africa. It may very well be that there is still more to come about the manner in which the final was won and lost. I hope not, but even by their own inconsistent standards, Pakistan had had an unbelievably horrendous day and then perhaps began to protest too much.

CHAPTER THIRTEEN

Tiptoeing back to TMS

E ven if appearances may have been against them, I do not believe Pakistan threw the World Cup Final. They simply had one of those ghastly days. Had they won, it would have been such an honour for the country that the government would have set up the players in noble style for the rest of their lives, as they had done after Imran Khan's side won the World Cup in Australia in 1992/93. On that previous occasion the players had been given money and land and I daresay many other benefits in kind. If Wasim Akram's side had been persuaded to 'sell' the Final, the pay-out would have had to have been enormous for it to be worth their while. Moreover, there was no evidence anywhere from betting patterns or ridiculous odds that the Final had been fixed.

Of course, Pakistan's subsequent defeat was a profound humiliation and back at home it caused a furore. The Commander had told me a day or two before the Final that he considered that Pakistan had to be the favourites. The country needed an excuse and match-fixing was on everyone's mind. The defeat was to have repercussions across the whole match-fixing saga. For one thing, the celebrated Commission and its judge had been dragging their feet saying that its findings would not be passed on to the appropriate authorities until after the World Cup. I have not the smallest doubt that if Pakistan had won, it would have been conveniently forgotten about. I even heard the rumour that the judge had been preparing one set of accounts to be published in the event of Pakistan winning the Cup and another to be published only if they did not. Of course, far from winning, they had lost in the most horrendous way. The learned judge himself must now have bitterly regretted his involvement in this whole business. I am sure that by this time he was himself in severe danger of being match-fixed by the unscrupulous, who were determined to do all that they could to make sure the truth never saw the light of day.

Unless one has visited Pakistan, it is impossible even to guess at the impact the Final will have made on the entire country. In a matter of moments, disappointment will have turned to outrage and anger. Within a week it came out that the entire Pakistan squad had been carefully watched by their own government investigators. The players had apparently been living life to the full in the build-up to the Final. Casinos, drinking clubs, late night parties, birds and booze were all said to be very much on the agenda. The Pakistan government's anti-corruption squad, Ehtesab, put together a most damning report, we were told, and an inquiry was going on into all these frolics. Alcohol is of course forbidden under Islamic law. It was reported that Ijaz Ahmed, a key batsman, was spotted in a gambling club at getting on for four o'clock in the morning the day before the Final. When the main body of players returned to Pakistan, they were dismissed as 'gamblers and traitors'. At Karachi airport they were pelted with rotten eggs. The head of the government's intelligence bureau, Saifur Rehman, spoke at some length about the unsatisfactory behaviour of the players. It was all vigorously denied by the team manager, Zafar Altaf, and the captain, Wasim Akram, who had stayed in England to take up his commentary duties with Channel Four. The Chairman of the Board, Khalid Mehmood, also spoke out strongly in their defence. It was ironically perhaps in the players' favour that former seam bowler, one-time politician and espouser of lost causes, Sarfraz Nawaz, said that he was convinced several of their matches, including the Final, had been fixed.

The following week reports came from Lahore that no less than eight of the Pakistan players involved in the World Cup had retired from international cricket. The Lahore newspaper, *Jang*, reported that Saqlain Mushtaq, Wasim Akram, Salim Malik, Ijaz Ahmed, Waqar Younis, Mushtaq Ahmed and Inzamam-ul-Haq had all decided to call it a day as a result of the accusations which had been made. The Pakistan Cricket Board chipped in with the news that none of those concerned had so far been in touch about their futures although the players had met and held discussions.

In the meantime, Judge Qayyum had asked for help from the Prime Minister's anti-corruption bureau. If the papers he requested were forthcoming he would be able to submit his eagerly-awaited report on the 16 July. But the judge himself was now being queried. I heard it said in London soon after the World Cup was over, from a source as impeccable as it was unimpeachable, that some of those who had given evidence *in camera* to Judge Qayyum's Commission had been shopped in an appalling manner. The story has it that the details of their evidence reached the ears of a member of the Pakistan Board who proceeded to sell it for a not inconsiderable sum to an Indian journalist in Madras. It was then published in the February copy of a magazine called *Outlook*, of which I was given a copy. My informant also told me he did not see how Judge Qayyum from the High Court in Lahore could possibly overrule a decision taken by a member of the country's Supreme Court, Judge Fakhruddin Ebrahim. In 1994 the senior judge had thrown out the original case against Salim Malik, on the basis there was no evidence to convict, when the three Australians, Mark Waugh, Shane Warne and Tim May refused to return to Pakistan to testify. I was assured that no additional evidence had come to light.

The plot thickened yet again when Rafiq Tasar, the country's president, sacked the entire Board of Control replacing it with an *ad-hoc* committee presided over by Mujeebar Rehman and Javed Zamaan. Mujeebar is the brother of the aforementioned Saifur Rehman, the head of the anti-corruption squad, and Zamaan is the cousin of the former chief executive, Majid Khan, who had been certain that match-fixing had been going on and was determined to expose it. It is thought Majid strongly suspected the World Cup matches against Bangladesh and India were fixed. The *ad-hoc* committee began by digging out a report on match-fixing which was more than a year old and then they decided to flex their muscles and announced that they had suspended Wasim Akram, Salim Malik and Ijaz Ahmed from the Pakistan side.

It became even more confused when, during the Second Test between England and New Zealand at Lord's, Reuters reported from Pakistan that these three players had all been formerly charged with match-fixing. A somewhat restless but good-humoured Wasim Akram's comment at Lord's was, 'I certainly haven't been informed and I happen to know the judge involved [Judge Qayyum] is on holiday in America. We're used to this sort of thing.' Reuters later withdrew this report. It was entirely in keeping with the spirit of chaos that our learned friend Judge Qayyum should have taken off for at least a month to the United States. Maybe he had turned into Pakistan's equivalent of Gilbert and Sullivan's shameless nobleman. The Duke of Plaza Toro who 'led his regiment from behind. – He found it less exciting.' It was during the same Second Test at Lord's that Wasim announced that he was going back to Pakistan to clear his name. He would have had to have done it in record time because Channel Four were expecting him back to commentate on the Third Test at Old Trafford ten days later. I would have thought that clearing your name might take an uncommonly long time in Pakistan. Wasim had two days of interrogation in Islamabad and made it back to Manchester in time for the second day's play, but with plenty more clearing of his name still ahead of him.

Far from becoming clearer with the passage of time, everything was becoming daily more confused and confusing. The latest deadline for Judge Qayyum's report was 17 August, in the unlikely event of him having torn himself away from his in-depth researches in Las Vegas or wherever. By my reckoning he still had to examine the players who flew to London for the World Cup on the day he was supposed to see them. Then, apparently fast bowler Ata-ur-Rehmann was scheduled to have a return fixture in front of the judge. Small wonder that the handling of this whole saga has caused such merriment around the world. But if only it wasn't such a profoundly serious issue.

It was also at Lord's during the Second Test Match against New Zealand that I was told, again by a highly reputable source, a hair-raising tale about an ICC-appointed umpire who had apparently been involved in match-fixing in a recent Test series in the southern hemisphere. My informant told me the umpire had rung him nightly during a Test Match to ask him how it had looked each day from the outside. Of course, it is only to be expected that the ungodly will try and 'turn' umpires, who have such enormous influence on the game. If this is true, it is a pretty sizeable cat to have jumped out of the bag and I wonder if the dear old ICC are on the case. The fact that stories like this are being put around is a good indication of the stage that has been reached. This makes it even more transparently clear that the ICC and its constituent members must do all they can to wipe out this dark blemish on the game once and for all. This one must not be filed in the 'Too hot to handle' drawer. The very fabric of the game is at risk. If this is allowed to fester there soon won't be an international match where the result will be accepted by everyone as genuine. The games most vulnerable to match-fixing are those in the one-day tournaments which keep springing up in unlikely parts of the world. These sometimes produce the most extraordinary results. It is easy to see the hands of the ungodly here. This whole issue is the most difficult the ICC has ever faced and it is desperately important that the august body shows strong leadership, gets its priorities right and faces up to its responsibilities.

As we saw in Chapter Eight, in Christchurch the ICC had decided to put into place an apparently independent body to look into incidents of this nature. The country concerned would have the right to try and sort it out themselves as Judge Qayyum was struggling to do in Lahore. If the ICC then decided that the results were unsatisfactory or that the investigation had been improperly carried out, the Code of Conduct Commissioners, as they were now called, would give advice or even themselves take over the inquiry. Judge Qayyum had promised to deliver his findings on numerous occasions but by the middle of August 1999 nothing much had happened and there still must be a chance that nothing ever will. But if the three Commissioners who are appointed to deal with this issue in Pakistan decide that it has not been satisfactorily handled, will the Pakistan Board be happy to allow the Commissioners to take on the investigation? Having given the ICC teeth, it may be that they will be extracted at the first opportunity. Shades of the School Bully in Adelaide.

While all this had been going on, my bypasses and I, having begun life together in a state of more or less permanent and fairly painful armed neutrality, had become the greatest of chums with scarcely a cross word. By the end of June my long suffering surgeons and doctors felt it was time for me to start getting back to a normal life. During the early stages of the World Cup I had refused the chance to come onto one of Jonathan Agnew's many excellent programmes and talk about my progress, or lack of it. I had seen stress looming round the corner, the one thing I had been forbidden to consider. As the Cup reached its final stages, Peter Baxter rang me in Hoveton and asked me if I would be prepared to have a chat with him on air during an imminent lunch interval. By then, I was missing the adrenalin of the microphone like nobody's business and I couldn't wait to say yes. So, sitting in the hall with Bitten listening to the wireless behind closed doors in the kitchen, I had a go and was skilfully shepherded through the ordeal by Backers – a Johnstonian nickname, of course.

My opportunistic qualities came to the fore during these ten minutes and I made it clear that I was available to commentate on the series against New Zealand in the unlikely event of anyone wanting me. I feared the news may have had Backers reaching for the smelling salts but to my joyful surprise he was on the telephone again a day or two later and signed me up for the first two Test Matches, at Edgbaston and Lord's. Naturally I was thrilled but I was also a trifle apprehensive. Even though I had been commentating for an awful long time I did seriously wonder if I could still do it. A number of times I caught myself coming downstairs or lying in the bath and saying 'And it's Gough from the Pavilion End ...' At least my voice was back in mid-season form.

During those beastly operations I had had a huge pipe jammed an indecently long way down my throat until it reached my voice box and beyond. For two weeks I was only able to croak and sounded like a cross between a spasmodically highly-pitched chainsaw and Louis Armstrong on a particularly bad day. Christopher Lincoln, my surgeon, had assured me I would be warbling like a good 'un in no time at all and mercifully he proved right.

It has been years since I enjoyed a drive as much as that from London to Chaddesley Corbett the day before the First Test. It was almost as if nothing had happened since I had last travelled that way except that the trees appeared to have grown a few feet higher and that illustrious beehive or distinguished dovecote on the left of the motorway on the corner of the Blenheim estate came upon me with rather less warning. We were staying, as always, at that most pre-eminent of watering holes, the Brockencote Hall, presided over with an amiable and elegant five-star charm and efficiency by Alison and Joseph Petitjean. I felt a bit like a new boy. It was all so familiar and yet I had to pinch myself to make sure that it was really happening. There had been a time when I was lying in the Harley Street Clinic with my chest hurting like billio every time I moved or even breathed that I hardly dared think about broadcasting or *Test Match Special*. Quite a lot of things had gone seriously wrong then, probably because I was much closer to putting my cue in the rack than the assembled company of medics had appreciated at the time, and I was firmly convinced that there were one or two more surprises in store for me. In the bleakest of moments I had even thought I might never make it back in front of a microphone again. Can you imagine what it felt like to be arriving at the Brockencote with a Test Match starting the next day? I am bound to say that inside the hotel there were a number of my friends and colleagues who looked at me rather as if they had just spotted a ghost. They had kept my usual room for me, too, the delightful number nineteen called Flowering Cherry after the tree just outside one of the windows and I can assure you it more than lived up to its name.

The most touching moment of all came before dinner when I was sitting outside on the terrace drinking a glass of wine. Through the door came Graham 'Foxy' Fowler who had opened the batting for both Lancashire and England with considerable distinction, and is an old friend and a long-standing colleague on *TMS*. He had heard that I had not been very well and now stood dumbstruck looking at me. Then he gave me an enormous bear-hug. He remained speechless for sometime afterwards eyeing me as if he had just seen Mary Queen of Scots come through the door holding her head under her arm. In a funny way this brought home to me more than any other single thing how close to death I had been and how lucky I was to be alive, let alone at the Brockencote the day before a Test Match. Foxy's reaction also told me a great deal about friendship and how lucky I was in that respect, too.

At Edgbaston the next day I was greeted like a man who has just made it back from the outer rim and I suppose it should have made me painfully aware of my own mortality. But I am afraid I concentrated vigorously on the present and I have no doubt that I have never before enjoyed every ball of a Test as much as I did now. Having been commentating for more than twenty-five years it probably sounds silly, but when I sat down to start my first twenty-minute session, there was very definitely the odd butterfly or two. I am happy to say that by the time I had reached the midway point of my first sentence, they had flown away. By the time I handed over to Aggers at the end of my spell, I felt I had never been away.

The one blemish was the match itself, which ended after lunch on the third day when England won by seven wickets, thanks to a remarkable innings of 99 not out by Alex Tudor, who had come in on the Friday evening as nightwatchman. Tudor confirmed all the good things we had said about his batting at the end of the previous November in Perth when, in his first Test, he had made 18 not out in England's first innings of 127. It was thoughtless and a trifle niggardly of Graham Thorpe, who was batting with him at the end, not to have made sure that Tudor became the first England nightwatchman and the third in all to score a Test hundred. Thorpe had apparently spoken about it to Tudor who had properly replied that they should just get on with it and win the match. Fair enough. But Thorpe should then have taken matters into his own hands and it showed an unsympathetic lack of imagination that he did not. Tudor's bowling, which after all is what he is principally paid for, did not live up to his batting.

On the first two days under heavy cloud the ball had swung all over the place. New Zealand's seam bowlers had put it in the right place while England's did not. This accounted for New Zealand's first innings lead of a hundred runs. When the ball moves around contemporary batsmen are woefully out of their depths and the overall standard of batting was dreadful. It was now New Zealand's turn to bat disgracefully in their second innings. Then, when they came to bowl again at England, they had forgotten the length and line that had served them so well in England's first innings. The New Zealanders were unlucky, though, in that the atmosphere was fresher on the third day and there was less movement in the air, but they gave Tudor every chance to play some lovely strokes off the back foot square with the wicket on the offside. New Zealand should have won.

This was, of course, Nasser Hussain's first Test Match as captain and it was the first time since Bob Willis's against India in 1982 that a new England captain had got away to a winning start. Hussain's own second innings of 44 was a healthy contribution. But in the first he confirmed his reputation as a player who first and foremost looks after himself, when, without so much as a backward glance, he ran out Mark Butcher after his calling had left his partner stranded. As captain, Hussain had left his mark on the side before a ball had been bowled in a move which told us all a good deal about him. He had insisted on the selection of Andy Caddick and Philip Tufnell, who had both toured the West Indies under Michael Atherton in 1997/98. Alec Stewart had then taken over from Atherton and had refused to take either player to Australia the following winter, regarding them both as too difficult to handle. He will, I am sure, have had a ready supporter on the selection committee in Graham Gooch, whose unimaginative thinking is in such contrast to the way in which he batted and has not helped England since. Gooch was going to Australia as manager and he will have made his feelings clear about both players. It was a shameful admission of inadequacy by captain and manager that they were prepared to sacrifice England's best interests in this way. Caddick had taken a hundred wickets in England during the 1998 season while Tufnell was the best spinner in the country, some way ahead of the two who were picked, Peter Such and Robert Croft, and he also turns the ball away from the right-hander. That refusal to pick Caddick and Tufnell for Australia was an inglorious reflection of the attitude of mind of some of those charged with running England's cricket.

By the time of the First Test Match, the Zimbabwean, Duncan Fletcher, had been appointed to take over David Lloyd's job as England coach, but he was not going to start until the autumn. This was a nonsense. Fletcher should have been in the thick of it at once and it is yet another example of muddled thinking that he was not. As a result, David Graveney was now in charge in the England dressing room as well as being Chairman of the Selectors. He is the most charming and understated of men and has allowed himself to become a strangely grey figure. He appears to have been constantly outvoted at selection meetings and sees his role simply as the convenor. I believe that the chairman should insist on a considerable amount of clout of his own and by failing to do so, Graveney has allowed the views of Gooch and Mike Gatting to go unchecked when in reality they should no longer have been on the panel so irredeemably stuffy and conservative had they become. After England had lost the Second Test at Lord's playing just about the worst cricket anyone could remember from an England side, the selectors brought back three over-thirties, Mike Atherton, Graeme Hick and Peter Such. Do you wonder England has become the laughing stock of world cricket? These selections had Gooch and Gatting written all over them. I wonder if the chairman stood up and tried to make himself heard or whether he was persuaded to go along with this Neanderthal thinking.

Now that England had a new captain, it was extremely important that there should be a complete break with the past. Hussain had himself broken with the immediate past when he insisted on the recall of Caddick and Tufnell, but now here he was still surrounded by those whose names had been synonymous with failure and managerial incompetence. Fletcher had already let it be known that he wanted many fewer back-up staff in a dressing room which had come more and more to resemble Waterloo Station in the rush hour. It was essential for Hussain and Fletcher to start together. It would be interesting to know whose decision it was to agree to allow Fletcher to finish the season with his current employers, Glamorgan. The ECB should have insisted that he started straightaway and, if necessary, paid the county the appropriate compensation. In the light of England's predicament, Glamorgan's arm could surely have been twisted. If Fletcher had taken office at once I wonder, for example, if Alec Stewart would have kept his place in the side. Even if he had played at Edgbaston, where he contributed one run and two important dropped slip catches, I am sure he would have not have been in the side for Lord's. England's cricketing future does not lie in the hands of Stewart's age group.

I could not resist a snigger or two when I opened the morning papers for the rest of the summer or occasionally tuned in to Sky television. There was David Lloyd telling the world what the trouble was with England's cricket and what should be done about it. In view of his lack of success as England's coach, I would have thought he would have been much better advised to keep his mouth shut. In the old days before he took charge of the England side, he often worked with us on *TMS* and he was always the greatest of fun and loved a laugh. Now, he appears to feel that it's his duty to take himself so seriously that it's almost as if he is trying to outdo Geoffrey Boycott as he analyses, coaches, advises and censors. One day someone will ask him why he didn't do a few of these things himself when he was in charge. Or maybe his fellow commentators have been told not to.

We were back at the Brockencote the following weekend for the first of the Benson & Hedges Super Cup semi-finals. For 1999, the competition had been reduced to the top eight teams in the 1998 County Championship as part of an attempt to reduce the amount of domestic one-day cricket played in England. This was one of the changes proposed in that most celebrated of documents prepared the year before by Lord MacLaurin and the ECB, *Raising the Standard*. In a World Cup year with a fixture list which would have had the Brain of Britain scratching his head, the B & H raised scarcely a ripple. Edgbaston was not even half-full as Yorkshire put it across Warwickshire, although the much smaller county ground at Bristol was more thickly populated the following day when Gloucestershire beat Sussex. The sides that reached the final at Lord's had only had to win two matches each. It was a competition without giant-killers or much advance publicity and it all went off with about the impact of those fireworks which had declared the World Cup open. At least the principal objective of reducing the amount of one-day cricket was admirable – or so we thought.

Imagine the surprise that same weekend when Karen Earl Ltd, that splendid public relations company which had looked after the B & H cricketing sponsorship so successfully, issued a press release promising bright new frontiers for 2000. The Benson & Hedges Cup, to be played early in the season, was to be expanded to include all eighteen first-class counties. There would be group matches to decide the quarter-finalists and it would be a knock-out competition from then on. Ho hum. Except for the omission of the Combined Universities and the Minor Counties, it was back to the old B & H formula which had been kicked into touch the year before. So much for the new enlightened management of cricket in England, which had promised us fewer one-day games. It looked suspiciously as if the old farts had won that particular day. What's more, it has ensured that when the selectors have to sit down in 2000 to pick the first representative side of the summer for the extended programme of seven Test Matches, the first of which starts in mid-May, they will have desperately little four-day Championship cricket to help them. So much for the brave new world.

My favourite cricketing occasion of the year came two days after that match in Bristol. Bitten and I had been asked by Sir Paul Getty to spend the day on his ground at Wormsleigh, surely the loveliest in the world. Many of us hope to find the ultimate cricket ground in heaven, should we be lucky enough to proceed in that direction. We may well do so, but before planning it The Almighty will have sent St Paul and John the Baptist and one or two others down the M40 to pick up a few tips from Sir Paul. Even then it would be a close run thing.

On this occasion the Getty Eleven was taking on the New Zealanders. The weather was perfect and more than matched by the hospitality, and there were an enormous number of cricketing friends there as well.

After lunch Bitten and I were standing outside one of the big marquees when suddenly a familiar voice from behind me shouted out, 'Come here, Blofeld.' They were the ringing and unmistakable tones of none other than Keith Miller, who comes over from Sydney most summers to stay at Wormsleigh. In spite of his health, which more or less confines him to a wheelchair, Keith's spirited optimism and enthusiasm is still as great as it was when he was one of the game's greatest allrounders all those years ago immediately after the war. Like Peter McFarline in his wheelchair in Melbourne, Keith is a formidable example and lesson to all the gloomy guts of this world. How marvellous that the two of them are in touch. As I found now, five minutes with Keith is better than a bottle of champagne. We flipped energetically from cricket, to mutual friends, to the World Cup and then a couple of minutes of tribute to our remarkable host and his breathtaking ground. When I moved on, more old friends were coming up to greet him and his voice surged cheerfully on. When we later drove back down the M40 into London, we talked mostly of Keith. He had given us both a shot in the arm.

Lord MacLaurin was also at Wormsleigh and we spent some time talking about that much vexed subject, England's cricket. The former chairman of Tesco, who had tragically lost his wife to a sudden heart attack earlier in the summer, was now well into his second term as chairman of the ECB. How he must have longed to be back with the supermarket giant. He will have found Tesco much easier to run than English cricket for the simple reason that what he said went. At the ECB his hands were tied by the counties. Whenever the England Management Committee took a decision about the running of the game, it had then to be ratified by the First-Class Forum. As often as not, I expect it will have been thrown out or seriously modified by the brigade of old farts determined to put county before country. The chairman was currently grappling with the plan to contract England's best cricketers to the ECB and not their counties. At that particular moment England were leading New Zealand in the Test series; in just over six weeks time they had lost it 2–1 and the chairman must have then wondered if there were any players good enough to bother grappling to the Board.

I thought it wiser not to ruin a good day by asking him how in the name of all things above and below us, the old Benson & Hedges competition could have been reinstated in direct opposition to his wishes in *Raising the Standard*. Another of his problems, now that the two-tier system for the County Championship would be a reality in 2000, was how to give it the teeth to make sure it fulfils its principal objective which is to improve the standard of England's Test side. The two-tier system is only the first move in a belated attempt to concentrate excellence so that the best are continually playing against the best preferably on uncovered pitches, although there is about as much chance of that happening as there is of England regaining the Ashes in the immediate future. But then maybe the first might lead to the second.

Of course, some of the poorer and less successful counties may go to the wall as part of a massive realignment of the game in England. This change will surely one day happen just as the supermarket chains are crushing the smaller, more intimate village stores and grocer's shops. In the best of all possible worlds this would not come to pass but the world is changing. A new order will take over and will in time settle down into an acceptable alternative. It is the process of evolution. After all, a great many people made an awful stink when the internal combustion engine came along. If we try and hang onto old-fashioned attitudes rather than devote our energies to embracing new ideas and trying to shape them into an acceptable form, the game will be left further behind. Domestic interest is then going to be as difficult to maintain as international success will be hard to find in the twenty-first century, when England supporters may have to put up with the occasional victory over New Zealand or Zimbabwe. They may do so uncomplainingly for a while but sponsors and television networks certainly won't, and with no one to pay the bills the game as we have known it will soon be lost. It is no good cricket lovers running away from the reality of the present. That is the fast track to disaster.

It is essential, too, for the future wellbeing of English cricket that the benefit system is scrapped and a proper pension fund is put in place. Under the present system too many old players carry on past their sell-by date waiting and hoping for the benefit which should become their due when they have been a capped county player for ten years. Committees and administrators understandably take a sympathetic view and they are allowed to hang on in the first elevens keeping out youngsters who may even have played a part in, say, enabling England's Under-19 side to win a series. The young need to be encouraged and given every chance (as they are everywhere else in the world) rather than being shoved into county second elevens so that old Bloggs, to say nothing of old Jones, can have his benefit. The present benefit system helps perpetuate mediocrity and, in this day and age, is deeply humiliating for the cricketers concerned who, for twelve months, are turned into upmarket beggars. Mediocrity does not pay – the fact that the World Cup lacked four main sponsors made a powerful statement about this. A strong England side is what makes cricket in England vibrant and only the short-sighted would deny that. How long can the game go on affording a crowd of barely 4,000 for the Sunday of the Old Trafford Test, as happened against New Zealand in 1999 when England were being bundled unceremoniously off the park? I know money is not everything but as the second Millennium looms, it speaks in louder and more ringing tones than ever before and, like it or not, will continue to do so.

These are the problems that face Lord MacLaurin at the ECB and his colleagues on the England Management Committee. The greatest legacy MacLaurin could leave behind would be a system whereby the Management Committee has binding powers of its own. This would mean it would no longer have to go cap in hand like a recalcitrant schoolboy to the First-Class Forum for approval every time it comes up with a good idea. What cricket in England desperately needs is strong leadership and with this archaic system in place there is little possibility of that.

The morning after Wormsleigh I drove to Southend to see my first Championship match of the summer. I was intending to watch only the first three days but, as it happened, this was more than enough for Essex to finish off a Middlesex side who turned in a performance of quite remarkable ineptitude. Essex are lucky that their festivals at Ilford and Colchester and Southend are all so well supported. Southchurch Park in Southend may not be the most beautiful ground in the country but it was ringed with its usual handsome collection of marquees and deserved better than this. Southchurch Park attained immortality in 1948 for it was there that Essex became the first county side to bowl out Don Bradman's Australians in less than a day. By the time the last Australian wicket had fallen, they had scored a small matter of 721 runs.

After Middlesex had batted inefficiently for much of the first day, Essex plodded on and on through the second and built up a sizeable lead. Then Middlesex's batting again disappeared with all hands on board. The only notable point about this game was that Ben Hutton, the son of Richard and grandson of Sir Leonard, made his Championship debut. He made 27 good left-handed runs as Middlesex floundered in the first innings. He has a well-ordered defence and played two lovely drives through extra cover for four, which would have had Sir Leonard nodding in considered approval. While his inheritance on the male side of things is classical elegance, there is something more robust and exciting handed down by the maternal bloodlines. His mother's father is Ben Brocklehurst, who captained Somerset for a short time soon after the war and has for many years owned *The Cricketer*, the best and most successful of the cricket magazines. Brocklehurst, always a cheerful cricketer, hit the ball like a kicking horse. Perhaps his most famous single blow came at Bradford when he dispatched the Yorkshire and England left arm spinner, Johnny Wardle, far over the pavilion. He then suggested to the bowler, not unreasonably, that as he knew what the ball looked like, it might be just as well if he went and had a look for it.

By the time I had parked my car outside the synagogue in St John's Wood Road on the first morning of the Second Test Match at Lord's (with the spirited and cheerful cooperation of Ray Weatherhead, who mans the Grace Gates just across the road), I was beginning to feel in mid-season form again. I even began to wonder if those wretched operations had been a figment of the imagination after all. During the World Cup, *Test Match Special* had operated from their old position in the turret of the pavilion above the committee dining room so that the invading hordes from radio and television stations from overseas could all be accommodated in the new media centre at the Nursery End. There was a brief hope that we might be reprieved from having to move away from the pavilion, but word reached my ears that a very important member of MCC, who was once not unconnected with *TMS*, had stamped his foot most firmly upon that germ of an idea. So off we went to the media centre, which to my mind has the peculiar look of a particularly venomous cough lozenge lying on its side.

I have to admit I was darkly apprehensive and would have been only too happy to have disapproved, but on the whole I was pleasantly surprised. Our box is the only one to have a window that opens. This means that the atmosphere can filter through and we feel marginally less like fish in a goldfish bowl than the rest of our colleagues. It also has more room that I thought it would and we have an excellent view behind the bowler's arm. The two main problems are that it is too high, significantly higher than our old venue in the pavilion, and that as the sun goes round it becomes more and more like a particularly fierce form of oven. For all its exciting newness with its shiny fittings and new carpets, I am afraid I would still much rather have been back in the pavilion. When we had first been told we had to move we were informed that the old box was to be put to an alternative use and the wishes of the Westminster City Council were even invoked. To date, it remains the same as it ever was as we look nostalgically across the ground. I felt that there was about all this more than a touch of Thomas à Becket and Henry II and 'Who will free me from this turbulent priest?' Our venomous but futuristic cough lozenge had cost a small matter of £5.8 million and for underestimating that figure the treasurer of MCC, the delightful Brian Thornton, had done the decent thing and fallen on his sword. In spite of this, he still took the trouble to come up and see if we were reasonably content.

If we had had an exciting Test match we probably wouldn't have noticed what faults there are in this new building. While England were terrible, New Zealand played wonderfully well and must be roundly congratulated on winning their first ever Test Match at Lord's in thirteen attempts going back to 1931. For three and a half days, for that was all it took, they outplayed England from the first ball to the last. England were without their surprising hero at Edgbaston, Alex Tudor, who had been forced to pull out in extraordinary circumstances that served to illustrate the eternal dichotomy between counties and country.

The day before the Test Match began, on the Wednesday afternoon, Tudor went off to have a scan on his left knee without anyone in the England camp knowing anything about it. The England management were told late that evening that Tudor, who has tendonitis in his knee, needed rest. As a result, Angus Fraser, who was about to play the next day for Middlesex at Taunton, had to make a journey of 350 miles there and, as it transpired, back, in case he was needed as cover for Tudor. He had reached the Hammersmith round-about the next morning when the chairman of selectors spoke to him on his mobile telephone to tell him to continue on round the roundabout and to steer a course back to Taunton. Simon Pack got in touch with the Surrey management for an explanation about Tudor and he will surely have asked whether the player had been told not to inform the England management of the scan when the squad had met up on the Tuesday. Surrey's chief executive, Paul Sheldon, was quick to respond. He said, a trifle too indignantly perhaps, that England had been kept informed about Tudor's 'niggle'. He then registered surprise that the England management did not know the player was going for a scan on the Wednesday after-noon. The injury had obviously been regarded as so minor by England that at the press conference the day before, Hussain had barely seen fit to mention it. England had been told before the First Test at Edgbaston that Tudor had a niggling knee. He played and made 99 not out whereupon he was picked for Surrey in the County Championship match that followed immediately after the Test. By contrast, Stewart and Thorpe, both of whom had had a considerably less arduous match, were rested. David Lloyd's comments about the Tudor situation were interesting. He said that England would be most unhappy about another such incident of not being kept up-to-date by a county, and added that it was usually the same county. And he should know.

Throughout this Test Match there was something hopelessly unfocussed about so much of England's cricket. It was as though the players did not know what was expected of them. After winning the toss, their batsmen found the ball was moving in the air and off the seam on another cloudy day and they should have known they had to take it carefully, and then, as the conditions eased, build a good first innings total. But they played some dreadful strokes and were bowled out for 186. It then should have been the job of the bowlers to pitch the ball up to allow it to swing and to bring the New Zealand batsmen onto the front foot where they were at their most vulnerable. Also, when there were six men on the off side and three on the leg it was as well not to bowl at the leg stump. All of this should have been within the grasp of experienced professional cricketers. Then, when England began their second innings 172 runs behind, they knew they had to sell their wickets as dearly as possible, particularly as Nasser Hussain had broken a finger fielding in the gully and would not bat.

Yet what happened? Stewart and Butcher gave the innings a sound start until, in the last over before tea, the left-handed Butcher tried to sweep left arm spinner, Daniel Vettori, out of the rough and was caught off the top edge. After the interval Stewart was bowled trying to hit Vettori over the Grandstand and failing to get any part of his body behind a ball that pitched outside the leg stump and turned. Before the close that evening, to compound the hopelessness of it all, Mark Ramprakash, whose character becomes daily more enigmatic and contradictory, played a wild slash without any footwork at a ball he could hardly reach and was caught behind. Here was a man who is haunted by the fear of failure and of getting out – exactly the attitude England now needed – playing a shot which was as wild as it was absurd and irrelevant. Aftab Habib played a poor stroke the next morning which told more of a faulty technique than an over-hasty approach to the situation. Sanity was only restored when Chris Read and Andy Caddick showed what might have been possible in a stand of 78 for the seventh wicket but by then it was far too late. New Zealand were left with the formality of scoring 58 to win.

This was obviously an unforgettable occasion for the many New Zealanders at Lord's and no one will have enjoyed their victory more than the president of New Zealand Cricket, Iain Gallaway. A Dunedin solicitor by trade, Iain was for years their best ball-by-ball commentator on Radio New Zealand. He and his wife, Virginia, have always been wonderfully hospitable whenever international cricket has found its way to Carisbrook in Dunedin, and in all the years I have been involved in the game I can honestly say that I have never met a more splendid chap. I bumped into them both walking round Lord's before play began on the fourth morning and Iain could still not quite believe the day was going to bring his country's first ever Test Match victory at Lord's. Later that morning he paid us a visit in our new commentary box just as Read and Caddick were taking root and he was still apprehensive that the perfidious English might yet spoil a perfect day.

Commentating from high up at the Nursery End was a remarkable experience. Although it was wonderful for me to be back in business at Lord's, throughout the whole match I never felt that I was really back at Lord's. The new media centre gave us such a different perspective. It was magnificent looking at the pavilion and yet somehow it wasn't quite the *TMS* of old, even though Fred Trueman was with us and in his usual inimitable form. It was strange, too, being in a box at Lord's not inhabited by Brian Johnston's ghost. Lord's was of course his home ground. Even now, five years on, his memory is as strong and immediate as ever. Scarcely a day goes by without someone saying, 'What would Johnners have made of that?' Yet, mercifully perhaps, the cough lozenge came after him. I'm not sure he would have cared for it. For me, the saddest part of it was that there was hardly time to walk round to the garden behind the Warner Stand to have at least a drink with all one's picnicking friends. For those of us with *TMS* I am not sure it will ever be quite the same again. A lot of sad things happen in the name of progress. But we will be brave and resist the temptation to call for a special General Meeting of the MCC.

The selectors, bless their cotton socks, now excelled themselves even by their own standards. For selectors, I fear one has to read Messrs Gooch and Gatting. Nasser Hussain was very unlikely to play at Old Trafford and a new captain had to be found. So too did another spinner, for Old Trafford was now the temporary home of that eminent Sri Lankan off spinner, Muttiah Muralitheran, and by a strange coincidence the pitches had begun to spin. Aftab Habib had also not looked the part in the first two Tests. The dynamic selectors, after a lengthy round-table conference, made the decision to go back to Michael Atherton, Graeme Hick and Peter Such, all of whom were well past thirty. Atherton had just made 268 not out for Lancashire against Glamorgan and his back had at last been properly diagnosed and treated. So as a genuine class player, his return was welcome. Hick increased his number of come-backs to a total that probably exceeded Melba, Sinatra and Jeffery Bernard put together. He had never yet established himself as a permanent member of the side in spite of a Test average of 34 and being over thirty years old his day had now come. Such had gone to Australia the previous winter when Stewart and co. were too frightened to take Tufnell and had bowled well in the two Tests in which he had played. But he was now thirty-five and was hardly going to be the backbone of England's future. As far as the captaincy was concerned, they plumped for Mark Butcher on the slender basis that he had done a good job for Surrey when Adam Hollioake, their official captain, had been involved in the World Cup. One could see Gooch and Gatting looming large in the choice of the three over-thirties. David Graveney may have been either brain-washed or outvoted although I cannot see Hussain being all that happy with Dad's Army.

Old Trafford was as big a disaster as Lord's although the rain at least prevented another defeat for England. The team were as unfocussed as ever and only 35,000 spectators turned up over the five days. At the end of it English cricket was only one Test Match away from having to choose the squad for South Africa having learned almost nothing in the first three Tests against New Zealand. England had won the toss on a pitch which looked as bad as the groundsman, Peter Marron, suggested it might be. There are only four pitches at Old Trafford that can be used for televised matches. Two of these had been relaid only two years previously and needed a total of three years to bed down. The other two, which had been on World Cup duty, had been relaid at the end of the eighties and it had been hoped that they would keep going for fifteen years. But both had effectively 'died' after eight years and this Test Match was being played on one of them. England's brilliant administrators had chosen to play at Old Trafford on one of these two 'dead' pitches ignoring the claims of Headingley and Trent Bridge, who were both celebrating their centenaries of Test cricket, as well as local advice from Old Trafford. Whoever made the decision was hard pressed to escape a charge of culpable barminess.

The pitch was bare in parts and irretrievably cracked and on the first day was a real handful. Mark Butcher had won the toss and reasonably decided to bat. He can hardly have thought the pitch would improve. The ball swung under the cloud, seamed off the pitch and there was a most uneven bounce and England did not make a good fist of it as always seems to happens when the ball moves around. They were bowled out for 199 and by the time the last wicket fell, Peter Such had scored the second longest nought in the history of Test cricket, surviving for 72 minutes with Mark Ramprakash. As this suggests, the pitch played much better on the second day and thereafter. This showed that the moisture in the pitch from the late watering Marron had given it (in order to try and hold the surface together) had caused the difficulties on the first day. With Nathan Astle and Craig McMillan scoring good hundreds and Matthew Bell making a most adhesive 83, New Zealand built up a lead of 299. But the weather, which had caused problems on the first day, now came to England's help. By the time they had reached 181/2 in their second innings and Alec Stewart was 83 not out, it began to rain again and the game was drawn.

Although the many minions of the ECB tried to play it down as a routine get-together and a chance for Nasser Hussain to have a long chat with Duncan Fletcher, what was in reality an emergency meeting for England's cricket was arranged over dinner on the Sunday night. Those in attendance were Lord MacLaurin, Hussain, Fletcher, Simon Pack and David Graveney. One hears that it was a lively meeting and that, on occasion, voices were raised. What came out of it gave the lie to the routine-get-together line. The day after the Test ended, it was announced that both Gooch and Gatting had been sacked as selectors. This made excellent sense because they were both finishing their stints after the side for South Africa had been chosen. The new captain, Nasser Hussain, and new coach, Duncan Fletcher, obviously will have wanted to do it their way. These two both sensibly saw that the future of England's cricket lay more with the young than the over-thirties. The return of Atherton, Hick and Such had not been successful at Old Trafford and had wasted a golden opportunity to look at young players who are unlikely to have contributed much less. The only way anyone will ever know if the promising young players in county cricket are good enough at Test level is to give them the chance to prove it. No other country would have returned to the oldies in the way that the Gooch and Gatting inspired selections had done. I would be surprised if Lord MacLaurin tried to stand in the way of Gooch and Gatting's dismissal. One aim of the meeting was to try to keep faith with the public who had been dismayed first by England's extremely premature departure from the World Cup and then by a disastrous Test series against New Zealand, and finally by the call back to arms of the geriatrics.

There were one or two new faces for the last Test at the Oval where the bowling was good, but the batting as bad if not worse than ever. New Zealand won in less than three and a half days and England were unceremoniously dumped at the bottom of the unofficial table of Test cricketing countries. The next day the side for South Africa was to be selected and by then Thorpe had announced he was not available for the tour. Even if the quality of the country's cricketers does not exactly leap up at you out of the county grounds, the selectors have now to try and come up with a blend of youth and experience. The vitality and enthusiasm of youth has been missing from England's dressing room for much too long. This is where the future lies. The best that there are must be chosen and given a proper chance. The Under-19 World

Champions cannot all have turned into donkeys. England may not beat South Africa but we must hope that the experience gained there will enable Hussain's side to return and give the West Indies and Zimbabwe a real run for their money in England in 2000.

The cricket may have been disastrous for England at Old Trafford and then the Oval, but the Third Test Match was a particularly agreeable occasion for me as I had stayed, as always, at the Belle Epoque at Knutsford. My annual visit there is as joyful a part of my own season as any of the Test Matches and to think I had come perilously close to never seeing it again! The Belle Epoque has been owned and presided over for many years by Keith and Nerys Mooney. A month before my visit this time, poor Keith had been struck down by a beastly stroke but was now on the mend, even to the extent that on one of the days of the Test Match he was able to leave hospital and come and have lunch there. It may be a while before he is again greeting guests with his usual boisterous cheerfulness while wearing one of those wonderfully coloured blazers of his (which would have had Joseph taking a long, hard look at his Coat of Many Colours). But with David Mooney, their eldest son and head chef, rolling up his sleeves as never before, the establishment is thriving. The browsing and sluicing has never been better. The front of house is now presided over by Nerys, who remains as elegantly unruffled as ever, and Mark Walkden, also indomitably cheerful and, as you would expect after sixteen years, an expert on his ample wine list. I always look forward to my visits to the Belle Epoque.

My three and a half week visit to the Harley Street Clinic was becoming a more distant memory. Old Trafford and the Oval flowed into Edgbaston and Lord's and only the odd twinge in my chest and the pills I had to take reminded me of the boring start I had made to the summer. Even my scars were looking more friendly. Then I woke up on the Sunday of the Old Trafford Test feeling lousy, even though I had gone to bed at half past nine the night before. I struggled through two poor commentary spells in the morning and at lunch Peter Baxter suggested I went back to my hotel. I did – the first time I had ever left the microphone – and I slept and slept. I had been told that I would occasionally have a bad day. Perhaps I had been going too fast and my body was telling me to slow down. I reminded myself that, all told, I had spent something like 58 hours under anaesthetic. That Sunday I had perhaps been given a warning. It made me remember only too well how my chest had tightened as I had walked down the King's Road that evening in April and how desperately lucky I had been to see another summer.

On the Monday I felt fine again.

HCB 25/8/99

Picture Credits

1. Bill Sykes – author's own
2. Geoffrey Boycott descends on Grasse – "PA" Photos
3. Brian Lara and Ali Bacher – "PA" Photos
4. Nelson Mandela's letter – "PA" Photos
5. Gooda's Gold – author's own
6. Shane Warne – "PA" Photos
7. Alan Mullally – "PA" Photos
8. Darren Gough – "PA" Photos
9. The Commander – author's own
10. Bitten Blofeld – author's own
11. Arthur Mailey cartoon – author's own
12. Laurie Bryant – author's own
13. The Valley of Peace – author's own
14. Arjuna Ranatunga – "PA" Photos
15. & 16. Muttiah Mulitheran – Empics (both pictures)
17. Alec Stewart – "PA" Photos
18. Anil Kumble – "PA" Photos

Index

Index

Index

Index

Index

Index

Index

Index